Stanford in Turmoil

Stanford in Turmoil

CAMPUS UNREST, 1966–1972

Richard W. Lyman

STANFORD GENERAL BOOKS
An imprint of Stanford University Press
Stanford, California

Stanford University Press
Stanford, California

Printed in the United States of America on acid-free, archival-quality paper.
Library of Congress Cataloging-in-Publication Data
Lyman, Richard W.
  Stanford in turmoil : campus unrest, 1966-1972 / Richard W. Lyman.
    p. cm.
  Includes bibliographical references and index.
  ISBN 978-0-8047-6079-9 (cloth : alk. paper)
  1. Stanford University--History--20th century. 2. Student strikes--California--Stanford--
History--20th century. 3. Student movements--California--Stanford--History--20th
century. 4. Stanford University--Students. 5. Stanford University--Presidents. I. Title.
  LD3030.L96 2009
  378.794'73--dc22   2008043087

Typeset by Bruce Lundquist in 10/14 Minion

To Jing,
without whose loving support and gentle but persistent prodding
this book would never have been completed

CONTENTS

PREFACE

THE STUDENT UPRISINGS of the late 1960s and early 1970s continue to stir controversy. The causes of those events remain the subject of debate, and there is frequent speculation as to whether they could recur. I have no intention of ending these controversies, only a desire to contribute my perspective to them.

I undertook the writing of this book more years ago than I would like to admit. I finally began to make real progress during a three-month stay at the Rockefeller Foundation's Villa Serbelloni, a conference center at Bellagio, Lake Como, in 2001. There have been many fallow periods since then. I would like to thank the foundation, and particularly the head of the Bellagio office in New York at the time, Susan Garfield, and the director of the Villa, Gianna Celli, for their help and support.

Back at Stanford, the university archivist, Margaret J. Kimball, and her staff have been unfailingly helpful, cheerful, and patient with a user whose visits were unpredictable and whose demands were sometimes unreasonable.

Bob Rosenzweig and Paul Robinson read the manuscript in draft and offered many valuable suggestions. Needless to say, they are not responsible for the errors and omissions that remain. Kelly Richter, a graduate student in American history, has been diligent, creative, and persistent in pursuit of missing facts and dates. Both she and I are grateful to the President's Office at Stanford for supporting her work for me. Former Stanford president Gerhard Casper was among the first to urge me to write this book.

My family has been patient and supportive. I have tried to describe the roles of our four children, Jennifer P. Lyman, the Rev. Holly Lyman Antolini,

Christopher M. Lyman, generally known as Cricket, and Timothy R. Lyman. Their mother, Jing Lyman, has been, of course, my partner in all the struggles in which we were involved during the years. She has been gently persistent in encouraging me to get the job done. She and our children are no doubt as surprised as I that the book did get done—finally.

Stanford in Turmoil

INTRODUCTION

THIS BOOK is a cross between a case study and a memoir. It does not purport to be either a history of Stanford in the relevant years or a study of "the Sixties," a period that has been written about in countless venues and forms. Instead, this work concentrates on the campus unrest that Stanford, like many other institutions, suffered from in the late 1960s and early 1970s.

In some ways Stanford's experience in those years resembled that of other universities, especially the so-called elite ones. Our troubles were not as widely noticed as those at Columbia, Berkeley, Harvard, and Cornell. People are surprised to hear that we had a half-dozen major cases of arson, suffered significant damage to campus buildings, principally in the form of broken windows, and during the notorious "Cambodia Spring" of 1970 had to summon police to the campus repeatedly to end sit-ins or deal with other disruptions; dozens of police and students were hurt. One Stanford president had his office burned, with the loss of a lifetime's mementos; his successor was forced to resign after just nineteen months in office for his inability to cope with the uproar.

At the same time, although some faculty sided wholeheartedly with the protesters, they never became as bitterly divided as their colleagues at Harvard did after a police bust there in the spring of 1969. And unlike what happened at Cornell, the local Palo Alto community was never terrorized by black students; we offered no photo opportunities like the picture of blacks leaving Willard Straight Hall with automatic weapons at the ready.

In fact, one of the remarkable facts about Stanford's experience was that the rise in prestige and all the indices of academic strength that had begun in the 1950s under President J.E. Wallace Sterling and Provost Frederick E. Terman continued unabated throughout the period of crisis and threats to institutional integrity.

Whether that came about through particular things that we did or refrained from doing is hard to say. There was some well-executed structural change, the leading example being the creation of the University Senate to give the entire faculty a representative assembly of manageable size, and one which, by the device of giving the president, provost, and deans ex-officio seats without vote ensured that the chasm that so often separates faculty from administration could be bridged. At each Senate meeting the president and provost had a place on the agenda to make statements and to respond to questions raised by Senate members.

But it cannot be said that the Senate's existence enabled us to escape troubles. In fact the stress level at Stanford in this period was intensified by the university's startling progress. The university began shedding its parochialism; a system of providing a European experience through overseas campuses contributed to this, as did the civil rights movement in the South. The faculty, docile in the early Sterling years, began to assert itself. Alumni from earlier times found it hard to recognize their alma mater in this burgeoning institution.

.   .   .

Stanford was one of the wave of late-nineteenth-century institutions, such as Johns Hopkins, Cornell, and the University of Chicago, born as full-scale universities that included postgraduate work and professional schools as well as undergraduate colleges. Bit by bit, Ivy League institutions evolved from undergraduate colleges, with the exception of Dartmouth, which never quite completed the development, though it did create both business and medical schools.

The newer universities, except for Johns Hopkins, were coeducational from the beginning. Some of the older ones had coordinate colleges for women. Coeducation only became the norm for the Ivies after World War Two.

Stanford was an interesting crossbreed between the old East Coast private institutions and the great state universities that flourished in the West and Midwest. The Stanfords' emphasis on practical education resulted in a strong engineering program, while the creation of the Graduate School of Business and the School of Earth Sciences after World War One continued this tradition. Perhaps Stanford should have been called the Cornell of the West rather than the Harvard of the West; Cornell, of course, was and is a crossbreed itself between a private college and a land-grant institution run by the state.

Stanford began with a mixture of advantages and disadvantages. A clean slate was in many ways an advantage: Stanford had no traditions to stand in the way of constructive change; no alumni body as yet looking over the president's shoulder and lamenting any departure from the old ways; a huge endowment, at first held up by a lawsuit but soon successfully claimed; ample space, conveniently near but not in a major city; and no rival private university west of Chicago. Despite all this, as an early observer noted, a visitor found "teachers and pupils going through the same old lessons in the same way as everywhere else. . . . It shows the power of educational heredity, that a university unique in its origin should grow up to be so much like its older sisters."[1]

Partly this derived from the tug-of-war between the surviving founder, Jane Stanford, Senator Stanford having died in 1893, and the first president, David Starr Jordan. Mrs. Stanford always had in mind the university as the memorial to her son, and she was much more interested in constructing buildings than in what went on inside them. This meant that even when the lawsuit was decided in the university's favor and an income began to flow from the endowment, she wanted to see it spent on more buildings rather than on faculty salaries or support for research and teaching. And no sooner had she died than the great earthquake of 1906 left many of her buildings destroyed and in need of replacement, a further drain on the endowment.

Perhaps equally damaging was the Ross case. Edward A. Ross, sometimes described as a sociologist and sometimes an economist, incurred Mrs. Stanford's wrath, first for his public support of the free silver movement and the presidential candidacy of William Jennings Bryan and later for his advocacy of municipal ownership of the street railways in Oakland (clearly socialism!), and second for his opposition to Asian immigration, which Jane Stanford saw as an insult to the Chinese laborers who had built her husband's railway. She urged President Jordan to dismiss Ross from the faculty, which for several years he resisted. Finally, fearful that Mrs. Stanford would withdraw the endowment and destroy the university, Jordan gave in. Ross, however, protested his dismissal, infuriating Jordan.

The Ross case quickly became a cause célèbre, and seven other Stanford faculty members either resigned in protest or were dismissed for vocal criticisms of Jordan's action. The American Economics Association investigated the firing and censured the university. It was one of several similar cases around the turn of the century that eventually led to the creation of the American Association of University Professors to fight for faculty rights. And it cast a pall over Stanford's development that only lifted gradually with the passage of time and the end of the Jordan presidency.

The interwar years were those of the long presidency of Ray Lyman Wilbur, who held office from 1916 to 1943. Stanford, during that period, was more notable for its football prowess than its academic standing. Although the university was among the charter members of the Association of American Universities, founded in 1900 to bring together all those institutions that offered graduate work, it was certainly not among the more prestigious members before World War Two. At that time it might have been described as a respectable regional university, not in the same league with the Ivies or the University of Chicago.

1 THE STERLING-TERMAN ERA

STANFORD UNIVERSITY in the early 1960s was a peaceful, bucolic place, often referred to (without conscious irony) as "the Farm," in recognition of its origins in the place where Senator Stanford raised trotting horses. When I arrived there as a nontenured associate professor of history in 1958, one colleague told me that anyone in search of intellectual excitement would have to journey fifty miles to Berkeley. Another asked, in a conversation about Stanford's role in the world, whether we were "going to go on educating the children of the middling rich of Los Angeles" or find more exciting things to do.

But just under the placid surface, plenty of excitement brewed. Since 1949, J.E. Wallace Sterling had been Stanford's president, and since 1955, the former dean of the Engineering School, Frederick E. Terman, had been provost. Together, by 1960 they were well on the way to converting a respectable but largely regional institution into one of the world's great universities.

They were an odd couple. Sterling, a huge bear of a man—*Time* magazine said he "looks like a heavyweight Jimmy Durante, sounds like Edward R. Murrow, and thinks like Tycoon Stanford"—the son of a United Church of Canada minister who was a recent immigrant from England, worked his way through the University of Toronto pitching hay, stringing telephone wires, and serving "as an advance man for a Chautauqua show," inter alia.[1] He also played football until suffering a permanent back injury, and he met a student body vice president named Ann Marie Shaver, who went on to teach dietetics and who in 1930 became Mrs. Sterling.

In 1928–30 he coached football and basketball while earning his MA at the University of Alberta. He was about to turn down an offer to coach the professional football team at Calgary in favor of purely academic pursuits when Ann intervened: "If you coached at Calgary during the fall, you could study at Stanford during the other three quarters," she said, adding that then they could get married.[2] This plan suffered a setback when on arriving at Stanford in December 1930 they got the news that Calgary had cancelled its season because of the Depression. That Christmas, Ann's gift to her new husband was several history books from the Stanford library, wrapped in cheerful Christmas paper.

Sterling found employment as a research assistant at the Hoover Institution on War, Revolution, and Peace; in 1935 he became an instructor in history at Stanford, and in 1938 got his PhD and an assistant professorship at Caltech. During the decade he spent there, he rose to be made chair of the faculty and developed a second career as a news commentator on CBS radio. In 1948 the Henry E. Huntington Library and Art Gallery in San Marino made him its director. That berth must have seemed ideal—a prestigious position with enough flexibility to allow him to continue with scholarship, with more news analysis, or both.

Back at Stanford, Donald Tresidder, president in succession to Wilbur in 1943, had died unexpectedly. Sterling had scarcely settled into the Huntington when Paul C. Edwards, president of the Stanford University Board of Trustees, showed up to ask him to take on the university's presidency. Despite Stanford's rather precarious position at the time—or perhaps in part because of it—Sterling accepted, and in 1949 began a nineteen-year stint as Stanford's fifth president.

Like most colleges and universities, Stanford had had to scramble to survive during World War Two. Its problems were exacerbated by the cap on enrollment of undergraduate women imposed by Mrs. Stanford in 1899 when she had feared the development of a female seminary in place of her "University of high degree." As elsewhere, training programs for the armed forces supplied replacements for students who left for wartime service. But the university that emerged in 1945 was an institution with serious financial and morale problems. Donald Tresidder, who had been chairing the Stanford University Board of Trustees before succeeding Wilbur, never won the full support of the faculty.[3] Although, like Wilbur, he had been trained as an MD, Tresidder's career was in business. Some of his notable achievements were of a kind that faculty seldom fully appreciate; for example, exploiting the confidence that he had from his board colleagues, Tresidder ended the decidedly weird arrangement under which the business manager reported directly to the trustees, rather than through the university president.

Financially, Stanford's once dazzling endowment had long suffered from lackluster management and inadequate attention to fund-raising. Faculty salaries stagnated well into Sterling's presidency. In a striking memorandum to the board of trustees, written several months before taking office as president, Sterling wrote:

> The standing and progress of any university is directly dependent in the first instance upon the quality of its faculty and derivatively in the second instance upon the quality of its student body. I recognize that financial conditions directly affect the attainment of high quality in these related fields, but assuming that financial conditions are such as to place no real barrier in the way of high attainment, then every stress should be placed on effort to build a faculty not merely of good men but of the best men, and to attract and sustain a student body capable of high academic performance. Stanford has ground to gain in both these particulars.[4]

This seemingly casual assumption about finance cannot have reflected the incoming president's real view. He devoted much time and energy to fund-raising, involving the trustees more than had previously been the case, and working with the Stanford Associates, a body created in 1934 when a group of alumni, concerned that the university's early wealth had bred a complacency that was no longer justified, waited upon President Wilbur to offer their help in fund-raising. In 1955 Sterling made a key appointment on the management side in the person of Frederick Emmons Terman as vice president and provost, the number two official at Stanford.

Terman had Stanford roots; his father, the psychologist Lewis Terman, was among the most eminent of the early faculty, known nationally as the father of intelligence testing.[5] Trained as an electrical engineer at Stanford and MIT, Terman gained invaluable experience (and broadened his own outlook) when he went to Cambridge during World War Two to head the Radio Research Laboratory at Harvard.

He and Sterling were a study in contrasts—and complementary talents. The real wonder of Stanford's phenomenal rise in the later 1950s and the 1960s, and a fact that is hugely to the credit of both men, was their ability to work together. Terman was what one can only call intensely quantitative in his approach to all problems. Smilingly gruff, he wasted no time on small talk or discussions of context. He talked a great deal, however, and often didactively. Yet he understood his own limitations better than many people of great ability. He used to remark, ruefully but without resentment, that someone whose request was turned down by Sterling would emerge from the President's Office happier than the same person with the same request would feel upon Terman's acceding to it. Sterling told warm and funny stories; Terman analyzed numbers. Sterling played the piano and sang popular songs for relaxation; it is difficult to imagine Fred Terman engaged in any comparable activity. He would insist on receiving budget requests for the coming year on Christmas Eve, so that while others were celebrating he could get a head start on the next year's work.[6]

Fred Terman fully shared Sterling's determination "to build a faculty not merely of good men but of the best men," and he had a degree of ruthlessness in the pursuit of this objective that was lacking in the president. The oft-quoted phrase that denotes Terman's approach was the construction of "steeples of excellence." By this he meant that one went about building a given department or program by first attracting one or two truly preeminent scholars, and then giving them free rein to go about the task of appointing junior colleagues, building research programs, and so forth.

If to concentrate the resources necessary to do this required downplaying or even eliminating established programs or academic emphases that lacked promise for the future, Terman did so with equanimity. Thus in biology the traditional study of taxonomy got short shrift in favor of modern molecular biology, much to the anguish of the taxonomists.[7]

All of this depended to a considerable extent on success in pursuing the vision of scientific and technical progress that Fred Terman derived from his World War Two experience—including years spent in close proximity to such models as Harvard and MIT. Convinced that the federal government would retain its role, taken over in wartime from the philanthropic foundations, as chief funder of research in technology and the sciences, and that in the United States, in contrast to most of the world, such research would take place preponderantly in universities rather than in federal laboratories, Terman saw the implications for Stanford. His faculty of "the best men" would have the best chances of success in attracting federal research monies.[8] The recovery by the university of its indirect costs would help to provide support for the university's infrastructure in general.

Building the financial base for Stanford's rise involved more than the search for federal research support, of course. One huge but dormant asset when Sterling took office was the 8,800 acres of mid-Peninsula real estate that constituted the heart of its endowment. The Founding Grant forbade the alienation of any of this land—it could not be sold and the money put to work for the university. But with an entrepreneurial spirit that has become a shibboleth at Stanford, a way around this inconvenient (but wise and far-sighted) restriction was developed: long-term (up to ninety-nine years) leases. In due course, the land became a significant source of unrestricted income. Seventy acres of the land became the Stanford Shopping Center, which in its year of completion, 1957, included half-a-million square feet of retail space and brought in nearly $1 million in profit to the university. (The retail space was expanded significantly in the 1970s, and by 1990, the center was bringing in roughly $5 million per year.)[9]

By the early 1960s, some five hundred acres were devoted to an industrial park replete with companies generated directly or indirectly by the energies and ideas of inventors and entrepreneurs bred in the formidable School of Engineering—and especially its Department of Electrical Engineering—built by Fred Terman. The word "built" is used here in the most direct sense: David Packard and William Hewlett were but the most celebrated of the many for whom Terman had served as mentor.

The 8,800 acres were helpful in two more respects. They made it possible for the new Center for Advanced Study in the Behavioral Sciences to become $1-year tenants just across Foothill Boulevard from the main campus, and in these disciplines it became a rueful national joke that a scholar would be exposed to the joys of life at Stanford (climate, proximity to San Francisco, and so on), then wooed (successfully) by the relevant Stanford department. And once a tenured member of the Stanford faculty, she or he could build a home with money borrowed from the university on campus land leased from the university.

But if Sterling's and Terman's vision was to become a reality, something more was needed, beyond learning how to profit from the inalienable land endowment. By what turned out to be a masterstroke, in 1959, the administration launched a pioneering study of its funding and costs, with careful projections of its future needs. The study, "Stanford's Minimum Needs in the Years Ahead" (otherwise known as "The Red Book"), was the product of years of financial forecasting by Ken Cuthbertson (vice president of finance and development), Robert Moulton (presidential assistant for long-range planning), and Ken Creighton (university controller). It recommended that Stanford establish a stronger salary structure and steadily recruit more faculty, that it increase and renovate its physical facilities, including improving student and faculty housing, and that it create means for long-term financial growth. Essentially, the study argued that Stanford, although it had made admirable gains in prestige, would need to increase substantially its resources if it wanted to compete with the Ivy League. The university would need at least $150 million beyond existing income and gifts to accomplish these goals.[10]

Fortunately, the timing was perfect; higher education nationally was enjoying growth but was concerned about its durability. The Ford Foundation, the country's biggest organization of its kind, had an embarrassingly large monetary surplus to dispose of and was casting about for ways to push large sums out the door in a way that would be responsible but quick. To no small degree on the strength of Stanford's self-study, Ford offered the university an unprecedentedly large challenge grant: $25 million to be matched 3-to-1 by Stanford's fund-raising from other sources. Better still, while the matching money could come from anyone (except government) and be restricted as to purpose, the Ford dollars were unrestricted. They could therefore truly serve as the financial foundation for the Sterling-Terman adventure in institution building.

The ensuing campaign bore the Madison Avenue title Plan of Action for a Challenging Era (PACE), but Vice President for Finance Kenneth M. Cuthbertson saw to it that the faculty was engaged to the extent possible. He met with one academic department after another, explaining how the campaign would work, what its success should make possible, and how faculty members could participate. Cuthbertson, a polio victim who walked with a cane, a Stanford graduate of the class of 1940 and student body president whose ebullient wife, Coline, had been student body vice president, was uniquely attuned to faculty mores and ways of looking at things. Sterling's 1948 memo to the trustees remarked, "It is common knowledge that large faculties are frequently too readily given to . . . cliqueishness and sniping at trustees and administrative officers. . . . I venture the opinion that the broader the base of responsible faculty participation, the less the bickering and the less the deleterious effects of grapevine apprehensions."

Sterling did not always act in accordance with this insight—I recall his racing through a quarterly meeting of the Academic Council (tenured and tenure-track faculty) so fast that the following quarter he had to apologize for having failed to call for "any new business." But turning to Cuthbertson to run first the self-study and then the campaign itself fit the doctrine of enlisting faculty participation perfectly. All but the most determinedly contentious felt that PACE was in a real sense theirs.

The campaign lasted from 1961 to 1964 and exceeded its $100 million target, the largest to that date in the history of higher education, by $9 million. Meanwhile various other things were going on that brought Leland Stanford Junior University to the point of "trembling on the edge of greatness," as the novelist and Stanford professor Wallace Stegner famously put it.[11] The faculty was expanding rapidly, often by raiding other institutions for superstars.

The History Department recruited four future presidents of the American Historical Association within the space of a few years. The Medical School, moved to Palo Alto from its deteriorating San Francisco quarters—a move derided by some as "Wally's folly" because of the expense, the resistance of many clinical faculty and their spouses, and questions as to where the patients were going to come from amidst the apricot orchards of the Santa Clara Valley—recruited Nobel Prize winners Joshua Lederberg and Arthur Kornberg from the University of Wisconsin and Washington University in St. Louis, respectively.

Stanford, again turning its abundant acreage to advantage, secured the Atomic Energy Commission's contract to build and run the $114 million Stanford Linear Accelerator Center (SLAC) that stretched for two miles and brought leading high-energy physicists from around the world for research visits. For some years conflict between the university's Physics Department and SLAC caused the blessing to be seen as somewhat mixed, but *Time* called this "Sterling's most audacious 1962 coup."[12]

Before World War Two "half or more of the graduate students at Stanford had received their bachelor's degree at Stanford, and most of the rest came from western and particularly California institutions."[13] By 1958, the university was eighth in the number of National Science Foundation (NSF) fellows it attracted, ahead of Yale, Columbia, and Cornell. Between 1960 and 1963, when the graduate enrollment went from 3,636 to 4,781, the number of NSF fellows increased from 44 to 151, while the number of Woodrow Wilson fellows went from 33 to 81.[14] In 1951, Stanford admitted seven out of eight who applied. It was calculated that applicants in the lower half of SAT scores in the 1951 freshman class would not have been admitted five years later. By the mid-1960s, the university was admitting about one in five applicants (and by the 1990s, one in seven).

By 1965, the dean of admissions was compiling data on the nonacademic credentials of incoming freshmen to enable the President's Office "to give 'ammunition' to one or more major gift volunteers to use in combating the charge that Stanford University is now admitting only 'egg heads.'"[15]

By the mid-1960s, then, Stanford was becoming recognized as a university with high aspirations and moving rapidly to fulfill them. The exact nature of the institution that its leaders proposed to achieve was not clear; there were few signs that Sterling and Terman thought in terms of making Stanford a different *kind* of university from its competitors; the competition was seen in conventional quantitative terms: a growing endowment; ever more selective undergraduate admissions; a growing graduate student body; successful raiding of the faculties of others to increase the number of stars in Stanford's firmament; and further increases in federal research support.

On the most general issues concerning higher education after World War Two, Sterling did have fairly clear views. He distrusted the broad call for democratization backed by massive federal funding that came from President Truman's commission of 1947. In 1951 he expressed concern that

> Higher education today faces the danger of watering down intellectual performance—through a lowering of standards—by responding to demands that it embrace every American boy and girl. It is not ordained that because there is equal opportunity, or should be, and because there is equality before the law, there is any such thing as equality of talent. There is no such thing. Each of us is differently endowed and we should be measured individually in terms of how we make use of our selective individual endowments.[16]

Within the broad diversity of higher educational institutions in the United States, Sterling considered the roles of public and private to be "complementary," but saw the independent colleges and universities as having "more opportunity to set the pace and set good standards." In both word and practice, he urged "the essential unity of all education," and he maintained cordial relations with the University of California. His distress at the dismissal of Clark Kerr as president in 1967 was palpable, and he sought to maintain, past the point where it was really tenable, the "gentleman's agreement" by which UC would refrain from major public fund-raising (beyond ordinary alumni giving) while Stanford would not push for public funding of independent colleges by the state. But it was clear throughout his presidency that he believed that the independents were the natural pacesetters, as well as the indirect protectors of public sector institutions: by flourishing under conditions of freedom, they made regulatory incursions in the public sector more difficult to sustain.

Beyond this, Sterling's views of higher education consisted largely of a pervasive individualism that generally led him to talk about education as a mechanism for maximizing human potential. In what a commentator described as a "somewhat anthropomorphic conception of the university," Sterling declared that "a university will, indeed, be influenced by society's expectations and demands, but it should not permit itself to be shaped by these influences alone; rather, it should shape itself by its own choice of values and purpose."[17] This left a good deal to be spelled out—the point at which being "influenced" becomes being "shaped," for starters. Just such questions as these were about to be raised in dramatic fashion.

By the early 1960s, it was beginning to become clear that Stanford's rapid rise in academic quality would bring changes in the university's overall climate. In 1959, the Academic Council objected rather vociferously to a new statement of purpose for the Hoover Institution, drafted at the insistence of its founder, former President Herbert Hoover, in which it was stated, "The purpose of this Institution must be, by its research and publications, to demonstrate the evils of the doctrines of Karl Marx—whether Communism, Socialism, economic materialism, or atheism, thus to protect the American way of life."[18]

Wally Sterling quieted the fuss by hinting broadly that if the faculty would be patient, the former president, who was eighty-five years old, would no longer be interfering in the affairs of the university and all would be well. Still, a fuss had erupted, though it was succeeded by many a quiet meeting in which the main item of business was the report of the president.

· · ·

In 1962, the placid round of student politics, in which a fraternity man would run for student body president against a man from the dormitories, suddenly gave way to the election of a graduate student named Armin Rosencranz. His campaign had spoofed the process—his slogans were "elect Charmin' Armin" and "send a man to do a boy's work." But he talked about student power, and a referendum run by the Associated Students of Stanford University (ASSU) called for replacing the existing total prohibition of liquor on campus with current California law prohibiting alcoholic consumption only to anyone under twenty-one. The trustees rejected the ASSU's proposal, but recognized the irrationality of trying to maintain the existing policy in on-campus apartments inhabited by graduate students—the first of many adjustments to university rules that would result from changes in the composition, distribution, and disposition of the student body.

Prohibition of alcohol on campus was but one of an array of regulations usually summed up under the heading "parietal rules." Dormitories were of course segregated by sex, and the regulation of visits by members of the opposite sex in any "living group" (a term widely used at Stanford) was detailed and precise. A dress code was in effect; women students were not to wear the slacks known as pedal pushers in the Inner Quadrangle. Even the enforcement of rules was segregated, at the student level by consultative and judicial groups called the Men's Council and the Women's Council, and at the administrative level by the presence, under the dean of students, of a dean of men and a dean of women. Beyond the regulation of social life, there were requirements that placed any student activity connected with politics under the Political Union, which was responsible to the Associated Students of Stanford University and their Legislature (LASSU). This was to ensure balance in the invitation of speakers and to prevent the flowering of issue-oriented organizations among the students that might somehow appear to represent a departure on the part of the university from the nonpartisan stance required by the Founding Grant.

In the spring of 1962, LASSU tested these political restrictions by trying to charter the Forum for the Discussion of Non-Violent Alternatives to War. The administration vetoed this, on the grounds that the forum was a partisan organization and its creation would violate the monopoly enjoyed by the Political Union. The legislature passed a resolution claiming the primary responsibility for the creation, dissolution, and conduct of student organizations and expressing "its profound disappointment that the University administration . . . has overruled the Legislature's decisions and responsibility in this area of student activity."[19]

Responding, Sterling charged LASSU with being "ready to take an action which, if approved, would destroy the mechanism—the Political Union—by which student responsibility has been exercised," and he asserted that its "delegated authority does not extend to the modification of basic University policy as determined by the Board of Trustees, nor to the alteration of the Founding Grant under which the University was established."[20]

It may not have been wise to respond by resorting to such heavy artillery as the Founding Grant and the authority of the board of trustees, since less than a year later the administration had to beat at least a partial retreat. Armin Rosencranz showed what could be done with a deft choice of issues. When it became known that the Federal Communications Commission was withholding the renewal of the public radio station KPFA's license pending an investigation by the Subcommittee on Internal Security of the U.S. Senate, Rosencrantz wrote a letter, on ASSU stationery as president of the student body, protesting that these actions threatened free speech.

Reporting on this, and Armin's intention to ask LASSU to pass a resolution supporting his action the next evening, Fred Glover, executive assistant to the president, wrote, "Don [Winbigler, dean of students] feels that nothing short of a verbal or written order from you will stop him, and even then he will no doubt make an issue of the matter before Legislature. Want to blow the whistle?" Next to this query Sterling scribbled "Yes—& now."[21] Accordingly, Winbigler wrote to Rosencranz:

> The resolution which has been proposed for action by LASSU regarding the Senate Security Subcommittee represents an improper involvement of the University's name in a matter which, according to official policy, is not delegated to student organizations. The President and the Board of Trustees have begun a review of the University's policies relating to institutional participation and identification with political and social action. At the request of the President of the University, I am writing to inform you that pending the policy review and until further notice, Stanford student organizations may not take public stands on issues affecting affairs beyond the Stanford campus without prior University approval. This provision applies also to officers of Stanford student organizations in their official capacities, although it does not limit the right of any student as an individual to participate in undertakings which are not identified with the University.[22]

The Legislature went ahead and voted seventeen to one, with two abstentions, "affirming the right of the Associated Students to speak out on public issues," and by two-to-one margins, it passed resolutions approving Rosencranz's letters to officials in Washington and "expressing concern that the right of free speech is being threatened by the Senate's investigation of KPFA."[23]

Editorially *The Stanford Daily* blamed the administration's "paranoid" stand on worries about potential donors to the PACE campaign, concluding harshly, "In its very great efforts to raise enough money to become the Harvard of the West, the University has set forth a policy more appropriate to a second-rate state university."[24]

In the end, the trustees did approve a liberalization of the rules that allowed voluntary student organizations registered with the university through the Student Affairs and Services Committee to take stands on political issues, provided they made it clear that the members of the organization were speaking only for themselves, not for the ASSU or the university. The trustees also approved a new ASSU constitution.

Armin Rosencranz greeted the trustees' actions with a euphoric letter addressed to the presidents of the board and of the university. Although "many student leaders, including myself, will feel that the new policy does not go far enough and that there are matters of national and international student concern upon which it seems appropriate for the student body to speak out collectively," he declared, "The new University policy will no doubt be a landmark in the history of student rights and privileges at Stanford. It is a tribute, too, to what can be accomplished when students, faculty, administration, and trustees work together to form sound educational policy and to provide a liberal education for all who come to study here."[25]

In the next few years, faith in such collaboration was to be sorely tried, sometimes validated, but often found wanting on Leland Stanford's onetime farm.

2 EARLY VIETNAM STIRRINGS, DEAN ALLEN'S DEPARTURE, DAVID HARRIS'S ARRIVAL, AND STANFORD'S FIRST SIT-IN

WITHIN A FEW WEEKS of Armin's limited but significant success in opening up political life for Stanford students, activism relating to the Vietnam War began.

During spring recess, 1963, notices went up in eighteen campus locations denoting fallout shelters, each supplied with such necessities as water, biscuits, and first-aid and radiological-monitoring equipment, courtesy of the federal government. Critics of the war immediately viewed this as "an essential part of American military posture."[1] By cooperating with the government in preparing for war, the university tacitly condoned the war policy.

To many, this seemed far-fetched; the connection between providing fallout shelters at home and assisting the South Vietnamese government against the Viet Cong was not apparent. Fallout shelters were seen as public services, not distinct from any other protection against potential disaster.

On April 2, members of the Stanford Peace Caucus met with Fred Glover to "invite a representative of the university administration to participate in a public discussion of the advisability of having fallout shelters on the Stanford campus." The administration refused, whereupon the caucus declared that its members would "directly confront President Sterling by means of a permanent vigil. For an indefinite period of time beginning April 18, we intend to be present at his office during the day and at his home at night."[2]

Thus the procedural issue replaced the substantive one, a pattern that would become familiar. Whether one agreed with the administration's decision to accept the shelters, surely one would find unacceptable a total unwillingness to discuss the reasons behind the decision. The implication of the refusal, no doubt well understood by both sides, was that students and faculty had no legitimate role to play in such decision making.

The vigil began as announced, but the issue quickly became the legitimacy of carrying such tactics into the residential area of the campus. On April 26, Sterling issued a statement, declaring:

> 1. A vigil may be held on the campus in areas which are generally available to the public, provided it is conducted in an orderly manner and does not interfere with classes or other educational processes and business of the University.
> 2. A vigil may not be conducted in the private residential areas of the campus or in any manner which represents harassment of any person on the campus.[3]

This policy had the unanimous endorsement of the Committee on University Policy, a body comprising the Executive Committee of the Academic Council (elected by the tenured and tenure-track faculty), the president, and the deans of schools. But the president's statement went on to spell out the decision-making structure of the university:

> The policies of Stanford University, and the procedures by which such policies are formulated, are established by the Trustees of the University. In the formulation of policy recommendations to the Trustees by the President of the University, the Faculty of the University has extensive participation. No University policy-making function has been delegated to the students of Stanford University. But students have means of registering their views on University affairs through student publications, through scheduled discussions with the President of the University, through representation on several Committees of the Faculty, through public debate on University platforms, and, indeed, through a "vigil" on the campus other than in private residential areas.[4]

The vigil did take place, and the enforcement of the president's ban on extending it to the residential areas (in this case, the vicinity of the president's residence, the Hoover House) was accomplished somewhat clumsily. Stanford security officers lifted student body cards. "The peaceful atmosphere of the Farm was violently upset last night," the *Daily* reporter wrote of these skirmishes, not anticipating how the experience of real violence would expand in the years ahead.[5]

One critic wrote that a student found guilty of plagiarism, a serious offense against basic principles of the university "is likely to be suspended at worst (if caught). And yet someone quietly living up to sincerely-held principles is threatened with the ponderous machinery of dismissal. It seems to me that a serious distortion of values is involved here."[6] Of course no dismissals ensued, and a meeting at which members of the administration engaged in a public discussion of the issues surrounding fallout shelters took place on May 15. Speakers included meeting chairperson H. Donald Winbigler, dean of students; Alf Brandin, vice president for business; Lyle Nelson, director of university relations; and Wolfgang Panofsky, director of SLAC. Even before this, on May 1, the Peace Caucus, "impressed with the attempt on the part of the Administration to reach a solution to our problem," ended its vigil.[7]

Six weeks later, one of these "spokesmen," Kit Havice, a graduating senior headed for medical school, provoked an episode at Stanford's commencement sufficiently dramatic to get front-page coverage in the *San Francisco Chronicle*. The speaker that year was retired Air Force General Lauris Norstad, a former commander of the North Atlantic Treaty Organization forces. Ms. Havice notified the President's Office beforehand that she intended to protest against this choice. She was warned that, although she was free to demonstrate outside Frost Amphitheater, "to use the formal ceremonies themselves as a platform for advertising personal opinions violates the spirit and privacy of the occasion for 10,000 students, parents, and other invited guests."[8] She nevertheless showed up to march in the academic procession armed with a placard reading "Non-Violence, Not NATO" on one side and "I welcome Mr. Norstad, Not NATO" on the other. Lyle Nelson, director of university relations, confiscated the placard, at which point Ms. Havice got in her car and drove around to the opposite entrance to Frost Amphitheater to try again with a duplicate sign. This time two security officers "pulled her out of line and took the placard. When one of the officers said, 'Let's get her out of here,' she went limp," as the procession marched past her and into the amphitheater.[9]

By the standards of what was to come just two or three years later, this was the mildest of episodes. But the reactions of some Stanford trustees provide an indication of how unprepared some were in 1963 to encounter even the slightest challenge to decorum. A memo to files (copied to the dean of students) from Fred Glover dated June 21 read, "There is no question but that the Kit Havice incident shook Trustee confidence in Medical School admissions standards." Both Mr. Herman Phleger and Mr. Donald J. Russell questioned staff vigorously June 19 on how the university could justify giving a medical education to a young woman whose judgment was in serious question as evidenced by her actions. "Should a student with such an obvious lack of balance be permitted to practice medicine?" was one of the ways the question was put. Again the question was asked "whether a bright mind was our only criteria [*sic*] for admission at the graduate level. No attention to character? To stability? No attention to judgment and integrity?" This was the tone of the questions.

It was clear that Kit's performance did the Medical School no good in the eyes of the trustees, or the general public for that matter, judging from comments reported by trustees. Ten days later, Glover wrote again to the files, "On July 2 I relayed to Dean Alway the purport of my June 21 memorandum. Dean Alway said he does not believe that Kit is going to continue her work at the Medical School but if she does he will keep in mind the fact that the Trustees do have questions as to her eligibility." Perhaps fortunately, Ms. Havice did not pursue her application, so the carefully noncommittal response of Dean Alway was not tested.

The war in Vietnam was not yet the dominant focus of student activism, however. Interest in civil rights grew steadily. Thirteen Stanford students went to Mississippi in November 1963 to work on voter registration there, having been inspired by a charismatic former assistant dean of students named Allard Lowenstein. In April 1964, Martin Luther King Jr. addressed a packed-to-overflowing Memorial Auditorium, and the following summer Stanford led the nation in the number of students making the pilgrimage to Mississippi.[10] Some faculty were also involved.

During 1964, a variety of student-life issues engaged the attention, at least of the politically attuned, in and around LASSU and the *Daily*. Two of these issues deserve attention as illustrative of how far the university had to travel before the kinds of freedom and student participation in governance that might now seem fairly obviously appropriate could be attained. One involved religious practice and policy on campus and the other related, if indirectly, to accelerating the dismantling of the doctrine in loco parentis.

On January 30, 1964, the Committee on Religion of LASSU issued a report calling for changes in the university's role in supporting religious activities. Appointment of the committee was triggered by a $1.2 million contribution to the PACE campaign from Mr. and Mrs. Lowell Berry of Oakland to support religious activities (excluding both academic programs and buildings). The committee's ostensible purpose, then, was to offer suggestions for how to spend this money. The document began by pointing to the remarkable success of the academic program in religious studies developed under the academic umbrella of the interdisciplinary Humanities Special Programs. In 1962–63, there were a total of 888 students enrolled in these courses, "taught by an excellent and popular faculty."[11]

But this obvious evidence of interest in religion was not matched by growth in attendance at Memorial Church. According to a survey carried out by the committee "only 3% of the sample attended Memorial Church 'regularly,' 16% came 'occasionally,' 24% 'seldom,' and 57% 'never.' (At least 30% consider themselves religiously active)." According to the report, this lack of interest stemmed principally from the monopoly of religious services enjoyed by the nondenominational Protestant Christian program of Memorial Church. Students wanting other kinds of religious exercises had to go off campus to churches and synagogues in the surrounding communities, where the services were geared to older congregations and not to concerns of relevance to Stanford undergraduates. Two-thirds of those describing themselves as "religiously active" said they would attend services of their particular denomination in Memorial Church if such services were offered.

"The program and spirit of Memorial Church need to be given a more vibrant and active direction," the report argued, and it called for engagement with community issues through "work projects in different parts of the world, projects to help needy citizens in East Palo Alto, a student exchange with Negro universities." To organize and coordinate such a program would require more staff. Although he was not mentioned in the body of the report, Chaplain Rabb Minto was the target of the criticisms. "Many people go to Memorial Church only when there are guest speakers." The contrasting of what went on in the church with what went on in classrooms where religion was the topic was no accident. The report's appendix excerpted interviews with various knowledgeable people. Minto's was rambling and confused, ranging from his "dream" of restoring a spire to Memorial Church (if this was infeasible, "perhaps there could be a low dome or octagonal roof"), to a blunt expression of his real position: "I'm not in favor of change. I don't see the need for it. The major problem is that most students don't care for religion."

Even granting that change might be desirable, was it possible under the restrictions of the Founding Grant and of various expressed opinions of Mrs. Stanford? The report quoted her address of October 3, 1902, amending the Founding Grant: "The University must be forever maintained upon a strictly nonsectarian basis. It must never become an instrument in the hands of any political party or religious sect or organization. . . . [It must be] entirely free from all denominational alliances, however slight the bond may be."[12] But it also quoted the views of the counsel for business affairs, Cassius Kirk, who stated, "There is always leeway for expanding a trust unless the wording is very explicit. I believe there is some leeway in Mrs. Stanford's wording." The LASSU committee argued that the meaning of such words as "nondenominational" and "nonsectarian" had changed since her day and quoted a member of the religious studies faculty as saying, "Mrs. Stanford lived at a time when she really thought it would be pan-sectarian to have this type of church." The committee's report closed with a plea for student involvement in "the final decisions about the use of the money and in the operations of any program and activities established with it."

President Sterling gave the LASSU report a guardedly positive welcome; reading the articles on the committee's work in the *Daily* had prepared him for it. "I shall be discussing the use of the Berry fund with faculty and Trustees in the near future, and I shall see to it that the student recommendations receive full consideration," he wrote.[13]

There ensued a long hiatus, in which students became occupied with other matters and the president was taken out of action in March by a severe attack of diverticulitis complicated by a rupture and subsequent peritonitis. He returned to duty in the fall, and in October he created a presidential committee, consisting entirely of faculty, to consider the state of religious activities at Stanford in the light of the Berry Fund's potential for making improvements. He named me as chair of this new group, I then being a professor of history and part-time associate dean of the School of Humanities. To the *Daily* I framed the committee's agenda as follows: "What aren't we doing that we could be doing to provide a richer religious life on campus?" I made it clear that our agenda would be inclusive: "We will be involved in a range of questions, from fairly sophisticated issues about the place and purposes of religious activities on campus, to specific issues, such as how exactly to spend the increase provided by this generous gift [the Berry Fund]."

The LASSU committee report had paved the way; we soon found ourselves in agreement with them on the need to open up religious observance on campus and used the same reasoning to reconcile this conclusion with the provisions of the Founding Grant: the nondenominationalism of the Stanfords' day corresponded to a broader pan-sectarianism of the 1960s. By January we had provided a "Draft Statement on Religious Freedom at Stanford" very much in line with the earlier student recommendations.[14] We began to pursue immediate practical steps such as conversion of the off-campus unofficial chaplains to full-time (but unpaid) "chaplain's associates," and the development by the Counseling and Testing Center of a seminar in counseling "meeting weekly throughout the year" and offered to "all full-time and part-time campus ministers."

According to handwritten notes for his January 1965 presentation to the Committee on Academic Affairs of the board of trustees, Sterling did review the subject and made clear that he saw a need for changes. The chaplain's was "a big job—too big, I think, for present staff." The academic program in religious studies "by intellectual standards is qualitatively superior to the fare offered by the Chaplain. I mention this," he continued, "because whatever may be the problems related to the program of the Memorial Church, they tend to be intensified when that program is compared with the academic program—a comparison which is, I assure you, readily made by students."

While he referred to the work of the faculty committee, Sterling did not put forward our "Draft Statement." Rather, he introduced the topic by saying that he found "the language of the Founding Grant is difficult to interpret and apply—not least of all during a cycle of ecumenical interest." But he thought "Mrs. Stanford's desire for the university 'to avoid all denominational alliances, however slight the bond may be' could [be taken to] imply a desire to avoid restrictions, an implication which would be somewhat reinforced by the stipulation that religion is not to be a criterion for the admission of students to the University." He urged the Committee on Academic Affairs to "readdress itself to these problems at an early date," and he promised to assist by providing a staff review of previous trustee actions.[15]

In March I wrote Sterling that the members of my committee "stand ready to help in any way they can towards presentation of the 'Draft Statement on Religious Freedom at Stanford' to the forthcoming meeting of the Board of Trustees."[16] By April the tone was getting more urgent:

> I wonder whether the May meeting [of the board] is likely to be any more free to consider the . . . draft? We're getting a good many queries as to the products thus far of the Committee's deliberations, which I'm stalling off as best I can. Eventually, though, we're going to have to say something about our views on the subject, and I still think we'll emerge with a happier result if we can put this to the Board before the campus community returns to the question of its own accord.[17]

In the summer, a memo went from Fred Glover to his boss under large handwritten capital letters, "URGENT." Unless the president moved quickly to renew the mandate and membership of the Committee on Religious Activities, Chaplain Minto "will have picked many of the preachers for 1965–66." (The implication is that the quality of these appointments will suffer if the committee is not involved.) Glover continued, "I suspect that if much of 1965–66 goes by without some obvious accomplishments on this front, Mr. Berry is going to be unhappy—if he is not already—and certainly he is going to hit the ceiling if the only visible accomplishment turns out to be Trustees OK of Jewish and Catholic services being held on the campus!"[18]

By late September, Glover was telling Sterling: "Dick Lyman would like very much to have a chat with you about the work to be done by the Committee on Religion [sic] during the coming year. Sandy [Dornbusch, professor of sociology and a member of the committee] has reported to Dick concerning your discussions with Trustees on the issue, but he'd like to get his instructions first hand. . . . Dick also asked whether you had set up a search committee for a new person to work with or over Rabb [Minto]."[19]

What Dornbusch had communicated to me was that the trustees wanted a full description of the program of religious activities after the proposed reforms, before they would act on our "Draft Statement" of January. This delaying tactic caused something like consternation on the committee, and during the fall matters moved rapidly toward confrontation.

In October, I received a letter from LASSU requesting the addition of student members to our committee. At our first appointment in 1964 I had defended the absence of such representation, arguing, "It is better for committee members to consult and co-operate [with] student groups themselves than to count on their representation by, say, two student members, who may be ineffective and non-representative."[20] By October, this was clearly an untenable position, and after due deliberation the committee forwarded LASSU's request to the president with its endorsement; presidential approval was quick, but it did not avert LASSU's proceeding to vote a resolution asking the trustees "to change present policy to recognize the right of freedom of worship for all groups."[21]

With the passage of the LASSU resolution, our committee felt its collective back to the wall. Accordingly I wrote two letters to the president on its behalf. The cover letter thanked him for his prompt action on student membership—LASSU was to submit six names from which he would select three—and then

I explained why on the eve of a board meeting we were forwarding such a strongly worded argument for trustee action on the issue of freedom of worship. I wrote:

> For one thing, it was suggested that it would be unfair to send you this just *after* a meeting of the Board of Trustees, rather than just before it. Not that we expect that you can rearrange the agenda at this eleventh hour, but that you ought to have maximum freedom to make some mention of the matter if you saw fit, and to take into consideration our views in planning ahead to further Board meetings. We also wanted to take our stand *before* the new student members joined us, to establish that we were not simply responding to the pressure of their presence.[22]

The longer letter stating our position was indeed strongly worded. We described how circumstances had changed since we made our initial recommendation ten months earlier. Then things had been quiet; now there was "a substantial revival of student concern, as witnessed in the *Daily*'s series of articles and its editorials, the actions of LASSU, and the forceful and constructive advocacy of a group of students led by Messrs. Clark Brown and Bruce Campbell, and comprising representatives of the existing religious organizations on campus." There were more radical voices, too, but no "suggestion of intent on anyone's part to try to stretch 'worship services' to include socially or morally dubious activities that would be inappropriate for a major university in the contemporary world." The letter continued:

> We appreciate the concern for their fiduciary responsibilities that led members of the Board of Trustees to ask for fully detailed plans for the administration of a modified religious policy before they could consider modification of the ban on worship services. We believe, however, that it is impossible to draw up a complete blueprint in advance of the facts. . . . Scheduling of services, either in Memorial Church or elsewhere, in advance of any assurance that relaxation of the rules is forthcoming presents further difficulties, and indeed might have the effect of begging the basic question at issue; surely it will not be possible for the Board of Trustees to say, in effect, "We were prepared to act favorably on the recommendation to permit religious worship on campus, with suitable safeguards, but we find we cannot do so because of some scheduling difficulties." In sum, continuing doubts and frustrations on this broad issue of principle are having the effect of blocking intelligent planning and progress in

matters of day-to-day religious activity at Stanford. We find it difficult if not impossible to discuss other matters with the underlying issue undecided. To make recommendations for the expenditure of moneys allocated to "Memorial Church and related activities" becomes impossible when we do not know how the University intends to define this phrase.[23]

Indeed, we were too late to influence the November board agenda, but at the next meeting, in January 1966, Sterling finally pressed the trustees on the issue. After setting the stage with the development of religious studies on the academic side, the creation of the Berry Fund, and the presidential committee "exploring opportunities for . . . enrichment" of the program at Memorial Church, he informed the trustees:

> Growing out of last year's Committee work, a search is now underway—and it is about to zero on a target—for a top-flight man to be brought to the Church. The new man would have top responsibility for the program and activities centering on the Church. The search is for a man of eminence as a preacher and of effectiveness in relationships with students. It is hoped that the "Dean of the Chapel" would be an appropriate and agreeable title—one which would make possible continuation of the title of Chaplain for Mr. Minto. Also growing out of last year's Committee work was a recommendation "that worship services by any campus group (defined as consisting primarily of members of the Stanford community—students, faculty and staff and their families) be permitted in Memorial Church or elsewhere on campus, insofar as is practicable and consistent with the carrying out of the University's educational functions, and with the preservation of the main Sunday service in Memorial Church, free from conflicts of scheduling."[24]

He went on to remind the trustees that these recommendations had been reported to the board "last Spring and were again discussed last August and September," at which time the trustees' request for "specific details as to how facilities would be used and scheduled" was made. He reported the committee's conclusion that such a "complete blueprint" was impossible and that action now was required. With a sure tactical touch, he argued:

> I should like to see Stanford move in the direction of the Committee recommendations, and I believe that it would be helpful in the recruitment of the person whom we need for the Church if a decision could be made at an early date. I think that the recommendation of worship services "by *any* campus

group" . . . is too inclusive, and that this evaluation is implied in the Committee's recommendation that a Presidential Committee should be responsible for "recognition of campus religious groups and the scheduling of worship services."

Thus Sterling introduced a fresh reason for action, unrelated to student pressures: the need to be in a position to tell a prospective dean of the chapel what the job would entail henceforth. To reassure the trustees he found a way to amend the committee's (and LASSU's) recommendations in a conservative direction: "any campus group" was too broad and would have to go. Finally, he dealt with the portions of the Founding Grant that might seem to constitute obstacles and dismissed them readily—no leasing of facilities was being suggested and no "alliances" contemplated. He stated, "Indeed, the implication of an 'alliance' would seem to be greater when only one type of service is available and when that one type is conducted by a denominational minister—and I know of no desirable ministers who are nondenominational."

Faced with a board reluctant to undertake the unpleasant task of amending Mrs. Stanford's arrangements, the president had obviously proceeded cautiously—until caution lay in the direction of action to forestall rapidly building pressures on campus. When he did make his move, however, it was decisive.

There were further delays for consulting attorneys and others. As late as September 1966, the dean of students, Joel Smith, listed as number nine in a list of fourteen issues that he anticipated might arise in "crisis" form during the forthcoming academic year: "Non-Christian Worship. While I understand that it is virtually certain that this question will be completely resolved in advance of the beginning of Autumn Quarter, I believe it should be added to the list, because, should there be any difficulty to developing facilities for major non-Christian faiths, there would be very substantial faculty and student reaction."[25]

Not the least of the immediate consequences of all this was the arrival at Stanford of the Rev. B. Davie Napier, the master of Calhoun College at Yale, to be dean of the chapel. Ironically, worries about Lowell Berry's impatience to see some tangible results of his PACE contribution soon gave way to worries about his reaction to the flamboyant success of the new appointee, success deriving from his eloquent association of Memorial Church with a variety of activist causes on campus, particularly opposition to the war in Vietnam. While Napier's advocacy never stepped over the line separating violent from nonviolent protest, his acute sense of the cultural as well as political trends among students led him to be a very different kind of campus minister from anything a conservative businessperson like Berry could have imagined, much less encouraged. Indeed, he did ask that his funds be moved out of Memorial Church and used for something else.[26]

One reason why there were not major on-campus pressures for a decision on freedom of worship in early 1965 was the absorption of the community in a much more exciting controversy. In February, Stanford made lurid head-lines across the country—"Sex At Stanford," said *Newsweek* (March 1, 1965).

The origins of this were small-scale indeed. Some time in May 1964, the dean of women, Lucile Allen, had an informal lunch meeting with the as-sistant dean, Elizabeth Avery, and the Women's Council, an advisory, super-visory, and judicial group that linked the Dean's Office with student life in the dormitories. All but one of the eight members of the council were present. Ex-actly what was said at this meeting will never be known; no minutes were kept, and the matter only became the subject of serious investigation nine months later, when recollections differed on various points. But it is agreed that the deans raised the issue of the sexual content in courses taught by the English Department, which had been brought to their attention by undergraduate stu-dent dormitory counselors, called "sponsors" at Stanford. Council members responded with instances in which class discussions or theme subjects had embarrassed women students. But they did not feel that the English courses caused significant changes in the sexual value structures of the students, that there was any general overemphasis on sexual materials, or that the material presented was erotically stimulating.[27]

It is clear that Dean Allen "suggested that Council Members inquire among students about theme topics with sexual content and report to her. . . . The students' reports would be kept confidential and would serve as docu-mentation for any reports by Dean Allen to the department head." According to the recollections of most council members present, these reports were to deal with the content of classroom discussions as well as theme topics; other members, and the deans, thought they were limited to theme topics.

There apparently was not a lot of discussion of this; the two council mem-bers responsible for the freshman dormitories offered to cooperate, but the chair-elect of the council, Nora Crow, objected, saying if she ran into a prob-lem she would prefer to take it up directly with the instructor.[28] At this, Dean Allen "said that the investigation should not be pursued in view of the opposition of the Chairman-elect. Accordingly, no action was ever taken on Dean Allen's proposal, and there was no mention of the suggestion at subsequent Council meetings."

Relations between council members and the dean, never easy, deteriorated in October in controversy over a proposed series of articles for the *Daily* concerning the council. On October 28, at a regular appointment with her honors adviser, Bliss Carnochan, who was an assistant professor of English, Miss Crow poured out some of her grievances, including the May proposal for reports on English Department courses. Professor Carnochan asked her to write an account of the May meeting. On November 12, Miss Crow brought him a statement signed by three persons who were present at that meeting. The students included in their version all events that were recalled by at least two of the three signers.

Carnochan reported all this to a senior colleague, Albert Guerard, who was a member of the Executive Committee of the Academic Council; neither man thought that he had an obligation to take the matter further, but the students meanwhile were awaiting action by the faculty members. In January, Nora Crow and a former chair of the Men's Council, Darrell Halverson, decided to prepare a report on the student judicial system, to include an account of the May episode. After learning of this, Guerard informed the Executive Committee of the plan, and things escalated at an accelerating rate. The students discussed possible publication of their report with several members of the faculty and administration; virtually all urged them not to publish. On January 30, Crow and Halverson showed their report to Sanford Dornbusch, professor of sociology and a member of the Executive Committee, who told them "that the Executive Committee should be requested to investigate these serious allegations and that publication prior to investigation would be irresponsible." But by this time rumors of the report's existence and garbled versions of its content were rife. Although the Executive Committee did launch an investigation on February 2, Crow and Halverson, together with the editor of the *Daily*, decided to publish, "based on their judgment that disclosure of the allegations in their full context would do less damage to the English Department, Dean Allen and the Women's Council, and would direct greater attention to issues in student judicial process, than would the dissemination of a somewhat garbled and anonymous publication."

In the *Daily*'s thundering editorial on February 4 (in the same issue as the publication of the report), no worries about doing damage are discernible: "In suggesting the instigation of an almost 'Kafkaesque' system of informing, the Dean of Women has clearly overstepped her prerogatives and, in some measure, has simply abrogated her right to a position of authority. . . . The Dean's action suggests disrespect for the intelligence and dignity of both students and faculty. It also calls into question an administration which would, by ignorance or apathy, permit a climate within which such a breach of academic freedom could occur." The report of the ad hoc committee of the Executive Committee was submitted to the parent committee and the president on February 12.[29] This was a remarkably clear and scrupulously careful narrative and analysis, especially for a document on so complicated a subject produced in ten days. Even Dean Allen, in a "reply" ten days later that ran to three-quarters the length of the document on which she was commenting, could produce scarcely any rebuttal on the facts. She claimed that her suggestion would have applied only to theme topics, not classroom discussions, but on this the recollections of a majority of the council members disagreed with hers. Strains between her and council members she saw as "inherent in the very nature of the relationship between students, faculty and administration; they are completely normal and they are to be expected."[30] But here, too, she was in the minority.

The ad hoc committee's conclusions, endorsed by the parent committee, were clear and forthright:

> 1. Neither Dean Allen nor the Women's Council members allege that the general level of attention to sexual materials in English Department courses is excessive or inappropriate. 2.There are no allegations of sexual misconduct between faculty and students in the English Department. 3. Dean Allen's proposed investigation of the teaching of English courses was not in accord with what we regard as proper procedures in an institution devoted to academic freedom. 4. The working relationship between Dean Allen and the Women's Council has been, and continues to be, marked by ineffective communication and mutual mistrust. We do not believe that there is a reasonable prospect of establishing satisfactory working relations between Dean Allen and the Women's Council. 5. Our observations confirm the importance and urgency of the ongoing student-faculty-administration efforts to clarify and revise the Stanford judicial process.

That there was actually controversy about whether to publish the report illustrates how easily Stanford leadership could now be rattled. Apparently Robert Minge Brown, trustee and university general counsel (a conflict of interest that escaped the attention of everyone for years), believed it was "libel-ous on its face." He went on to point out that if malice can be proven, even a defense based on truth is useless, and that the "truth" of assertions about such things as just how bad relations between the dean and the Women's Coun-cil had become would obviously be pretty difficult to establish beyond ques-tion. He noted "that the possibility of a libel action is not remote, as he has confirmed—through conversations with Vin Cullinan—that Dean Allen has indeed consulted Vin."[31]

Fortunately, cooler heads prevailed. Gerald Gunther (a member of the ad hoc committee) and two distinguished Law School colleagues, Professor Marc Franklin and Dean Bayless Manning, worked all night to produce an argument against any attempt by the university "to buy the Dean's resigna-tion and promise not to sue in exchange for an agreement not to publish the report. . . . Existence of the report is widely known, and suppression would inevitably produce suspicion and rumor. The healthy atmosphere created by the University's prompt appointment of the Committee would be largely dis-sipated." Other reasons advanced included the judgment that "without Pub-lication, Dean Allen would be under a worse cloud than with publication. Many would infer serious guilt from suppression." Besides, "libel and slander suits are rare because they are exceedingly dangerous to the plaintiff. (Re-member Oscar Wilde.) Any trial of the present matter would be apt to be far more harmful to the lady than to the University. The report is most circum-spect, given the testimony received."[32]

The three urged immediate resignation by Dean Allen, and if she balked at that, prompt dismissal. Her resignation was announced February 15, as shortly thereafter were those of both the associate deans who had accompa-nied her at the May 1964 meeting and the two assistant deans, in protest at the university's handling of the matter.

Sterling's relief at her decision not to pursue legal remedies is apparent in his letter of February 17 to two San Francisco lawyers, John Bennett King and Charles F. Jones, which read in part, "I am profoundly grateful to you and Chuck. Dean Allen has my gratitude for her service to Stanford and my sym-pathy for recent events. Those put her under very great strain; even so, she retained her dignity and composure—no mean accomplishment! I'm sure that you and Chuck helped her immeasurably to do so. . . . I shall remember always your good offices." In a letter to someone apparently considering of-fering a position to Lucile Allen, Sterling gave a mixed report on her abilities, but concluded, "I regret greatly the circumstances leading to her resignation here. Two students wrote a report about her which was published (despite our efforts to the contrary) in the student newspaper. The allegations in the report were not altogether justified, but her effectiveness here, already in doubt, was undermined."[33]

It seems a fair summary. But in hindsight it seems clear that, whatever the strengths and weaknesses of Lucile Allen as dean of women, the structure of which she was part was doomed by changes in the broader society from which Stanford could no longer be a refuge. Separate deans for men and women had no future—Allen had no successor—and the Men's Council and Women's Council would be swept away in the long, tangled struggle to reform the mechanisms for holding students accountable for their behavior at the university. It might have seemed a change of subject, but it was not surprising that the ad hoc committee's recommendations in the Allen case wound up stressing "the importance and urgency of the ongoing student-faculty-administration efforts to clarify and revise the Stanford judicial process."

Nor is it surprising that the *Daily*'s fulminations against the administration for tolerating "a climate within which such a breach of academic freedom could occur" concluded with a demand for greater communication: "The administration, which holds the largest share of practical power in this community, has rarely, if ever, participated in a[n] open, public discussion of university problems. . . . It is to be sincerely hoped that in dealing with this document [the Crow/Halverson report] the administration, students and faculty will set a precedent for open, free, and public discussion as is befitting a great university."[34]

A direct outcome of the Lucile Allen controversy was the creation of the Committee of Fifteen (C-15)—five faculty chosen by the Executive Committee of the Academic Council (and later, when the Senate came into being, through its mechanisms), five administrators appointed by the president, and five students, chosen through LASSU on recommendation of the ASSU president. On February 19, 1965, the *Daily* editorial called for "a student-faculty-staff committee to study the problem of intra-University communications." On March 29 the *Daily* spoke of the C-15 having been created on March 10 to consider the LASSU Judicial Competence Bill.[35]

In mid-April there was a flurry of activity involving C-15 that seemed to show Stanford solving problems that were baffling others. On April 19, the *Daily* congratulated Sterling and his administration for their "determined effort . . . to avoid the kind of paralysis of understanding which, at Berkeley, left men of general good will on all sides no choice but to go for each other's throats."[36] It is easy now to say these felicitations were premature—the reform of the student judicial system that led to the editorial proved far from satisfactory in the event—but the creation of C-15 was an important step in enabling Stanford to deal peaceably with at least some campus issues that might otherwise have exploded.

An example was university policy on open houses in the dormitories. Efforts to relax regulation of the hours during which men and women might be permitted in one another's rooms without wholly abandoning the principle of such regulation had by the end of the academic year 1965–66 led to an impasse between the University Committee on Student Affairs and Services and LASSU. The latter, preempting the authority of the former to make recommendations to the president in this area, adopted its own variant of reform as an ASSU by-law, superceding university policy and creating a "conflict-in-law" that threatened to paralyze the enforcement system.

The issue was referred to C-15, which arrived at a proposed resolution of the issues in November 1966 that probably pleased no one but appeased nearly everyone—perhaps the best to be hoped for in such times of rapid change and ceaseless controversy. It adopted a "basic regulation," but it allowed departures by individual "living groups" (Stanford-ese for dorms); the regulations could be made more restrictive for the house by simple majority vote, but could also be made more liberal (within an overall prohibition of open houses between 2:30 a.m. and 10:00 a.m.) by a three-fourths vote. In other words, there was to be a local option with protection against peer pressure.

In 1965, the emphasis of campus activism shifted decisively to the war in Vietnam. There had been rumblings, such as the controversy over bomb shelters and Kit Havice's lonely protest at commencement in the spring of 1963, and sufficient concern on the part of the administration and the Committee on University Policy to produce a comprehensive statement of policy on demonstrations in February 1964. This read as follows:

> Because the rights of free speech and peaceable assembly are fundamental to the democratic process, Stanford supports the rights of students and other members of the University community to express their views or to protest against actions and opinions with which they disagree. The University also recognizes a concurrent obligation to maintain on the campus an atmosphere

conducive to academic work; to preserve the dignity and seriousness of University ceremonies and public exercises; and to respect the private rights of all individuals. The following regulations are intended to reconcile these objectives: Campus demonstrations may be conducted in areas which are generally available to the public, provided such demonstrations: 1. Are conducted in an orderly manner; 2. Do not interfere with vehicular or pedestrian traffic; 3. Do not interfere with classes, scheduled meetings and ceremonies; or with other educational processes of the University; 4. Are not held (a) within University buildings, stadia, amphitheaters or fields while University functions are in progress therein, or (b) in the private residential areas of the campus.

While not blatantly unreasonable, these regulations constituted a more restrictive code than might be obvious on their face, as an episode a few weeks later made clear. At the annual review by the university president of the ROTC graduates in the Sunken Diamond, half-a-dozen students standing in the rearmost row of the bleachers attempted to hold aloft the flag of the United Nations. As one of them wrote later, explaining his decision to leave Stanford, "Our purpose was to protest the maintenance of the Stanford R.O.T.C. program in its present form by contrasting the U.N.'s efforts towards a peaceful world (symbolized by the flag) with the glorification of military forces taking place on the field."

Despite the fact that the students were silent and blocked no one's view of the ceremonies, their flag was seized and removed from the stadium by a Stanford police officer. Apparently, raising the flag in the stadium constituted a violation of the fourth regulation. Just a few years later Stanford administrators would have been happy to settle for so innocuous a "demonstration."[37]

The year 1964 was "Freedom Summer" in Mississippi, and students from Stanford and Yale, recruited by the charismatic Allard Lowenstein, constituted the core of an effort that produced frequent headlines back on campus. Their experience contributed significantly to bringing "the Farm" into the real world of political strife. Antiwar efforts took various forms over the two years that followed: rallies, teach-ins (including one in May 1965 that lasted from noon into the wee hours of the following morning), a campaign against United Technologies' plans to build a plant to manufacture napalm in Redwood City, in which Stanford students took part, as did a couple whose names would become better known shortly, H. Bruce Franklin, associate professor of English, and his wife, Jane. But opinion was still divided; the May 1965 teach-in included spokespeople favoring the war as well as critics.[38] A student group calling itself CONSCIENCE collected sixteen hundred signatures on a petition backing the existing Vietnam policy in November 1965, and a Stanford Political Union poll showed "that 63% of the Stanford community favored U.S. policy."[39]

In March 1965, a Stanford chapter of Students for a Democratic Society (SDS) quietly received approval as a campus student organization, after filling out the requisite forms. The applicants offered a list of members totaling sixteen, of which only one was female. Their purpose was "to prepare students to build a truly democratic society in America, beginning with the university & the ghetto," and the group indicated that "the structure and procedure of SDS shall be according to the principles of 'participatory democracy.' "[40]

In late February 1966, Selective Service Director Lewis B. Hershey announced that standardized tests would be offered as a means for college students to persuade their draft boards that they deserved continued deferment. This was by way of a return to policies that had been in effect until 1962, and at first it stirred no reaction at Stanford. But in April the faculty at San Francisco State voted to oppose administration of the examinations, and interest in the topic picked up. Still, the test was scheduled to be offered at Stanford to those interested on May 14 and 21, and not until May 12 did the Stanford Committee for Peace in Vietnam (SCPV) raise objections to it. On May 14, SCPV distributed copies of two documents produced by SDS nationally: a "National Vietnam Exam," a catechism concerning the horrors of the war, and a "Call for an Examination of Conscience," which told the test-takers, "When you kill a man, you kill a man. And we think you'd better know what you're doing when you do it."[41]

Administration of the Selective Service examinations by the university was attacked on several grounds. It represented cooperation with the hated war effort. It served a privileged class—those well enough off to be in college in the first place. Together with providing grades and class ranking to Selective Service (which the university did upon request by the individual student), it had the effect of distorting one's academic process: "Professors cannot escape the knowledge that the grades they assign their students may condemn them to the front lines."[42]

At least retroactively, SCPV explained its failure to take more drastic action against the first round of the exam on the grounds that the special meeting of the Academic Council set for May 17 would be taking up the matter. How they reconciled this with their charge that "the Academic Council in effect abdicated its responsibility in a life and death matter to students by shelving the decision until after one of the deferment tests was to have been given" was not clear; had SCPV not "in effect" joined this "abdication" by withholding action on May 14? On May 17, more than three hundred faculty debated the university's role in relation both to the draft and to classified research for almost two hours. In the end, they voted overwhelmingly to direct the council's Executive Committee to take up both matters and make recommendations to the next meeting of the council, no later than June 10.

On May 16, SCPV wrote to the president requesting that the forthcoming exam be cancelled; the next day they wrote again, to "invite" him to attend an open meeting on May 19 to discuss the outcome of the Academic Council meeting. Sterling replied that he would be in San Francisco at board of trustees' meetings on May 19, but would be happy to meet privately with leaders of SCPV. SCPV meanwhile was phoning local news media that there might be acts of civil disobedience at Stanford, possibly including occupation of the President's Office, following a noon rally in White Plaza the next day.[43]

At the rally, John Black, director of the Counseling and Testing Center, sought and was denied a chance to speak. No doubt he wanted to say publicly what he had written SCPV privately: being willing to send academic information "to a draft board at a student's request is a service to the student and certainly constitutes no endorsement of [the] Selective Service System or the war in Vietnam." To refuse to do so "would be to coerce the student into accepting one point of view about the draft system."[44]

From the rally, around one hundred marched to the Inner Quad and into Building 10, which housed the President's Office. Secretaries went on with their work as best they could; Miss Lillian, at Stanford since the 1920s, told one protester, "This is darned tomfoolery. You ought to be ashamed of yourselves." Some protestors brought in pet dogs, others guitars and radios. The leaders met with Robert Wert, dean of undergraduate studies, who told them the president would not meet "under duress" and would not promise an open meeting as a condition of their ending the sit-in. The protestors voted in favor of disrupting the tests if they were held and against holding a student referendum on the issues.

With the end of the normal business day, students relaxed in their new environment. By 8:30 p.m. the lobby looked like the setting of an informal party rather than a protest against university involvement in the Selective Service test. Placards declaring "I am just unexpendable" and "Uncle Sam needs cannon fodder" had been propped against the door as students listened to rock-and-roll tunes and Joan Baez folk songs.[45]

The next day things got more intense. Students protesting against the sit-in marched outside Building 10 with placards reading "Down with Mob Rule," "We support President Sterling," and "Academic Freedom and Responsibility." Inside, the demands shifted. As usual, the procedural began to dominate; rather than seriously hoping to prevent the test from taking place, the sitters-in concentrated on the president's refusal to meet, or to promise an open meeting later. The procedural focus allowed both a narrowing and broadening of the issues—narrowing in that substantive changes were no longer stressed, broadening in such statements as this, issued from the protesters Friday morning: "We believe that students do not exist for the university, but that the university exists for its students. Consequently, it must recognize our rights to a major role in making policy. We demand the right to make decisions which affect our lives. This protest initiates our campaign to democratize the university."[46]

For its part, the administration distributed copies of the 1964 policy on demonstrations and declared the sit-in a violation of that policy; the process of prosecuting violators was under way. Friday night the protesters tried to engage members of the faculty Executive Committee in pressing Sterling for an open meeting. The answer delivered by law professor Herbert L. Packer Saturday morning on behalf of himself and three other Executive Committee members was clear: "As several of us assured you at various times during the day yesterday, the Executive Committee is planning to hold open hearings [on the draft]. Unless you disbelieve these assurances, there is no impasse. We urge you to terminate your defiance of university regulations."[47] The other three signers were Kenneth Arrow, Gordon Wright, and Albert Guerard.[48] Saturday morning, too, the draft exam was taken by some eight hundred students, and administrators began taking the names of those sitting in.

At 2:30, SCPV declared itself defeated: "We have met with harassment and intimidation. The punitive process of the university's judicial procedure has been set in motion. Our several concessions were met with no willingness whatsoever on the part of President Sterling to negotiate with us."[49] In a leaflet, the protesters whined: "During the sit-in no more than seven faculty members bothered even to appear before us to ascertain what they could do to help, or even to get accurate information on the issues and negotiations that were under way. . . . At a time when united action was called for between faculty and students, the faculty acted not independently but in effect as an arm of the Administration."[50]

Initially, the *Daily* editorialized, "The dissenters are unjustified in demanding that the University foist their moral code upon the entire male segment of the student body." But the editorial on May 24 was headed "Intransigence Forever?" and, while it remarked that the protesters' demand that the university cease cooperating with Selective Service "had little popular support," the editorial went on to describe Sterling's gradual loss of contact with ordinary students over the preceding five years, for which the writers blamed his increased burdens during the PACE campaign. "Last weekend's protesters made several attempts to compromise, and by Friday evening were demanding only that the President *or* his representative participate in an open meeting to discuss decision-making at Stanford. Sterling's arrogant refusal demonstrated once again the intransigence that has become peculiarly his when asked to deal with students on any but his own terms."

The Student Judicial Council held hearings quickly—the end of the academic year loomed. At a "marathon eight-hour session" on May 26, the council received pleas of nolo contendere from thirty-six students involved in the sit-in. The council's verdict, however, raised as many questions as it resolved. First, while the council did find defendants guilty, to avoid the possibility of a conflict between university regulations and LASSU legislation, it based its verdict not on a violation of the university policy on demonstrations but on the "Fundamental Standard." This caused President Sterling to write to the council's chair "to make it clear that, if there be a possibility of conflict, the University regards its regulations as being paramount to LASSU action, in accord with the resolution of the Board of Trustees, 21 March 1963, in approving the ASSU Constitution."[51]

Second, the penalty imposed by the council created fresh difficulties. Defendants were placed on probation, but with an additional requirement that they take part in a series of seminars "with individuals representing the administration and faculty . . . to investigate the existing decision-making structure of the University, and to reach consensus recommending possible improvements."[52]

This created all sorts of obvious problems and was rejected by the president as basically infeasible. Amidst the confusion, the deadline for the university to appeal the council's decision to the Interim Judicial Board, an all-faculty body, was allowed to pass, and members of the administration found themselves debating whether to ignore the deadline and appeal anyhow—obviously a distasteful proceeding that would provide all sorts of undesirable precedents for subsequent deadline violators.[53]

Small wonder that Robert Minge Brown called regretting "that it has not been made abundantly clear that the university's regulations must and will be enforced; and that if the students don't enforce them, the University will."[54] Mail poured in from fund-raising volunteers, saying things like this, from a veteran Stanford supporter in Los Angeles:

> I am sick about the conditions at Stanford and the image they have created in the minds of the public. Unfortunately my feelings seem to be shared by all of the Stanford alumni with whom I have come in contact. Many of them have been loyal and effective workers in raising money and most have been contributors. One of these volunteered last week—"I'm through." He was one of those large potential givers upon whom I have been hopefully working, who is capable of making our [athletic] pavilion campaign a success.[55]

University Relations was reduced to pointing out that the sit-in . . . failed to achieve its announced goal, that of stopping the Selective Service examination. It also failed in a secondary objective, that of goading the university into removing students from the President's Office by force before national television cameras.[56] Probably this "secondary objective" was simply a plausible conjecture on Nelson's part. I have encountered no evidence of discussion, either of calling in the police or of "goading" the administration into doing so during the sit-in.

No one can have emerged from this episode with much feeling of achievement. SCPV's statement abandoning the protest admitted that they had been "defeated," but claimed that this was "the first round of a wider struggle to democratize the university's power structure—a defeat which clearly exposes the moral failure and the intransigence of the administration, as well as the irresponsibility of the faculty."[57] In the numerous letters published in the *Daily* on May 25, criticism of the sit-in exceeded support. The belatedness of the protest was repeatedly condemned (as indeed it was in the text of the Judicial Council's ruling): to one letter writer it was striking "that the demonstrators' moral revulsion to the test had materialized overnight." Civil disobedience must meet a stern test: "As an appeal to the public conscience, it must carry such moral justification as to overcome the democratic presumption against extra-legal methods of protest."[58] In failing to use "normal channels (such as the Committee of Fifteen)" over the months since the scheduling of the draft exam had become known, the protesters had clearly not exhausted their remedies before resorting to coercion. Furthermore, and ironically, the same students who had protested the university's failure to provide condoms at the Health Service for those students who wanted them were now protesting the university's willingness to provide the draft exam for those students who wanted it.

The Executive Committee held its promised public hearing on June 1; about one hundred people attended, mostly veterans of the sit-in. In a session full of repetition—the university's false claims to "neutrality" being the favorite theme—the most powerful attack (to judge from copious notes taken by the head of the Stanford News Service, Bob Beyers) came from one who would be heard often in the next few years: H. Bruce Franklin, associate professor of English.[59] Providing transcripts of grades to Selective Service was one thing, but

> computing class standing and providing that to draft boards was "outrageous. . . . It converts the University into a jungle where academic performance places [one's] classmates in a position of vulnerability . . . to make this class standing a matter of life and death seems indefensible. . . . There's a very good likelihood that if college people were being drafted in this war, the war would not continue." Part of the popular support for the war stems from the fact that those in most influential positions are least likely to suffer personal losses.

On June 10, some two hundred members of the Academic Council spent four hours finding ways to touch all the bases on the draft controversy. "The grading system may be distorted by pressures extrinsic to the purposes and function of a university," they said. "We feel that the long-term loss to the nation attending such pressures will outweigh their short-term contributions to our military effectiveness." But at the same time they "expressed general approval of the university's present Selective Service policies" of making class standings available and providing the site for the draft examinations. They nevertheless urged Sterling "to join with other university presidents in urging the government 'to explore alternative arrangements for meeting the nation's military requirements.'"[60] For good measure the council applauded Sterling's "tactful and patient" handling of the sit-in. Obviously the faculty had just begun to tap into its capacity for squaring the circle.

For many at Stanford the more striking event of spring 1966 was the election of David Harris as student body president. Harris was a 6'2", shaggy, bearded, jeans-wearing major in social thought and institutions from Fresno. In the spring of 1962, Harris had been chosen Fresno High School's "Boy of the Year."[61] But in three years at Stanford he had changed considerably. No sooner was he in college when Allard Lowenstein's recruitment drew thirteen Stanford students to Mississippi to help in holding the "Freedom Vote," a mock election carried out simultaneously with the actual polling to dramatize the extent to which blacks had been denied the franchise in Mississippi. Although he did not attend the campus meeting where the project was described, half an hour of discussion in the corridors of Wilbur Hall was enough to convince freshman David Harris that he should go. He phoned home to convey this momentous news: "My father responded in the voice that always signaled me that he was pissed off, saying I should stick to studying and make sure I got to my job waiting on tables in the dining hall punctually. He hoped Mississippi Negroes got to vote, but he was not about to pay Stanford tuition in order to supply them with a campaign worker. I went back upstairs and unpacked my bag."[62]

The assassination of John F. Kennedy the following month jolted Harris definitively out of his conventional self, though it took another year before he took any definitive action. Then, in late October 1964, he reenacted the going-to-Mississippi decision—again not attending the recruiting meeting, again deciding on the spur of the moment to go. Nearly twenty years later he wrote, "I still don't altogether understand why, out of nowhere, I jumped at that opportunity. Part of it must have been an urge to adventure, to be tested. Part of it was being bored with life at the university."[63]

This time he did not call home. With four others he drove to Jackson, arriving early Sunday morning, October 18. On the evening of October 21, the senior who had driven the car went out to mail a letter. His car was forced off the road by four whites in a truck who then beat, kicked, and urinated on him. When this story hit the California newspapers, police in Mississippi told Harris he was a suspect. Harris wrote of the experience, "This was too much for us. Twenty minutes later Morse [the senior] and I fled across the state to the town of Columbus, rendezvoused with the other two Stanford sophomores, and headed back to school the next morning."[64]

They arrived Monday morning, October 26, having been away just ten days, about four of them in transit. Yet this brief and fruitless Mississippi adventure became a central feature of the Harris legend, to which he himself returned often as an explanation for all that followed: "Essentially, when I was in Mississippi it wasn't as big a thing as when I got back, because when I got back I really started thinking about what I'd done there. I got involved in the whole antiwar activity, from there it was a natural educational progression. The South wasn't just a boil on the face of America. The hate and brutality there were indigenous to the way America lives."[65] During the next year and a half, David Harris spent some time spinning his wheels. He later wrote, "My brief Mississippi adventure had flooded my life with new and unsettling information and provoked an irresolution that would plague me for several more months. I was no longer sure how I felt about the country I lived in. I still wanted to pursue something 'meaningful' and 'worthwhile,' but nothing of that order seemed even remotely within reach. That feeling wouldn't change until I finally met Allard Lowenstein early in 1965."[66]

Lowenstein's appeal was simple and direct: individuals mattered; "the course of history could be shaped by a single person." Each person should therefore take life seriously and seek to make a difference. Continued Harris, "My own adolescent sense of worthlessness was rampant enough so that to hear that I mattered was a need as great as any I then possessed. Allard hooked into it right away."[67]

He became one of the long succession of Lowenstein protégés, driving him on his endless errands of advocacy, heeding his advice to move into Stern Hall at Stanford, the dorm in which Allard, during his year as a Stanford assistant dean, had instilled pride in leading an activist nonfraternity life. A bit later Harris became a sponsor in the freshman dorm, Wilbur, and began to make a name for himself in student politics by engaging in battles with the university administration over the degree of autonomy that such student dorm assistants should have. He also began to take part in antiwar protests, veering quickly to the simplest available position: total opposition without concern for tactical advantage. He later described his outlook and that of his friends as follows:

> We treated all our thoughts as discoveries of immense magnitude. . . . People, we agreed, were no more and no less than what they acted out. Explanations were bullshit. What mattered was what you did. Means and ends were the same thing. You either embodied your values fully in the present, or you didn't have any. Hypocrisy, we agreed, was pernicious and everywhere, disguised as the ethic of deferred gratification and the politics of compromise.[68]

Such was the young man who reluctantly agreed in late March 1966 to run for president of the ASSU, after being assured that his would be "an educational campaign" and that he would "be lucky to get 200 votes."[69]

His platform minced no matters. He called for the elimination of the Board of Trustees and of fraternities, legalization of marijuana, the option to take all classes on a pass-fail basis, and "the end of all university cooperation with the conduct of the war in Vietnam."[70]

Such, at least, is his recollection; the *Daily* did not publish the platforms of the various candidates. But it did pose a series of questions to them, one of which was, "What do you think the government's policy should be on drafting students out of college, and how do you foresee that you might attempt to have this policy brought about at Stanford?" Most candidates had little to say about this, and none launched a serious criticism of the draft as it stood, except for this somewhat whimsical reply from the Harris/Collins ticket:

> We see little reason why, if America must blow the brains out of its youth, it should use the best brains. College attendance is not really a good measure, though, since it discriminates *de facto* against minority and poverty-stricken groups, and is more a badge of socio-economic status than much else. Rather, we propose a rationality test, made up of a law allowing conscientious objection to a particular war. Anybody who would support a war as irrational as the one in Vietnam would obviously flunk the test.[71]

It is not hard to see how the Harris candidacy baffled contemporary observers.

Eschewing the coats and ties and campaign paraphernalia of the other candidates, Harris was clearly the maverick. The *Daily* was unimpressed. In an editorial headed "A Non-endorsement," it classified the eight candidates as flyweights, bantamweights, welterweights, and middleweights. Harris and a fraternity-row candidate were welterweights. "Harris is not running to win but rather to protest. He has presented a platform of ideas, most of them laudable, but a few of them laughable, in a commendable attempt to promote discussion of significant issues among the remaining candidates. He is too radical to win, however, and if he were to win, too unrealistic and dogmatic to accomplish anything."[72] Finding no heavyweights in the race, the *Daily* held itself aloof. But win Harris did, emerging from the first round as the leading candidate with 26 percent of the vote, and then winning the runoff with 56 percent of the largest vote in the history of student body elections at Stanford.

Within weeks, the sit-in against Selective Service examinations took place. The ASSU president-elect was not prominent in the preparation for this event; in fact his attitude was ambivalent—opposed to university collaboration with the war effort, yet reluctant to deny fellow students the opportunity to secure deferment. During the sit-in, he was reported to be attempting, in vain, to mediate the dispute.[73]

This inglorious beginning aside, Harris's election was indeed a galvanizing event. It added fuel to the fires of alumni discontent, as headlines across the country proclaimed the victory of an unkempt radical in what had been supposedly one of the more conservative campuses—Berkeley's opposite number, so to speak. At Stanford expectations rose rapidly as this outspoken exception to all the normal rules of student politics came suddenly to the fore. Wrote Harris looking back, "My life would never be the same. In an age when students were on everyone's mind, I had been suddenly transformed into California's most notorious student-body president. I pictured myself as the messenger for a whole list of truths, and by embodying them I hoped to act as the vehicle through which they gained ascendancy."[74]

In a letter to the chair of the Executive Committee of the Academic Council, he was a good deal more down-to-earth, though ambitious enough:

Dear Professor Hilgard: Needless to say, there has been great confusion surrounding my election since I became a fit topic for national journalism and alumni paranoia. As I stated during the campaign, my central concern is with bettering Stanford as an educational institution. Such an indistinct goal would hardly seem to conflict with anyone's perspective on Stanford. Looking at next year, three efforts hold particular value in my mind: 1. Extensive reformation of the requirements surrounding academic work, 2. Involvement of students in *all* the University decision-making processes concerned with the community at large and particularly student issues, 3. The establishment of an experimental college to explore new approaches to education. I hope that we might be able to meet and discuss these problems and speak to the prospects of next year. Sincerely yours, David V. Harris, ASSU President, 1966–1967[75]

Harris worked on all three of these objectives, with mixed success. He stimulated the creation of "The Experiment," a student-run program that offered a variety of very nontraditional "courses" and that eventually evolved into the Midpeninsula Free University, but meanwhile was soon active in pushing Harris's antidraft effort, "The Resistance." He never got to the battlefield in reform of the curriculum, but found himself at loggerheads with Herbert L. Packer, vice provost and chair of the administration-sponsored Study of Education at Stanford (SES), over the method for appointing the three student members of its eight-person steering committee. Packer, while willing to consult with ASSU and others about candidates, insisted on appointing them himself. It is fair to say that Harris's interest in this whole project was limited, since he inevitably regarded it as a creature of the Stanford establishment. The SES steering committee was among the last to evade the ASSU nominations mechanism for students on committees. By 1969, with the expansion and reform of the board of trustees carried out under John W. Gardner's leadership, ASSU was placing students on most of the committees of the board, though actual trusteeship was not extended to anyone employed by or enrolled in Stanford. This would surely have happened without David Harris (he was gone by 1969, of course), but it is fair to say that he did add energy and determination to the movement for formal recognition of a role for organized students in university governance.

Ironically, however, the Harris presidency ran into its greatest difficulty in conflicts with the legislature of ASSU. By mid-October, less than a month into the academic year, David Harris's nominees to the Committee of Fifteen came under fire for being a solid bloc from the New Left. He admitted that they were not broadly representative of the student body, but maintained that they were "cognizant" of the full range of views on campus— a defense that he would hardly have tolerated from any other appointing body. LASSU approved four, but balked at the fifth, Jan Handke. (The fact that she was the only female among the five does not seem to have been raised by either side in the argument.) He refused to withdraw her nomination, charging the legislature with indulging in "petty little political games." The *Daily*, which had called for "a slate of students who represent the entire student body, who have the respect to act freely [rather than as delegates] within the Committee, and who are not constrained to view the Committee of Fifteen as a center of political confrontation," was now caustic: Thursday night Harris challenged the independence of the legislature when he told the legislature that he viewed the Committee of Fifteen nominations as "a vote of confidence," and again when he informed the body that he would resubmit the name of the unconfirmed nominee at the next session.[76]

On October 20, Harris yielded and appointed Sara Syer in Handke's place.

As he was walking away from the LASSU session that evening, he was way-laid by a gang of Halloween-mask-wearing Delta Tau Delta members (one of the "football fraternities"), who dragged him into the shadows and forcibly shaved his head. Apparently disappointed that he did not struggle or cry out, they acceded to his request to spare his beard, but photographed the scene and sent the picture to the newspapers. Reactions were mixed, but largely negative. While some thought it humorous, a letter from twenty-three fraternity men condemned the attack as "unacceptable behavior in the university commu-nity," and one student called it "tantamount to symbolic castration."[77] One of the Delts told the *Daily*, "Harris really showed the Delts a lot of class. He made us feel sorry we did it."

Recalling this incident years later, Harris remarked, "My visibility in-creased. The David Harris presidency now had a slightly heroic tinge. Frankly, it had also peaked. Dealing with the university bureaucracy was like wrestling with a vat of Jell-O, and my 'radical' proposals were all soon lost in a morass of committees and commissions, being 'studied' into oblivion."[78]

The "peak" came about one month after the start of autumn quarter at Stanford. The "commissions" to which he refers no doubt mean the Study of Education at Stanford, which in the end produced a "reform" of graduation requirements amazingly close to Harris's own campaign proposal to abolish any requirements other than completion of 180 units of coursework: SES fa-vored allowing students to study what they want to study and faculty to teach what they want to teach.

For the rest, one's impression reading the *Daily* for those few weeks is that David Harris was having at least as much trouble with the rest of student gov-ernment as he was with the university hierarchy. He was also distracted. Dur-ing Christmas vacation he received notice that he had been reclassified as 1–A in the draft. On January 12, the same day that his draft board called him up for his physical exam, he told a crowd of four hundred at Stanford that they had "no right to send others to do your butchering" and urged them instead to "join me in jail." From that moment, building the Resistance became para-mount in David Harris's life.

The *Daily* was quick to pick up on this. Noting his White Plaza statement as personal, and noting also his silence recently about the issues of educa-tional reform that had dominated his campaign, the paper urged Harris to give "a status report on his two largest commissions, housing and education, and his efforts [to] promote 'real education.'"

In his first public statement this fall, the student body president put forth a challenge: "Anyone who has a hold on this University must justify his position in the face of the students. It is time for David Harris to answer that challenge in public."[79]

On February 23, 1967, the campus was startled to read the huge headline in the *Daily*: "Harris Resigns Presidency." His statement was brief:

> To the students of Stanford University: I am writing this letter to announce my resignation from the position of student body president. I have done all I am capable of doing for the realization of education at Stanford. I feel my contribution in the context of the presidency has been made. A response to the questions I have raised over the length of my term remains in the hands of the community.—David Harris

His remarks in an interview were slightly more revealing: "All the motivation for me being student body president, all the things I had hoped to say, I have said, I've said a number of times, and I don't think I can add to them anymore." And again: "My contribution has basically been to say things to the community that up to this point the community was afraid to say to itself. I was just a spokesman for a basic way of seeing the university that I felt had to be articulated if there was going to be any healthy notion of education."[80]

Some months later, in an interview with a writer for *Esquire*, he was more revealing still: "The job had become a trap for my mind. . . . I'd done my bit for education, I'd given over two hundred speeches at Stanford and was repeating myself. I'd lost real communication with students because they treated me like a famous figure, they'd just sit and watch me do it and weren't putting themselves on the line."[81]

What is striking about all of these explanations for his sudden action is that they are all about talking. One would never guess from reading them that being president of ASSU involved anything other than making speeches. As for what he had been trying to say about education, the *Esquire* piece is as good a source as any. Describing his election campaign, Harris says:

> The platform was a long list of changes based on the attitude that Stanford is not educating and has no understanding of what education is. Students have no right of control over their own lives. It's a system calculated on the impotence of the students in that it makes everything the student does something outside himself. What that does is teach people to be powerless. We started

from the initial statement that education is something that happens in your mind, the mind learning itself, learning how to use itself. It's a very inner process and the function that teachers traditionally serve in most of the cultures of the world—where they haven't gotten to modern industrial teaching which is essentially a training mechanism—is one of spiritual guidance. Not only should a teacher know things but also he should have an understanding, wisdom about things, beyond simply knowing them. So that a teacher provides himself as a mirror to the other person's mind and gives that person a glimpse into his own mind so that he can then start educating himself. The Stanford faculty makes a show of promoting intellectual inquiry, but in fact most people who teach at colleges are doing it for very simple security reasons and they don't like people to rock the boat even though they make a big thing about intellectual inquiry and all that. A professor will allow you to put down the administration but will get offended if you say the faculty is irrelevant, which they are, by and large, except for maybe ten people, and they're relevant as people because they've developed a style of living that really has relevance to other lives.[82]

As a critique of American higher education in the late 1960s this may seem a strange amalgam of the obvious ("Education is something that happens in the mind") and the not-so-obvious—the point about faculty being happy to hear students decry the administration but tetchy when their own performance is called into question. It is clear, however, that David Harris in person had a significant impact on people. The editor of the *U.C.L.A. Daily Bruin* met Harris at the 1966 National Students Association Congress and recalled:

I was confronted by him and he blew my mind. Dave's views on educational reform, on the Vietnam War, on the draft, are not based on political expediency. They follow naturally from his life-style, his mentality. His concern for his "soul," for his values, and for himself as a valuable person are manifested in his concern for the communities that he exists in, whether they are his school, city, or nation. He confronts you with this mentality, this concern for community, and you just can't pass over it without some self-examination, some thought on your role as a human being and how you're going to relate to other human beings. You can't meet Dave Harris and not change your life in some way.[83]

The commentary in the *Daily* when he quit office included this characteristic effusion from the dean of the chapel, Davie Napier: noting Harris's "authentic qualities of greatness," he went on, "How often do you see a man who, in being himself, can help you be and find yourself; in whom you are able to detect no deviousness at all; whose compassion is no less compassionate for being unsentimental; who cares like hell about the world he live[s] in, and can somehow go on loving and believing in the people who inhabit it, even while he protests the ways we go on lousing it up?"

Jan Jacobi, head of the ASSU Housing Commission, a David Harris ally, said, "David Harris's greatest contribution to Stanford has been that he, and he alone, by the strength of his convictions and the vision he holds of the ideal educational community, has changed the atmosphere of this University from one of stagnation to one where change is indeed possible."

My own comments as provost at the time were, I trust, understandably if also characteristically, more astringent: "David Harris is a man of many talents. I disagree with much that he has said and done, but there is no doubt that he has stimulated people—both opponents and supporters—to think about education at Stanford. I do not believe, as his brief note of resignation would seem to imply, that he has exhausted the possibilities for constructive leadership inherent in the office of student body president."[84]

After his resignation, David Harris, together with Dennis Sweeney, devoted himself to the frustrating task of trying to make the Resistance the key focus of the antiwar movement. Even Harris's charisma and Sweeney's reputation for heroic persistence in Mississippi could not make anything remotely resembling a mass movement out of the idea of going to jail for totally resisting Selective Service. The hope was that success would starve the armed forces and force an end to the war. But recruits to the Resistance were single individuals here and there. One marvels at Harris's faith and his courage—after all, each speech he gave urging others to follow his example exposed him to conspiracy charges that could (at least in theory) result in a five-year prison sentence. Between January 1968 and his incarceration in July 1969, he gave "over 500 speeches in 20 different states."[85]

It was also a time of great distraction in his personal life. His "infatuation" (his word) with Joan Baez, whom he had met in the course of fund-raising for the Resistance, grew apace and contributed to his gradual alienation from most of his old associates, Sweeney among them. Such things as her effort to clean him up and make him look more respectable played a part, as did the general disparity between them in age (she was five years his senior), as well as her fame and fortune. His later description of their mutual attraction has the ring of truth:

> She was treated as a legend wherever she went. Having a woman everyone else seemed to want was, at age 22, an overwhelmingly seductive proposition. Two months away from a felony trial at which I knew I would be found guilty, I felt as if I had little to lose. For her part, she reportedly thought I was the best speaker she had ever heard. I was something of a hero, too, and that charisma had its effects. Linked with me, she was now the beneficiary of the credibility generated by The Resistance's willingness to sacrifice for what we believed in.[86]

On March 26 David and Joan were married in New York City. As Harris wrote a dozen years later, "The entire course of the Sixties would be littered with strategies that had been given six months to succeed and then abandoned for something a notch more obstreperous."[87]

. . .

Such was the fate of the Resistance. Its high point was the turning in of more than two thousand draft cards nationally in mid-October 1967. According to Harris, by January 1969, the organization was split between "the proto-Leninists, [who] wanted to give up draft-resistance organizing and turn to something more 'militant' and 'working class . . . [and] the space cadets [who] wanted to give up draft-resistance organizing in favor of 'alternative life-styles.' They talked about founding communes in New Mexico and co-ops in Mendocino County and commencing the new world immediately."[88]

David Harris finally went to prison on July 15, 1969.[89] While he remained a hero to many on campus, Stanford's "movement" had moved on, essentially without him. Though there turned out to be quite a number of people on campus who were prepared to take part in brawls or hurl rocks through university windows, not many were ready to make the personal sacrifice that Harris made in going to prison. By the summer of 1968, as Harris wrote, "the formerly radical people such as I who broke the law by practicing civil disobedience rather than violence were considered 'moderate.' From 'radical' to 'moderate' was a long distance to come without ever once having changed your stance, but it was typical of the times."[90]

3 HOW I BECAME PROVOST

I CAME TO STANFORD IN 1958 to teach modern British history, after five years at Washington University in St. Louis. I had no thought of a career in administration. But at Washington University I had been more active in faculty affairs than assistant professors generally are. In 1962, I got a letter from Thomas H. Eliot, who had been a mentor to me in St. Louis, and who had become chancellor of the university meanwhile, inviting me to return as professor of history and dean of the college at Washington University. I was enormously complimented, but ambivalent: after all, if I found that I did not take to administration I would find myself back in the position I had decided to leave a few years earlier.

The eminent psychologist, Robert R. Sears, who was dean of humanities and sciences at Stanford, urged me to stay, pointing out that opportunities were bound to come along to try administration on a part-time basis at Stanford, with tenure in the History Department secure if I found I did not like it. To no small extent on the basis of that, I decided to stay. In the fall of 1963 the dean called to offer me a one-third-time associate deanship in his school. I accepted, took office on January 1, 1964, and, though the one-third-time turned out to be more like two-thirds (and I was still teaching four courses a year in history), I found it interesting and invigorating to be working to strengthen a number of humanities departments at Stanford during a time of growth and dramatic overall progress.

One of my areas of responsibility was an entity called the Institute for Hispanic American and Luzo-Brazilian Studies. This turned out to mean in practice the teaching and research life of one faculty member, Ronald Hilton, a professor in the then Department of Modern European Languages. Hilton despised what he called "belles lettres" and thrived on contemporary affairs in Latin America. A charismatic figure—tall and broad-shouldered with a leonine head and penetrating gaze—Hilton was also notoriously difficult to deal with administratively, and fierce in the defence of his little empire. This was disconcerting, since it seemed to us in the Dean's Office an unacceptable situation to have degrees so largely in the control of one person, especially since he was reported to follow such practices as giving academic credit to football players essentially for clipping the newspapers of the day for his convenience. When I began having to deal with him, the university was in the process of applying to the Ford Foundation for a massive grant in support of strengthening international studies across the school. The assistant dean, Raymond F. Bacchetti (later a Stanford vice president) and I decided to try to deal with Hilton not simply by nipping at his heels with bureaucratic attempts at reforming institute practices, but by giving him a real stake in the Ford largesse in return for conforming more adequately to school norms in academic matters. This seemed to be going well for a time, until we got a peremptory demand from the director for a bigger share of the Ford bounty, bigger than we were prepared to offer. After a very nasty telephone conversation, I received a curt letter from him resigning his position as director.

Ray and I believed that this was a power play to get more money for his institute. We also came to the conclusion that constructive cooperation with him was unlikely to succeed. We knew that there would be some uproar if we accepted the resignation, but we decided that it was worth it to clear up this long-standing source of trouble and academic embarrassment. I sent Hilton a note thanking him for his service and accepting his resignation.

It soon became obvious that he was totally shocked by this. The uproar was somewhat greater than we had anticipated; between two and three hundred letters supporting Hilton and upbraiding the university arrived in the next few weeks, largely from his former students. But word of Bacchetti's and my having dared to brave the lion in his den soon got around. I found myself invited to the president's staff meeting to describe how we had done it. The prevailing tone was one of bemused admiration; all of a sudden I had an unsought reputation at the highest level of the Stanford administration for having the courage of my convictions.

The redoubtable Fred Terman retired as vice president and provost in 1965, and a national search for a successor began. A couple of offers to distinguished outsiders were turned down, and the search seemed to lag; rumor had it that Sterling was not entirely displeased to be free of Terman's stern discipline, and in no hurry to find a replacement. Meanwhile, I was getting feelers from Haverford College, neighbor and rival of my alma mater, Swarthmore, in connection with their presidency, and also from the University of Washington about the deanship of arts and sciences there. In June I withdrew from the Washington search, but Haverford persisted. My expectation was to retire from the Dean's Office at Stanford at the end of 1966–67 and return to British history; I enjoyed teaching and fared well in student reviews. But my spouse said, "I don't think you've got administration entirely out of your blood just yet." In October we visited Haverford, met board members and such relevant neighbors as Katherine McBride, the president of nearby Bryn Mawr. Shortly thereafter I had a call from the board chair saying, "We'd like the next President of Haverford to be a Swarthmore man!"

I had decided that Jing was right, and since nothing seemed to be happening about the provost's position at Stanford, I planned to accept the Haverford offer. I happened to be paying a visit, on routine business, to the office of the associate dean of students, Joel P. Smith (later dean of students at Stanford, then president of Denison University, and later vice president for development back at Stanford), one afternoon. As I was about to leave, Joel asked, "Have you decided about Haverford?" I indicated that I was about to accept the job. Joel said, "Does Wally [Sterling] know about your decision?" I said no, but that he was aware that I was seriously considering it because I had been to see him during my cogitations, mainly to ask him how many presidents of liberal arts colleges he knew, and how he knew them, as I was wondering whether I would be cutting off any possible return to a research university if I took on the Haverford presidency. (It turned out that Sterling was only acquainted with liberal arts college presidents he had known through some channel other than higher education administration—such as having played football with them.)

Joel said, "Before you say 'yes' to Haverford I think you ought to let Wally know that you've decided to go—for your own sake and for that of your colleagues here." So I wrote a brief note to Sterling, thanking him for his time and conveying my decision. Within hours he called, saying that he was putting together a new top team in academic administration and that I should hold my decision until we had had a chance to discuss this. It turned out that he was prepared to present a package deal to the trustees in which

Herbert L. Packer and I would come in as vice provost for academic planning and programs and as provost, respectively.[1]

I told the Haverford board chair that I had been offered the provostship and had decided to accept it. There remained only the approval of the Stanford University Board of Trustees. Herb Packer and I paid a visit to a group of them (probably a subset of the Committee on Academic Affairs) at the board offices in San Francisco. David Packard, the towering (both literally and figuratively) chair of Hewlett-Packard and future deputy secretary of defense, was among those present. The session seemed uneventful, and we awaited the forthcoming November board meeting without undue apprehension.

On the appointed day, a Thursday, we remained on campus, awaiting word from Sterling that we had indeed been appointed. The afternoon wore on without any word, and only when dinnertime was looming did we get a call requesting us to go to the Hoover House to talk with him. When we arrived, Sterling, looking grave, greeted us with, "Boys, we have a fight on our hands." David Packard had vetoed Herb's appointment. Eleven years earlier, Packer had been under fire from the popular right-wing radio commentator, Fulton Lewis Jr., for having accepted support from the Foundation for the Republic, a liberal offshoot of the Ford Foundation, to write his book on Whitaker Chambers et al. entitled *Ex-Communist Witnesses*, though the book turned out to be a scrupulously balanced study and not a polemic against its subject. The same cloud had hung over Packer's initial appointment to the law faculty in 1956, but at that time Sterling had fought successfully for approval.

But if the trustees had then been unwilling to challenge academic freedom in a faculty appointment, even though Herbert Hoover himself had wanted them to, it now appeared that they were prepared to follow Packard's lead: my appointment was approved, Packer's was not.

Herb Packer's towering anger and bitter humiliation have been well described in his son's remarkable book, *Blood of the Liberals*. He was determined to leave Stanford forthwith.

My reaction was also angry; Sterling's promise to work on the matter between then and the next board meeting and to secure a reversal, which he was confident he could do, struck me as woefully inadequate. There was no assurance of success. Besides, how could we just sit quietly on campus awaiting the outcome meanwhile? Word of a veto from the political Right would surely be out in days, if not hours, and trouble on a massive scale was bound to ensue.

But our first task was to persuade Herb Packer not to do anything precipitous. This was far from easy; I recall enlisting the help of that most respected and loved faculty colleague, Robert McAfee Brown, in our living room on campus to argue the case. It is apparent from George Packer's account that the crucial role was played by Nancy Packer, whose sound political instincts told her that it would be disastrous to turn tail and run. Herb calmed down a bit. I paid Sterling a visit to tell him that, although I had burnt my bridges at Haverford, he must understand that I would refuse to serve as provost if Herb Packer's appointment was not approved.

Soon a formidable deputation waited upon Sterling at his home: the deans of all seven schools of the university, led by the dean of the Law School, Bayless Manning. I do not know exactly what was said at this meeting—for example, whether there was an explicit threat of mass resignations—but the deans made it clear that waiting a month would be intolerable: Sterling would have to summon an emergency meeting of the trustees the forthcoming weekend and get the veto reversed.

However melodramatic that may seem, it is exactly what happened. An emergency meeting of the trustees at the Hoover House that Sunday approved both appointments, and the crisis passed without ever hitting the newspapers. George Packer, who does not appear to know of the deans' deputation to Sterling, speculates that the whole thing may have been a bluff. I do not find this credible. Recalling the Stanford board as it was in 1966 I am sure that the threat was in deadly earnest.

Not long after becoming provost I found myself increasingly absorbed in crisis management, which created interesting problems for our family. Our eldest daughter, Jennifer, soon left the nest, becoming a freshman at Berkeley in the fall of 1968, when the campus there was clouded with tear gas over the People's Park affair, and next year transferring to Yale just in time for the Black Panther trial, which for a time seemed likely to pitch the university into chaos. She recalls being interviewed by the *Yale Daily News* and remarking that the Stanford University Board of Trustees made the Yale Corporation look like a chapter of SDS, not realizing that this choice quotation would traverse the continent quickly; Parmer Fuller, our board chair, phoned me about it, shall we say bemused.

Jenny's sister, Holly, was still at Gunn High School until her departure for college at Hampshire in Massachusetts in the fall of 1970 as I was becoming president. An episode involving her illustrates the tensions and stresses of those times for our family. She was baking cookies in the kitchen at the Hoover House one afternoon when police cars arrived and officers were on the doorstep asking why they had been summoned. Apparently one of the children's friends had lifted the receiver of an emergency phone on the ground floor, curious as to why there would be a phone tucked away down there with no dial. This was sufficient to set off an alarm at the campus police station. Holly had no idea this had happened. When it was explained she apologized to the police, who returned to their offices anything but pleased. Holly thought that taking them some of the cookies she was baking would be appropriate; it turned out that the police were wary of eating them for fear they might have been laced with marijuana. Holly also recalls riding her bike to Gunn and worrying that she might be kidnapped as Patty Hearst had been.

Our two sons, Christopher (Cricket) and Timothy, took sharply contrasting paths in dealing with the fact that their father was a controversial figure about whom many of their friends at school were curious. Cricket went to every radical meeting he could attend, never taking an active part but observing all that went on. He also accompanied me to the KZSU studios in the basement of Memorial Auditorium when I was broadcasting a news conference. Tim, by contrast, distanced himself from the uproar, telling schoolmates that he was not responsible for his father's actions, good or bad. Distance was not always possible, however. One day when we were out of town, Tim got home to find that he did not have his key. He undertook to scale the walls to find an open window and was seen doing this by a security guard who ordered him to climb down, threatening to arrest him. It took several phone calls to establish his identity and his right to be in the Hoover House.

We established early on the practice of telling the kids everything that was going on and trusting them not to divulge anything that might prove damaging. This worked well; at no point did a problem arise in connection with this policy of full disclosure. Indeed, it may have contributed to the fact that made possible a degree of family solidarity that enabled us to weather the storm without serious divisions. Remaining in good communication with our teenage children certainly helped us to understand how any given development might appear to the Stanford student body.

4 THE STAGE IS SET

IN RETROSPECT, the year 1966–67 seems, to some degree, a calm before the storm at Stanford. But it was a strange sort of "calm," not so much without event as without a discernible *pattern* of events. There were impressive gatherings from time to time, such as the four hundred–person rally in White Plaza where David Harris urged the crowd to resist the draft and join him in jail.[1] The noisiest event of the year, however, was largely a nonevent, an episode without much prelude or consequences.

On February 20, three days before David Harris's sensational resignation of his ASSU presidency, the vice president of the United States, Hubert Humphrey, came to campus for private talks with members of the Food Research Institute and to deliver a public address to a packed Memorial Auditorium. In fact the crowd was the start of the trouble; the administration, after saying that admission would be first-come-first-served, reserved a sizeable number of seats in the front of the auditorium for various distinguished guests, faculty, and administrators. The remaining seats filled rapidly, infuriating those who got there only to find they had to listen to the address broadcast over loudspeakers outside the building. Many who ended up outside the auditorium were critics of the war, including David Harris and Dennis Sweeney among them, and their contemptuous and noisy reception of Humphrey's talk made it hard for others around them to hear the vice president's speech.

Inside the hall the audience was orderly and for the most part respectful. There had been much discussion during the week leading up to the talk about the most appropriate and effective means of protesting. Some 219 faculty signed an ad in the *Daily* urging audience members to wear white armbands and to remain silent throughout, neither applauding nor heckling. Others advocated heckling or at least walking out. In the end, only one person heckled. But as one observer noted, "The tactic of silence was rendered futile. Between seven hundred and a thousand of those inside wore white armbands, but in a contest between noise and silence, even a minority of noisemakers wins easily."[2]

Those walking out totaled about 240 in a hall holding 1,900. Humphrey did nothing to diminish the critics' ire, at first ignoring the war in his remarks, then defending it in what the *Daily* described as "a barrage of clichés, generalizations and contradictions: . . . he should have known better than to talk down to his audience; some mention of the United States' foreign policy dilemma, for instance, would have been more appropriate for his opening remarks than his inane chattering on *Time* magazine's 'now generation.'"[3]

But what made headlines was what happened at Humphrey's departure. Many of those excluded from the auditorium not surprisingly wanted to shout at him as he left. Others merely wanted to catch a glimpse of him. The Secret Service foolishly tried to trick the crowd as to where Humphrey would exit the building. When the ruse was discovered there was a rush to catch up with him as he walked, surrounded by guards, to his waiting car. The likelihood of an orderly departure was thereby undercut, and there was a good deal of running and shouting—both pro and con, but cries of "Shame!" and "Murderer!" were the more prominent. Several protesters pounded on his car as security people pushed aside the crowd to allow the vehicle to proceed.

Given this fairly chaotic scene, it is not surprising that the "violence" was exaggerated, particularly by a United Press wire service account that dominated the coverage in some papers. Humphrey was described as "visibly shaken" by a reporter who later admitted he had not been in a position to see the vice president's face as he walked to his car. A private letter from an eyewitness gives what seems like a very careful and detailed account: "The Vice President was in full control of himself at all times during the incident. He damn well did not enjoy the taunts he could hear, but he kept up a slow, deliberate pace and if his expression varied from one of terse neutrality, it was only in the moments when someone called a friendly greeting. Without question, it was incorrect to describe him as 'visibly shaken.'"[4]

But the impression was left with the public that there had been a near-riot at Stanford, and that quite possibly the personal safety of the vice president of the United States had been at least briefly at risk. Reactions were fierce.

A former president of the Alumni Association wrote to the president of the board of trustees, "If any members of the faculty took part in the insults to Mr. Humphrey or in fomenting them during the previous night's activities or on the day of the visit, I believe they should be summarily dismissed from the faculty as having brought disgrace to our great university."[5] The director of university relations wrote to Sterling, "The letters of criticism have *far* exceeded anything we have on any other subject since I have been here."[6]

The Washington Post editorial declared, "Shame! Shame! Shame!" Wrote the *Post*:

> No group of critics has the right to send their roughnecks, rowdies and storm troopers into the streets or meeting rooms to intimidate those with whom they do not agree. If universities and colleges cannot assure officials of the Government or other citizens of safe conduct on their campuses, the orderly debate of public issues will have to take place on other forums and prudent public men will have to decline appearance in an environment where orderly discussion is not possible.[7]

Given such reactions, it is hardly surprising, though critics of the war resented it, that Sterling issued a public apology: "Stanford regrets this incident and offers its apology to the Vice President for any inconvenience or embarrassment that it may have caused him."[8]

Ten days later Sterling followed up with a statement "To All Students, Faculty and Staff," in which he noted the lack of consensus as to exactly what had happened, and then he gave a fairly straightforward account of the episode, including recognition that "the walkout of 240 people, while debatable as a gesture of protest, was carried out quietly and with minimum disruptive effect upon the proceedings." But, he continued, though early news accounts exaggerated the uproar:

> There is widespread agreement among eyewitnesses that there was a threatening degree of anger among many in the crowd. Shouts of "Murderer," "shame," "get him" and the like, hard elbowing and other physical acts among those rushing toward the car occurred on a scale which justifies serious concern. . . . The overwhelming majority of the Stanford community rejects violence as a means of argument and does not regard mob scenes as permissible incidents on a University campus. But it remains a ground for serious concern that we should have fallen even this far from our tradition of

fair and free discussion, and, further, that perception of the danger has not been universal among our community. The ease with which a crowd, in the sway of strong emotion, can become transformed into an ugly and dangerous mob—dangerous as much to innocent bystanders or to its own members as to anyone else—has apparently been overlooked by a disturbingly large number of people.[9]

The Humphrey episode had no sustained follow-up. Protests of various kinds occurred throughout the spring, including some aimed at the Stanford Research Institute (SRI), a contract research enterprise owned but not de facto controlled by the university, which was doing applied research and development for a variety of defense-related agencies. But if four hundred rallied in White Plaza against SRI on April 13, another four hundred rallied there on April 24 under the banner of "Concerned Students for Responsible Debate" to hear a classics professor, Brooks Otis, say, "I object to noisy intolerance on one side and silence on the other."[10]

· · ·

October 1967 saw a wild and many-splendored protest at the Pentagon in Washington. The crowd of thirty-five thousand ran a long gamut from respected figures such as the poet Robert Lowell and the critic Dwight MacDonald through the celebrated baby doctor, Benjamin Spock, to people waving the Viet Cong flag and signs proclaiming "Che Guevara Lives" and "Where is [Harvey] Oswald When We Need Him?" Novelist Norman Mailer, who later wrote a prize-winning book about the episode, *The Armies of the Night*, "described in detail his search for a usable privy on the premises."[11]

In the end, more than four hundred protesters had been arrested and a baker's dozen injured, and the innumerable divisions and internal conflicts of the antiwar movement had been on full display. The road from those urging a negotiated peace in Vietnam to those hoping to use the antiwar revulsion as a stepping-stone to bringing down "Amerika" in ruins was long and tortuous. The lively and quite comprehensive account of the Pentagon events in *Time* (October 27, 1967) noted, "The generally permissive reception accorded last week's demonstrations" by the American public as a sign of increased political maturity, but concluded, "There is a danger, nonetheless, that continuing and escalating disorders on the pattern of last week's outbursts could lead not to a freer and more constructive dialogue about the direction of U.S. foreign policy but to an increasingly emotional standoff between intransigent extremes."

Back in the Bay Area, the October protests centered on attempts to shut down, or at least slow, the process of induction into the armed services at the Oakland Induction Center. There was no agreement on tactics. David Harris describes "a tumultuous meeting in Berkeley," involving the Resistance and the two factions of Stop the Draft Week: pacifists, and "SDS types" who wanted to forget about nonviolence and "forge cooperation with Black militants" who would not be interested in "middle-class garbage about civil disobedience and moral witness."[11]

On campus, the line lay between those who were ready to commit civil disobedience and those who would only "participate in or support parallel legal demonstrations in the immediate vicinity."[12]

In the outcome, the Induction Center was certainly "interrupted," but scarcely threatened in any long-term way; some people were hurt, some ugly scenes recorded, and on one of the more peaceable days the Resistance collected some four hundred draft cards to turn in with the promise never to carry the card again, as well as "several Social Security cards, a City College of San Francisco ID, a leaflet about Rosicrucianism, several dozen signed letters, a set of army discharge papers, and an envelope with the ashes of 67 draft cards publicly incinerated in Berkeley during the previous week."[13]

Ten days later, when Selective Service Director Lewis Hershey suggested that local draft boards might consider reclassifying students with deferments who protest against military recruiting, President Sterling wrote a letter to President Johnson calling the suggestion "an unwarranted and dangerous evasion of due process and an infringement on free speech."[14]

A few days later, the Stanford SDS announced their intention of sitting in to prevent the CIA from holding job interviews at the Placement Center. The administration moved the interview site to Encina Hall, "so the rest of the placement service will not be disturbed by demonstrations." In a response to the SDS demand, as provost I wrote, "I can assure you that Stanford is not going into the business of thought control, on your behalf or anyone else's."[15] The sentence was picked up by the press nationally. Jack Gerson, speaking for SDS, responded that "as long as the U.S. government continues to channel thought and interfere with the affairs of other nations, it cannot seek sanctuary behind the 'free speech' line. In other words, free speech need not be accorded to those who do not accord it to others."[16]

The legitimacy of using physical force to prevent a university activity that some in the community considered immoral from taking place remained the central question over the next few days. The *Daily* took the unusual step of asking several prominent faculty members to speak to this question and published their replies the day the sit-in was to take place. Law professor William F. Baxter, a future assistant attorney general of the United States, argued against such tactics, for reasons ranging from the practical—"Assuming, then, that some employers are to be permitted to conduct interviews on campus, the question arises: Which ones? What are the criteria of selection to be? Who is to apply those criteria?"—to the philosophical: "I am particularly troubled, although I am no longer surprised, by the fact that those from whom the demand comes see themselves as, or at least posture as spokesmen for individualism and humanistic values. Either their perception or their integrity is strikingly deficient." The future Nobel Prize economist Kenneth J. Arrow was no gentler:

> As SDS speakers had made clear . . . the aim is not to stop the war in Vietnam nor to cripple the CIA; it is rejection of the whole system in all of its parts, and any particular occasion on which it is possible to mobilize support should be seized on. Since the legitimacy of existing authority everywhere is explicitly rejected, I presume that one of my lectures would be as acceptable a target as the CIA if only people were interested enough to care.

Nor was a prominent critic of the war, religious studies professor Robert McAfee Brown, any more encouraging to the protesters: "As one who has had occasion to practice civil disobedience, I would suggest that it is not an automatic panacea for all occasions, that the extent of its practice should be exceedingly restrained, and that the university campus is one of the last places where its exercise is appropriate. Those of us who request the privilege of free expression must be willing to extend that privilege to others." The same *Daily* reported an interview with me as provost: "Lyman said, 'There is a clear line between liberty to protest and physical force to impose your point of view on people who don't agree.' He compared the proposed sit-in at the CIA interviews with sit-ins in the South. 'The sit-ins in the South tested the constitutionality of racial segregation,' he said. 'Sit-ins here would only test the University's right to discipline sit-inners.'"[17]

That was prescient to a degree no one could have anticipated: the anti-CIA protest would indeed test "the University's right to discipline sit-inners," and for some time the answer to that question would be a resounding "no."

On the appointed day, the headline was "Protesters Block Encina; CIA Interviews Continue." Most of the time the sit-in consisted of "blocking the front door of the building's west wing." But at one point several demonstrators gained access to the building via a fire escape and "danced and stomped heavily in the room above that used for interviewing." When associate professor of English H. Bruce Franklin "tried to force his way into the interviewing room, Stanford Police Chief Bell grabbed his shirt and closed the door." Most of the protesters, including David Harris of the Resistance, remained on the grass in front of the building, talking and singing. "The TV camera men and reporters outnumbered the demonstrators for much of the time during the protest," which ended "shortly after noon." According to the *Daily*'s summary, "Of the six interviews scheduled for Wednesday morning, three were held, one was rescheduled, one was not held because the student failed to show up, and one because the interviewee refused to enter anyplace but the front door. Afternoon interviews took place as scheduled." An attempt to renew the battle the next day "turned out to be nothing more than a two-hour discussion by fewer than 20 people on Encina Hall's front lawn."[18]

Two weeks later, a columnist commented from the New Left perspective: "It has not been a slow news month. But here at Stanford many are disconcerted. The impact of the anti-CIA debacle, and the still-unresolved problems of the Oakland demonstrations have somehow bogged down the most articulate leaders of the local peace movement. The debate goes on over 'violence' versus 'non-violence.' Everyone searches for a new tactic. The radicals huddle in Cubberley and bewail their fate."[19]

A couple of bits of fallout from the episode deserve mention. On November 28, I found myself writing an angry letter to the then head of the CIA, Richard Helms. After describing our success in ensuring that "every student with a genuine interest in an interview had one with your representative," I wrote:

> Two subsequent developments have given us cause to ask ourselves whether our efforts to this end were fully justified. First, an article in the *San Francisco Examiner* reported that at least one of our students was required to sign a statement at the start of his interview, promising to divulge nothing of the contents of that interview to anyone. Inasmuch as we were at that moment defending the freedom of your recruiters, it came as an unpleasant surprise to find that your representative was resorting to methods more appropriate

to your intelligence operations overseas than to a placement interview on our campus. Is the signing of such statements an authorized Agency procedure? Second, within a few days of our effort to provide suitable facilities and guarantees of orderly procedure to the C.I.A. on our campus, the Agency announced its intention to cease holding such interviews on any campus other than those isolated from branch offices of the C.I.A. Thus the protesters whose announced aim was to bring such an interview to a halt were given a victory which, at least as far as Stanford is concerned, they had not won. Did the Agency give no thought to this in making the change of policy at this time?[20]

A reply from Helms two weeks later defended the policy of asking interviewees not to divulge the contents of their interviews on the somewhat cryptic ground that "widespread knowledge of the Agency's interest in an applicant may well limit the applicant's eventual choice of professional employment within the Agency," but said the option of requiring a written promise would be "discontinued." As for my second question, he wrote, "We do not believe our withdrawal from the campuses constitutes a victory for the militant groups, even though they may claim it, but rather the removal of a source of controversy and friction which serves neither the development of wholesome relationships within the university community nor the conduct of fruitful interviews between the Agency and applicants."[21] It is not hard to imagine the delight knowledge of this exchange would have given our radicals at the time. Probably the agency should never have set foot on a university campus, given the Hobson's Choices to which their presence could give rise.

The involvement of Bruce Franklin in the fracas in Encina gave rise to another episode that he has (quite understandably) misinterpreted. As provost, responsible for faculty matters, I thought we should be asking the Advisory Board, elected by the faculty as a whole to be the body that approved promotions to tenure and would handle a disciplinary case involving faculty should one arise, for guidance as to the standards to be applied to faculty behavior such as Franklin's in this instance. I was, as I recall, especially put off by his summoning his regular classes to meet at the sites of demonstrations, since that seemed to me to abuse the rights of his captive audience, which had enrolled to study Melville, after all, not Mao. I suggested that Robert R. Sears, my former boss as dean of the School of Humanities and Sciences (in which Franklin held his appointment) might ask President Sterling for such guidance. It was not my intention, contrary to Bruce Franklin's understanding of the matter, to initiate a disciplinary action against him at that point. We had a fairly clear and widely understood policy concerning demonstrations. But rescheduling one's class to the site of a demonstration was not, on the face of it at least, a violation of that policy. We lacked guidance as to what the limits of acceptable academic behavior were in such circumstances.

Sears agreed and wrote Sterling a memorandum, which, as I read it now, could have been interpreted as a request for disciplinary action. He begins with a description of the anti-CIA incident at Encina and of Franklin's participation, and his rescheduling two of his classes, with a total of 115 enrolled students, to the site that day. It continues:

> In my view, a professor has an obligation to conduct himself with dignity and propriety before students, and he has a duty to avoid exploiting students to satisfy his personal aims, political or otherwise. I suggest that Professor Franklin's reported conduct on Wednesday violated reasonable standards on both counts. I am writing to ask whether you consider my interpretation of the proprieties to be essentially correct. If so, I would welcome any suggestions you may be willing to give as to what responsibility the Dean of the School has for making known to the University community what proper standards of conduct are. I would also appreciate knowing your opinion as to how the Dean may be effective in ensuring the propriety of faculty conduct on the campus. Since standards of faculty conduct are normally established by the faculty itself, whether by formal intention or not, you may wish to refer my questions to the Advisory Board for consideration. I have not discussed these matters with Mr. Franklin, since there does not seem to be any question about the facts but only about what attitude should be taken toward them.[22]

Sears's having expressed a judgment on his own about Franklin's performance makes the final two paragraphs seem less open-ended than I would have preferred, though I still think that the memo was far from constituting a call for disciplinary action. Unfortunately it may have been read as the latter by its recipient; there is a draft note in the archives in Sterling's handwriting, which may or may not have been sent—but if it was sent, it did indeed sound like a call for disciplinary action:

> You are all aware of deep and widespread concerns about our national policy & performance in Vietnam. And we are likewise aware that this concern has

found [a] variety of expressions. Among these expressions of concern is one which I find inimical to a university. I refer to protests which do two things: (1) claim for themselves a right of free speech which they in the passion of their protest proceed to restrict or to deny to others; (2) attempt physically to obstruct or disrupt the business of the university and, in doing so, risk causing injury to person and property. I have confidence that Stanford's record would demonstrate that the university has provided students & faculty with opportunity, freedom & facilities by which to exercise the right of free speech on public issues, however controversial. It seems to me that the abuse of such opportunity & freedom is intolerable, and that neither faculty members nor students should be immune from discipline appropriate to the offence inherent in such abuse. The Dean of Students office has responsibility as regards the student members of the community. I suggest that the fac., beginning with Adv. Bd., has resp. In re fac.[23]

The draft has no date and no initials or signature. Clearly it loses sight of the question to which I, at least, most wanted an answer: that of the rescheduling of classes for political purposes. It would certainly not be hard to read it as an invitation to the Advisory Board to take action, as opposed simply to declaring policy. Since presumably Bruce Franklin had not seen the correspondence from which I have quoted so extensively, he was left to rely on hearsay and on the statement by the Advisory Board published on November 14, 1967:

> To the extent that the demonstrations (against campus interviews by the Central Intelligence Agency) at Encina Hall Nov. 1 involved disruption of University activities and restraints upon the movement of individuals, the Advisory Board deplores them. We urge our faculty colleagues to respect the provisions of the University's policy on campus demonstrations. This policy seems to us to provide essential guarantees for the preservation of freedom of expression and choice in the University community. We would therefore view violations of its provisions most seriously.

I was told at the time that the Advisory Board had declined to rule on the issue of moving classes around on the grounds that, if disciplinary action were ever undertaken for a violation of this kind, they would have the task of judging the case. Their view that by issuing an interpretation they would be prejudging some later case struck me as unwarranted at the time, but there did not seem to be anything we could do about it, short of charging Franklin and thereby forcing the Advisory Board to hear the case if he chose to appeal to the board, as he assuredly would have done. Clearly we were not prepared to do any such thing in November 1967.

It may not be surprising that Franklin continues to believe this whole episode to have been an early attempt to do what I, as president, and the Advisory Board did in fact do four years later, under very different circumstances, namely, to dismiss him from the faculty. But he is mistaken. To this day I do not know whether rescheduling a class for political purposes is a violation of academic propriety at Stanford.

5 THE MARTIN LUTHER KING JR. CRISIS

ON OCTOBER 8, 1964, by way of follow-up to a conversation the preceding summer in the President's Office, a small group of faculty and administrators met to discuss "the problem of bringing Negroes and other disadvantaged minority groups to a position of full equality in our society," and in particular how Stanford might play a part in attacking the problem.[1]

In a memo about the meeting, Robert M. Rosenzweig, associate dean of graduate study, described some of the efforts being made at universities around the country to tackle the issues:

> The striking fact about the current situation is that many institutions, among them the best in the nation, are engaged in a wide variety of activities to improve the quality of Negro education . . . as one might expect in an area as new and uncharted as this one is, the activity is large in volume and diffuse and experimental in character. There are some common threads, however. The most obvious, judging from the number and quality of the schools involved, is that we are in the midst of a major educational crisis which can be met only by the best efforts of the very best people our educational enterprise can muster.

The point of the memorandum was simply to ask President Sterling to put in motion a "more careful and systematic study, conducted quietly and without untimely publicity" as a prerequisite to the involvement of a wider group to "make specific recommendations to you about programs which Stanford can undertake."

The memo combined a sense of urgency with reminders that other leading institutions were hard at work on the matter. Yet in the end all that the memo urged on the president was the formation of a committee to study the concerns. "If, however, you would prefer not to appoint a formal committee, the group would propose to continue meeting informally with the addition of a small number of interested students, and to report to you, or whomever you might designate, from time to time on its progress." As Raymond Bacchetti scribbled in the margins of the draft for this memo, "Excellent! I like the 'do you want to say yes or yes' ending."

Altogether a very modest proposal, as was befitting an institution that felt itself groping, and quite possibly lagging behind others. By early 1965, Rosenzweig was chairing the Committee on Educational Opportunities for Disadvantaged Minorities, which was receiving memoranda from departments offering suggestions as to things that might be done. Some progress had been made. As recently as 1960, just six African Americans had applied for admission to the freshman class; three were admitted and two came. By 1964, these numbers were twenty-one, sixteen, and ten, respectively. But ten students represented about 0.6 percent of a Stanford entering class. As late as summer 1966, in a response to a questionnaire from the Association of Independent California Colleges and Universities, Stanford had to confess to having no "programs to encourage socio-economically disadvantaged students to undertake graduate study," no tutorial programs aimed at helping such students on campus, and no curricula designed to meet their needs. The Admissions Office staff made about nine hundred secondary-school visits per year. "One member of the Admissions Office is assigned the responsibility of supervising minority group recruiting, and visits a number of predominantly Negro or Mexican-American high schools every year."[2]

Not all of the problems had their origin within the university. A case in point was the fate of a federal grant to the Medical School of $59,273 in April 1967, to run the Upward Bound project during the summer. A group from East Palo Alto led by Syrtiller Kabat, a trustee of the Ravenswood School District, and including teenagers from that district, burst into a meeting of Medical School faculty who would be teaching in the program and made nine demands as prerequisites to cooperation from the source of students for Upward Bound, the East Palo Alto community. Among them was that homes be found in Palo Alto for all the students seeking to attend Palo Alto High School instead of Ravenswood High School. Another was that East Palo Alto would appoint and control half the seats on a sixteen-member board of directors for the project. News reports quoted the South San Mateo County NAACP as saying that it was "advising all parents to not allow their children to be used as guinea pigs to provide jobs for the rich." Its president, the Rev. Thomas C. Sanders, added, "We are bitterly opposed to Stanford's involvement in our community. Once Stanford was helping us. Now it seems to be a hindrance. We say, 'get out of our community.' "[3]

Unable to meet the demands, Stanford turned down the federal money and terminated the program. Thus did Stanford "get out," and thus did forty-six disadvantaged youngsters lose whatever opportunity to make progress out of poverty the program offered. The leaders of the protest rationalized the outcome ingeniously: "In an encounter like this, the East Palo Alto teenagers probably learned more about democracy (and incidentally about Black Power) than they would have in a whole summer of civics courses."[4]

No doubt the gulf that yawned between the university and East Palo Alto was hard to bridge; no doubt the university's most well-meaning people lacked the informed sensitivity that might have softened the attitude of people like Rev. Sanders. But it remains the case that many in the minority community were quick to adopt a strategy based on the belief "that if a situation gets bad enough people will eventually be forced to take drastic action to make it better. A more accurate assessment . . . would be that when things get bad enough they fall apart," as Rosenzweig said in a letter to the *Daily* on April 27. A couple of months earlier he had written a memo that began, "For about the last six months I have been involved in a series of discussions, maneuvers, controversies, fights, etc., centering on what is generally described as 'getting Stanford to do something significant about the education of disadvantaged minorities.' Rarely have I been involved in a cluster of issues that have seemed so poorly defined." He argued that the university could not make any sensible policy about the internal, academic aspects of the question (as opposed to the "peripheral," community-service aspect) until it had decided what its student body ought to look like: "There are at present about 90 African-American undergraduates at Stanford, and the number has been growing for the past few years. Other minorities are represented, but in smaller numbers. . . . Ninety is not self-evidently too low, nor is 1,000 self-evidently too high. The tragedy lies in having to ask the question at all, for to do so exposes the lack of a coherent picture of the kind of student body we want at Stanford."[5]

Before the fateful spring of 1968, then, Stanford was an institution uneasily aware of a gap between potential and performance in the matter of serving the disadvantaged. The university that had contributed the largest contingent of volunteers to "Mississippi Summer" was certainly not leading the way at home.

On March 9, 1968, an incident occurred, minor in itself, but emotionally fraught, that set the stage for the major upheaval that soon followed. On a day when hundreds of young people were on campus to attend a Stanford Repertory Theater workshop, some fifty children from the East Palo Day School, run by Mothers for Equal Opportunity, also came to campus with four of their teachers on a field trip to visit an exhibit of African art. Fifteen to twenty of them had lunch at tables in the patio at Tresidder Memorial Union (TMU), and from time to time small groups of the children went into the Tresidder store to buy more food or candy. Exactly what happened in the store could never be ascertained, but Gertrude Wilks, a fiery East Palo Alto leader and founder of the Day School, wrote a strong letter to President Sterling alleging that two named staff members "harassed and in some instances physically abused the black children." The specifics were hard to pin down: if a child is asked if he or she has paid for an item, does that constitute being "accused of stealing"? Probably so, if one is expecting to encounter racial discrimination.

Testimony from eyewitnesses was sparse and conflicting. Reviewing the existing documentation, including the extensive report of the newly created Human Relations Commission chaired by law professor Byron Sher, leaves one uncertain about virtually every aspect of the incident and convinced of just two things: (1) there was a lot of confusion around TMU that midday, with which TMU staff were trying to cope, and (2) the children involved "were made to feel uncomfortable because of the general attitude and conduct" of employees of the store.[6]

The university's response to Mrs. Wilks's complaint was to schedule a meeting at which she and about a dozen others from East Palo Alto, including an attorney, Thelton Henderson (who later served as an associate dean of the Stanford Law School and who is now a federal judge), met with Associate Provost Robert M. Rosenzweig and an administrative assistant. A reporter from the *Palo Alto Times* was also present.[7]

At this meeting Rosenzweig reported what he had been able to learn from talking with Tresidder staff and a Stanford police officer. Since he had not talked with those who had allegedly been accused of shoplifting, nor with their teachers, he was accused of accepting the version of events given by these individuals as the facts in the case. No such thing, he responded, "what he had written was strictly a review of the situation as it appeared to the Stanford personnel involved." But the attempt to have a dialogue from this starting point was doomed from the outset. Rosenzweig's interlocutors were only interested in getting at the alleged perpetrators of harassment and false accusation. It is grimly fascinating, knowing what we know now about the power of suggestion in such situations involving children, to read that:

> Mrs. Aarons [one of the teachers] firmly stated that she believed the students were searched. She commented that the children were hesitant to say that they had been searched by Mr. Evans, but that after further discussion they claimed that they had in fact been forced to open their purses and show the contents. (It is unclear whether she was speaking of a single child or of more than one.) Rather quickly the overriding issue became the absence from the meeting of the TMU employees whose behavior was being questioned. . . . Mrs. Wilks then stated again that she and her group are extremely concerned and serious about the incident. She expressed her feeling of being "insulted" because the "accusers" [of the children] were not present at the meeting. Mr. Rosenzweig replied that he (as a representative of the University) and Mrs. Wilks and her group (as representatives of the Day School) were both acting as agents for the principals involved in the March 9 incident.[8]

In the end the delegation from the Day School walked out of the meeting.

Two weeks later the world in which universities groped to find the right path of progress in race relations dramatically changed. On April 4, Martin Luther King Jr. was killed by a sniper while standing on a balcony of his motel in Memphis, where he had gone to give his backing to a strike by sanitation workers. Hopes for a peaceful transition to a condition in which skin color would no longer matter, frail at best even in King's heyday, dwindled. Dramatic confrontations came quickly across the nation.

At Stanford, a memorial colloquium was set for Monday, April 8. As provost I was the leadoff speaker; Memorial Auditorium was packed, with the members of the Black Student Union (BSU) sitting in the front rows, accompanied by Mrs. Wilks and the students of the East Palo Alto Day School. A crowd listened to loudspeakers piping the proceedings outdoors. My notes for that talk begin, "My 1st thought: Does it take a national tragedy of these dimensions to bring us together for serious discussion of this subject? Only now do many Americans who are not black or brown begin to see racism, no longer merely as the country's most serious internal problem, but as a fracture in our body politic so severe that it could bring about the downfall of our society."

My notes do not indicate exactly when it happened, but not long after I had begun to speak, the entire population of the first several rows of the audience rose as one person. I thought they were about to walk out in protest, but they walked up onto the stage instead. I stepped aside and one of the BSU leaders, Frank Satterwhite, took over the podium and read a statement that began, "Stanford University is guilty of denying equal educational opportunities to minority group members of the local community, the State of California, and the nation." He went on to accuse the administration of having "presented false information" and "completely misrepresented a supposed non-discriminating university policy." He spoke somberly of a "maximum quota system for minority group members," and he added, "The Black Student Union rebukes the administration for attempted deception and indicts Stanford University for shirking the responsibility for minority group education."

There followed ten detailed demands, starting with: "(L) That proportional representation of minority group members be implemented with the freshman class of the 1969–70 academic year to include recruitment of a substantial number of minority students from East Palo Alto, East Menlo Park, Santa Clara County and San Mateo County; that each subsequent freshman class be comprised of a proportional number of black students, Mexican-Americans, American Indians, and other minority group members; and that active recruitment of minority students be initiated at junior colleges." Also demanded was an experiment whereby "at least five 'marginal' black students and five 'marginal' students from other minority groups [would] be admitted for the 1968–69 academic year [and] that the Black Student Union be given exclusive jurisdiction in the selection and recruitment of the five black students. The 'marginal' students would be 'given a one-year period in which to adjust to the university environment' and 'the admissions officer and Black Student Union representatives [would] be allowed to determine whether these students are to continue.'"

The demands dealt also with recruitment of minority faculty members, though curiously, they said nothing about increasing the numbers of minority staff. They also demanded the creation of "a tutorial program . . . for *all* minority students on campus." With financial aid, grades were to be "excluded as a factor in determining financial aid for minority/poverty students," and aid was to be determined on the basis of a twelve-month year. They issued demands regarding full reporting of the acceptance and rejection of minority applicants as well as comparisons made with the data for whites, with "no deception or false information." The BSU further demanded "that the university not act upon any SES [Study of Education at Stanford] report relating to minority students without the official approval of the Black Student Union," which, since it is hard to think of any possible SES recommendations that would *not* one way or other be related to minority students, would appear to give the BSU a sweeping veto power over Stanford decisions.

The longest demand began, "That the University immediately dismiss any employee engaged in discriminatory acts while on the job; that the University establish a permanent committee with responsibility for investigating charges relating to acts of discrimination." The majority of the committee's membership was to be minority, and its decisions "binding upon the university." Specifically, there was to be "a full and thorough investigation" of the TMU episode, with "the right to confront the accusers" and "dismissal of the employees involved, if the facts of the investigation indicate any black child was wrongfully searched and/or accused of stealing."

Demand number 5 also grew out of the TMU incident:

> That Dr. Robert Rosenzweig, Vice Provost [*sic*] in charge of minority group affairs, be dismissed from these duties and replaced with a full-time, black administrator to be selected with the approval of the Black Student Union; that this individual be given a substantial budget to implement relevant educational programs for minority group members; and that all major decisions affecting any minority groups be subject to the approval of these minority group members.

The ire of the Day School representatives to the meeting in Rosenzweig's office was thus to be assuaged.

Finally, the BSU demanded that "the administration immediately consider the aforementioned demands [and] that a statement of acceptance and timetable of implementation be presented to the Black Student Union at 7:00 p.m., Tuesday, April 9, 1968, in open forum at Tresidder Union, Room 270." That is to say, the next evening.

With that, the BSU and its East Palo Alto supporters walked off the stage and out of Memorial Auditorium, to a huge ovation from the audience, both inside and out. I returned to the podium and resumed my remarks, most of which consisted of a survey of where we stood in admissions, creating relevant courses, and employment. I could report some specific signs of progress. For next year's freshman class, "every candidate deemed admissible (& I'm sure that all or nearly all were in the judgment area, so-called) has been admitted with full financial aid to the limits of demonstrated need. African-American applicants got first priority in $$ aid decision-making, for the first time." Also for the first time, this year we were going beyond "seeing to it that Univ. hiring policy was non-discriminatory," and we had begun to practice what came to be called affirmative action. Since the designation of someone in personnel to promote this policy, about one-fifth of new employees were from minority groups, "mostly negro." There were, I said, 234 African Americans working at Stanford, compared with 87 in 1964.

But much, much more remained to be done. Concerning the academic program I warned, "We don't do enough, and too much of what we *do* do is too oblique. . . . Traditionally, and for good reason, curriculum is shaped largely by faculty; a contemporary faculty that does not heed the call for a new & far greater effort to teach & to understand the phenomenon of racism in America is *asking* to have its curriculum-shaping power usurped. We cannot use their near-sovereignty as an excuse to do nothing."

One important new step I was able to announce serendipitously anticipated one of the demands just issued: the creation of a Stanford Human Relations Commission, its members "to be faculty and students, and to include negro appointees." It would "hear complaints against the University or its staff from persons inside or outside Stanford." It would also "conduct studies & make recommendations on ways in which the Univ. can improve its relations with members of minority groups."

I concluded by reading a few lines that were written 165 years ago, about another martyr to the cause of black freedom, the Haitian revolutionary, Toussaint l'Ouverture, betrayed to his death in a French prison by the agents of Napoleon I. The lines are from William Wordsworth's sonnet "To Toussaint L'Ouverture":

> Yet die not; do thou
> Wear rather in thy bonds a cheerful brow:
> Though fallen thyself, never to rise again,
> Live, and take comfort. Thou hast left behind
> Powers that will work for thee; air, earth and skies;
> There's not a breathing of the common wind
> That will forget thee; thou has great allies;
> Thy friends are exultations, agonies,
> And love, and man's unconquerable mind.

A panel discussion followed in Memorial Auditorium, followed by an evening of intense discussion among the president's staff regarding what kind of immediate response we could make to the demands. There had been no threats, no discussion that we knew of concerning what the BSU would do if we failed to respond adequately in their judgment. The reception given the BSU by the audience that afternoon made it obvious that if they wanted to cause trouble, to sit in or block entrances or whatever, they could do it with massive support. White radicals, suddenly reorganized as "Students Against White Racism," were clearly eager to attach themselves to this cause. As the *Daily* described it, "Behind-the-scenes warnings of a BSU 'contingency plan' in case of an impasse were given to administrators by excited whites." But if, as the same source went on, "Provost Richard Lyman was bluntly warned that university buildings would be shut down by demonstrators if he reached an impasse with the BSU," the warnings did not come from anyone in a position really to know what was in the minds of the BSU leaders. In any case we needed no warnings to recognize these ominous possibilities.

When situations of this kind are analyzed, it is usually assumed that the establishment—in this case the Stanford administration—aims to yield as little ground as possible—just enough to avert disaster. Applied to the hectic days of April 1968, the assumption is quite simply wrong. Our mood and attitude toward what we were doing were a strange mixture of fear and exhilaration: fear that big and unmanageable disruption might take place, of course, but also exhilaration that we were being compelled, by the force of history as much as by the pressures from the BSU and East Palo Alto and their on-campus allies, to do the best we could to begin the process of righting huge historic wrongs.

Stanford had been for the most part blissfully oblivious of the possibility that the university bore any responsibility for these wrongs. When it became clear that we were basing our policy on a recognition of Stanford's responsibility, protests poured in from alumni and others. How dare we argue that this was a situation in which doing nothing had amounted to doing wrong, that exclusion had not required that anyone *work* at it; merely failing to work *against* it meant incurring responsibility? We were maligning the reputations of all the Stanford leaders who had come before us. We were insulting the university they loved, the degrees from which they were understandably and justifiably proud.

The evening of April 8 we were working on a statement to be issued the following morning over the signatures of the president and the provost:

At Monday's colloquium, the Black Student Union made a presentation about minority-group problems at the University. It is the matter not the manner of what they said that counts. In our community, they are among the prime witnesses to racial injustice, and it is important that all members of the community listen to these witnesses. Much of what they advocate constitutes the basis for a constructive program of action. Goals toward which the University pledges itself to devote the necessary resources of time, thought and money include: (1) An effort to double over current enrollment figures the number of minority-group students enrolled by Stanford by academic 1969–70, through an accelerated recruitment and financial aid program. (2) A pilot program in 1968–69 for at least ten minority-group students who do not meet minimal Stanford academic requirements. (3) An effort to double the proportion of minority-group employment at Stanford over the next year, and to upgrade such employment wherever feasible. (4) Adequate staffing and funding to achieve points one, two and three. We call upon the members of the Black Student Union to work with us to achieve these goals and to carry on a continuing dialogue about them. Dialogue does not take place in mass meetings. It takes place when men of good will, recognizing that none of them has truth in his exclusive possession, resolve to discuss their common problems. To this end we invite them to designate five representatives to meet with a like number of faculty and staff members this Thursday, April 11 at 2 p.m.—J.E. Wallace Sterling, Richard W. Lyman

Some were troubled by our second sentence: "It is the matter and not the manner of what they said that counts." Professor William Rambo wrote Sterling and me, applauding the general substance of our response but adding, "It would seem that we have had the first successful demonstration on the campus, a classical demonstration in the sense of its being held in a University building and disrupting a University function."[9] There was, of course, no answer to that; the statement is factually true. But the circumstances were so nearly unique—and the realistic possibility of disciplining anybody for the disruption so slight—as to warrant the phrase. Or so it seemed at the time. And, for whatever it may be worth, I do not recall having had it thrown at us later as justifying other protests.

Sterling's brief acknowledgment, dated April 11, leaves the impression that he shared, at least to some extent, Rambo's doubts:

> Dear Bill: Thank you for your letter. I value your observations and counsel. There have been differences of opinion among the officers of the University on how to handle the situation created by the BSU "demands." After a thorough discussion, we decided that it would be wisest to talk with the students, although not on their terms. This we tried to do. I shall share your comments with others involved in the handling of this sensitive situation.

There remained the urgent question of what to do about the BSU demand that we meet with them in public that very night, armed with "a statement of acceptance and timetable of implementation" of their demands. Simple acceptance was out of the question. Although most of the demands provided some basis for accommodation, most also contained unacceptable aspects, often in the direction of yielding up specific areas of policy making or administration to the BSU. The demand for Rosenzweig's dismissal, backed by no argument, let alone evidence, to suggest a justification, had to be rejected.

Our published statement had declared, "Dialogue does not take place in mass meetings." We might have been better advised to say "negotiations" rather than "dialogue," for in the end dialogue is exactly what took place. Even that was not easy. Neither Sterling nor I attended the meeting; without us it would be pretty clearly impossible to expect final and binding commitments to be made. Herb Packer led a seven-member delegation; his six colleagues were Rosenzweig, Vice President for Finance Kenneth M. Cuthbertson, Associate Dean of Students Willard Wyman, and Professors Robert McAfee Brown, Kenneth J. Arrow, and Donald Kennedy. Speaking for the BSU were its cochairs, Kenneth Washington and Charles Countee, Frank Satterwhite, and Letitia Carter. Professor James L. Gibbs, at that time Stanford's only black member of the regular faculty, was also on the panel.

The meeting nearly came to impasse early on. After preliminary remarks from both sides, Washington asked Packer if he was "prepared to respond to the first demand," and Packer said no. "The complexities can be worked out at a later date, but we must have some discussion on these demands now," Washington insisted. Packer was adamant. "This is not the atmosphere. This is neither the time nor the place to discuss the points you have brought up. I've tried to give you a progress report, I'm sorry if that is not enough. We want to talk."

When Countee demanded either a statement of acceptance or a timetable of implementation for the demands, Packer replied, "We have already made a beginning. The meeting Thursday, if you want, is the beginning of the timetable for implementation."

Washington again questioned Packer's refusal to discuss the issue then and there, saying, "I don't see the problem here. These are students. They don't bite. They have minds. I don't think it's at all unreasonable to talk now."

Sensing an impasse, Washington called a fifteen-minute recess, during which both sides caucused. Countee's willingness to consider that *either* the substance of the demands *or* the timetable of implementation might form an acceptable basis for discussion strongly suggests that the BSU were reluctant to see the meeting collapse in acrimony—as of course were the university representatives. When the recess ended Wyman asked whether the meeting could proceed with broad discussion of the individual demands, but leaving the details till Thursday. Washington and Countee agreed.

The resulting format, with Washington reading a demand and then a member of the university group responding, led to the next morning's headline in the *Daily*, "Open Meeting: University and BSU Agree on Nine of Ten Points," and Washington felt a need to tell a noon rally that the university's response Tuesday night "was not completely adequate. We did not come to an agreement." On the "tenth point" (demand number five in the BSU statement), the dismissal of Rosenzweig, Packer gave a firm "no": "We're not going to fire Bob Rosenzweig. America suffers too much from scapegoating. There was applause and my mother [Nancy Packer] relaxed a bit. 'To move a university, you have to move the people in it. . . . We think we ought to do these things because they are the right things to do.'"

On Wednesday we worked intensely on the full response that we would present to the BSU delegation at Thursday afternoon's meeting—again in Tresidder, though this time in a conference room out of sight of the three hundred or so gathered outside to await the outcome. The "Response" took the form of a memorandum signed by me. For the most part, we "met the spirit, if not the exact detail, wanted by the BSU," as the *Daily* had said of Tuesday night's responses. But, while reiterating the pledge to try to double the number of minority students in the 1969–70 entering class and promising to go beyond that "to bring us in excess of 100 minority groups students for each entering class after 1970," I went on to say, "Proportional representation, or any other form of quota system, is antithetical to the spirit of this University and adverse to the interests of the groups who are its supposed beneficiaries but who end up being its victims." For the most part we held back from turning over actual decision making to the BSU, though accepting them in consultative or supportive roles—for example, in preparing a recruitment pamphlet and as "admissions aides" under the work-study program. The nearest we came to an exception was in the operation of the proposed experimental admission of ten "marginal" freshmen, where we asked "the Black Student Union to assist in recruiting the pool of students from which the ten will be chosen and to advise the Dean of Admissions in making the choices." We also promised "no student [in this program] will be dismissed from the University without consultation with representatives of the Black Student Union." In the end this mattered little, since the experiment was allowed quietly to disappear after encountering various difficulties.

On the ticklish demand number five, dismissal of Rosenzweig, I tried to walk a fine line, saying we needed more help and agreeing to an immediate search for a "Coordinator of Intergroup Relations" who would "work for the University with Associate Provost Robert Rosenzweig, the Human Relations Commission, and other relevant groups." The Black Student Union was asked "to designate one or more of its members to act as consultants for this search." But the *San Jose Mercury* on Friday carried the headline, "Rosenzweig Relieved of Duties," and I had to issue a statement that his authority was unchanged, and that there had been no delegation of academic decision making to "any group of students."

In a letter to the members of the Academic Council on April 17, 1968, summarizing the developments for the benefit of those who had not been present at the April 11 meeting of the council to hear my report, I devoted a paragraph to the Rosenzweig case, saying that refusal to lessen his authority

> goes far beyond the issue of confidence in and support for an able and dedicated officer of the University. That immediate issue aside, if the University once yields to pressure to discharge or demean any member of its staff, then no member of the University, be he professor, student, or administrator, can be safe from the attack of any group that can muster a sufficient show of force. The principle that commands resistance to such pressure has been under attack many times in the past and will be assaulted many times in the future. I want to assure you that it has in no way been compromised.

The Thursday afternoon meeting was not routine, by any means. The atmosphere was heated at times, cordial at others. I found myself saying again, as I had said in Memorial Auditorium, that it did not make a lot of sense to argue (1) that education for blacks has been starved, deprived, and ignored for generations, and (2) there is a plentiful supply of qualified black professional talent out there if we simply looked for it. It made about as much impression in the one place as it had in the other. I also had some more stonewalling to do about Bob Rosenzweig (who once again was in the room listening to the calumnies with as much patience as he could muster). We seemed to have reached an impasse, with the students threatening to break off negotiations and report failure to the crowd gathered outside. Impasse was only avoided by the intervention of Robert McAfee Brown, who told the students (as Rosenzweig recalls):

> I have been with you on most of the demands you have made, but on this one we must part company. Let me tell you why. Not long ago, I wrote an article for *Look* magazine in which I said that if students came to me for draft counselling, I would think it my responsibility to counsel them on avoiding the draft if I thought that was the right course for them. President Sterling was under heavy pressure to fire or discipline me on the grounds that I was advising students to break the law. The President, whatever his beliefs about what I had written, refused to do so, saying that to act against one faculty member for expressing an unpopular opinion would dramatically undermine the University's commitment to free speech and was therefore unacceptable. That was a courageous act because some of those who were angry were also donors to Stanford. The same principle applies to Bob Rosenzweig. The University cannot yield to pressure to deal with one of its members because some don't approve of him. I regret not being able to support you here, but that is the way it must be.

As Rosenzweig says, "I thought at the time that it was the most courageous act of moral courage that I had seen in my relatively short professional life. After a good many more years, I still think that. At a time when pandering to noisy protest was epidemic, not only at Stanford but on campuses across the country, Bob Brown's statement was an outstanding exception, and it carried the day."

In the end the response with which we entered the room survived with little amendment.

When we adjourned, Kenny Washington went out on the balcony of Tresidder and told the crowd waiting below, "All our demands have been met. There has been no watering down." As for me, I rushed across White Plaza to Dinkelspiel where the Academic Council was in session, to report on what we had concluded and to ask for the faculty's support against "the inevitable backlash."[10]

Middle-of-the-road faculty response is captured by the historian, Gordon Craig, in a diary entry at the time.[11] Describing the crisis, beginning with the seizure of the microphone in Memorial Auditorium, he wrote:

> He [RWL] kept his cool, in the modern parlance; and so did the administration in general, jockeying the BSU to a negotiating position and reaching an agreement which gave them virtually everything they wanted but in a way that did not jeopardize the University's decision-making power or its control over admissions. What the University is giving it should, I am sure, give, but it will cost a lot. . . . Still, we can probably get it. We shall also have to build into our system something like a dispersed junior college to handle the new customers effectively without hurting general standards. This won't be easy but it can be done without too great an effort, and in ten years it may pay off handsomely. Meanwhile, the very fact that we are doing it will have a favorable effect and may stimulate action on the part of institutions who can take care of greater numbers than we, as a private institution, can.

Craig found equally depressing "the intimations of a coming white backlash on the part of the alumni and the abundant evidence of overreaction and emotionalism on the part of many of our colleagues and many students . . . an 'amour de la boue,' a visceral satisfaction in guilt and atonement, an undignified scramble to demonstrate to our black brothers that we will invite abuse and excuse it."

Looking back at all this, one remarkable feature is our lack of hesitation in making such significant commitments of policy and resources without prior approval by the board of trustees, or even substantial consultation with members of the board during that week. Writing to a critic on April 30, board president W. Parmer Fuller III defended the seemingly hasty actions of the campus leadership:

> I was in touch frequently that week with Messrs. Sterling and Lyman and it is my judgment that opportunity for meaningful discussion depended on a prompt follow-through by the University. To delay would have resulted in increased tension in an already charged atmosphere. Positions would have been hardened and the chance for rational discussion minimized. I believe if we

had postponed meeting the issue firmly, promptly and reasonably we would have done far more harm than good.[12]

I nevertheless recall a conversation in the car en route to the next meeting of the board, held as usual in San Francisco, that suggests that communication must have been sparse. In it, William Hewlett was quoted as having said to someone (not me or the president) that "this time he and his partner [David Packard] were in agreement" in doubting the wisdom of our course of action. This was alarming, and we were greatly relieved when we got to San Francisco and nothing came of it. Although there were questions, no real antagonism was expressed at that board meeting, and recognition seemed general that we had hardly been free agents, that we had protected the things that needed to be protected and agreed to things that needed to be done. Given what had happened at the time of Packer's appointment as vice provost, it may seem surprising that Packard went along on this occasion. But it should be recalled that he was a leader in establishing the Mid-Peninsula Urban Coalition and in other moves to improve the condition of disadvantaged minorities. Our path was no doubt smoother overall because the existence of a national upheaval was obvious, and all sorts of organizations and institutions confronted crises not unlike ours.

·   ·   ·

The search that brought Jim Simmons to Stanford from the East Coast to be the coordinator of intergroup relations was quickly accomplished. He was appointed in May and visited the campus twice before taking office in September. From the start, he confronted an all-but-impossible set of expectations—or rather two such sets, strongly conflicting. As he later described it:

> The students very clearly saw the office and me as "Their Office and Man in the Administration," to lead their fight with the University for more Black students, faculty-staff and a wide variety of other changes and benefits they felt necessary to insure their survival at Stanford. My administrative colleagues saw the office and me as an instrument and/or buffer to "cool" an explosive situation and to give counsel and advice as to the best ways to carry forth a University commitment to changes.

He tried, by his own admission more forthrightly with his administrative colleagues than with the students, to tell each group that he could not be the person they were envisaging, and that he would need their help—that of the students to "establish and maintain credibility with my administrative and faculty colleagues," and that of those same colleagues to "establish and maintain credibility with the entire Black community." He could not "stand at the President's door," either "defiantly" on behalf of the students or "to prevent entrance" in defense of his colleagues.[13]

To a remarkable degree he succeeded in this fundamentally Janus-faced role. Highly intelligent, hardworking, courageous, outgoing, and gregarious, but very thoughtful and capable of seeing things in perspective, he managed to "establish and maintain credibility" with both camps. Nobody's perfect; we had repeated difficulties with him over financial matters. He was beset by supplicants, both individuals and groups, and his empathetic concerns far exceeded his capacity to say no. But even in his first year as assistant provost for minority affairs (his title was changed because on his visits he encountered student scepticism about a title that seemed removed from the regular lines of authority at Stanford), he coped with the unsettled conditions and continuing militancy with tact and integrity.[14]

From time to time there would be a fresh wave of "demands," many of which betrayed no signs of any improved understanding of how the university worked. The twelve issued in February 1969 included once again the dismissal of someone (a faculty member in the School of Education this time) who had angered blacks by allegedly racist behavior. The demands went on to include that "there be a black faculty member in every department by Fall '69," that "a black man be hired as Asst. to the president in the Financial Aids Dept. and be in charge of all black financial matters," and, just in case that did not cover the matter, that "a black man be hired as Vice-President of Stanford in charge of all black affairs, answerable only to the President." As a perceptive white student noted at the time, the common thread here was "don't put any white man in a position of authority over us":

> The black student at Stanford has a pretty awful dilemma. On [the] one hand, he wants to get the white man's diploma and collect top dollar for his black-ness (as Bazile said, "Niggers is in demand."). On the other hand, he must struggle to convince himself and others that he is not "becoming white" by slipping into a cozy student life. He fears losing touch with black militants and ghetto residents, who are the real guardians of the black identity.[15]

Understandably the BSU tried to test the new president when Kenneth S. Pitzer arrived to assume that role in December 1968. I sat bemused in his first meeting with their leadership and listened to them describing how they had developed a fine working relationship with the provost during the months since April and did not understand why the new president was not equally approachable. As a result of misunderstandings and miscommunication about scheduling a meeting of BSU leaders with Pitzer in February 1969, there was an ominous episode in which "about two dozen persons, mainly blacks, rampaged through the Stanford Bookstore sweeping hundreds of books off the shelves, breaking a few glass shelves, and pushing over art displays. No one was injured and there were no arrests."[16]

A few weeks earlier the president received a letter that deserves mention. The writer said:

> I am a Stanford student, a member of the Black Students Union, and am very concerned about the current leadership of the organization. I have never before written an anonymous letter, but the situation on this campus at this moment is so hostile and volatile that I am actually afraid to express my opinions openly for fear of violence to myself or to my friends who do not always agree with what the B.S.U. does. I mainly want to express the opinions of the "moderates" among the Black students on this campus, so that you will know that the militants do not represent a majority of opinion here. Unfortunately, the faculty and administration seem to think that every time they make a threat or demand that the BSU is speaking for all of us. They are speaking for a very aggressive leadership and the strings are being pulled by leaders in East Palo Alto, and not by the student leaders.

The writer went on to express opposition to various efforts to set up separate facilities and programs for blacks: "We came to learn how to get along with whites and other groups and we cannot do this if we are pressured to segregate ourselves." There is, of course, no way to assess the claim that the moderates constituted a majority of black students. The very fact that such an assessment is impossible does constitute a reminder that the pressure for black conformity (justified as solidarity) was a potent force then and has reasserted itself from time to time since.

The BSU did not claim responsibility for the bookstore rampage, and the reaction on campus to the violence was hostile, naturally, which probably accounts for its having been a single aberration in a year that was full of sound and fury but not, on the part of blacks, violence or even disruption. This was certainly not because of lack of capacity. Leo Bazile, the new BSU cochair, a big, handsome, clarion-voiced sophomore from Oakland, was probably more capable of arousing a crowd than any other leader, white or black, of the era of disruption. At times he enjoyed taunting the white radicals with their inaction. He was not about to join them or even to help them out. The BSU, he steadily maintained, would "take care of business," meaning they would fight for concrete changes that they thought would advance their ability to get the most out of their opportunities at Stanford. As has often been noted, blacks on campuses wanted to make use of the universities for their own interests; they had no interest in shutting the colleges down. There were never more than one or two blacks at rallies and meetings of "the Movement" against the war at Stanford.

At the end of the 1968–69 academic year, Simmons sent a report to the president, which began:

> Dear President Pitzer: I wish to express my appreciation for the confidence you and other colleagues have shown in my judgments during this past academic year. It was this knowledge that made me look ahead despite several tense and agonizing situations. The Black Community at Stanford remains relatively ambivalent—strongly desiring at times to push forward in positive and constructive ways the movement for equal opportunities and human dignity; sincerely wanting to be actively engaged in constructive efforts designed to eliminate racism in all its ugly forms, but at the same time listening and sometimes responding to the less constructive influences; doubting the sincerity and commitment of individuals and institutions which by nature respond slowly to change, and in their frustration turning away from even their own impulses for constructiveness.[17]

Simmons's memorandum went on to push for his own set of proposals, aimed at developing activities both on campus and in East Palo Alto that would contribute to the educational experience of blacks outside the classroom—and just incidentally (though the memo said no such thing explicitly) keep them busy on activities less threatening than rallies, marches, and sit-ins. His arguments were sound and perceptive:

> The BSU is extremely interested in utilizing the vast reservoir of talent and interest at Stanford toward the solution of economic, educational, and social problems of the East Palo Alto Community. . . . Most black students at Stanford, while conscious of their own advantages at Stanford still identify posi-

tively with their black brothers and sisters whose lives reflect society's failures. They are restless and defensive when they believe that our concerns are limited to their individual needs while a student at Stanford.

This "defensive" attitude reflected not only the fact that, as Stanford students, they were privileged, but most of them had come from solidly middle-class backgrounds. Kenny Washington's *grandparents* went to college, while Charles Countee's parents had "multiple college degrees" and Charles himself had graduated from the Kent School in Connecticut.[18] We were often criticized for "creaming"—bringing to Stanford middle-class students with reasonably good SAT scores, who were likely to get a college degree in any event. Our answer always was that we were not abandoning meritocratic principles just because we were making allowances for educational shortcomings rooted in race. We saw ourselves as contributing our small part to the creation, under forced draft so to speak, of an array of professionals and other leaders from minority groups. I sometimes referred to the criticism as "attacking us for making silk purses out of silk." But it is not surprising that the beneficiaries felt the ambivalence that Simmons described, and never more acutely than when some incident, such as the Tresidder store affair, brought town and gown into close proximity, or even made them overlap.[19]

. . .

At Stanford as elsewhere, the changes brought about by the response to King's assassination were by far the most important and lasting of any attempted in that era so often seen as one of revolutionary change. The complexion (quite literally) of Stanford began changing then, and it has continued to the point where non-Hispanic whites are a minority of the undergraduate student body. Stubborn difficulties remain. Partly because so many other (and more lucrative) opportunities have opened up in society for minority members, recruitment of blacks and Hispanics to faculty positions continues to present problems. And because other comparable institutions are trying to cope with the same situation, "raiding" of minority faculty is frequent even in periods of slack academic markets. Many minority faculty live in a revolving door, and their total numbers remain small.

The African Americans paved the way, but others were soon to follow. Chicano students organized in their counterpart to the BSU, MEChA—Movimento Estudiantil Chicano de Aztlan—ably led by a law student named

Luis Nogales, who soon became the assistant to the president for Chicano affairs and eventually a Stanford trustee.[20]

MEChA's political style differed from the BSU to some degree. There was always the added complication that, for many, being Chicano involved choice—they could "pass" as Anglos with little effort. Their relations with the blacks have been characterized by the same ambiguities that have arisen elsewhere. To the extent that the sum of resources that can be tapped for minority programs is not infinite, there will be rivalries. "Identity politics" by definition makes alliances fragile.

In undertaking to recruit American Indian students to Stanford, the university was not responding to community demands. Recognition grew among university leaders that in many ways Native Americans constituted the most disadvantaged of all minorities. Ray Bacchetti played a leading role in this. The grim statistics about health, employment, nutrition, alcoholism, and suicide were becoming familiar in the late 1960s. In 1970 Stanford committed itself to trying to recruit twenty-five Native Americans for the next year's freshman class. On the recommendation of Dean of Admissions Fred Hargadon, generally a sturdy defender of academic standards, we relaxed the hitherto inflexible requirement that to be admitted to the university, any candidate must, on paper, appear qualified to do the work at Stanford. Given the deprivations suffered by American Indians on the reservations, we thought it would be necessary, despite the unhappy experience of trying such an "experiment" with low-income blacks, to bend somewhat. The result was again unhappy. We achieved our target, but the twenty-five and their immediate successors were the only ethnic minority to suffer high dropout rates, and before long we had to reinstate the regular policy, even at the cost of some slowing of recruitment.

Of course our decisions and policies regarding minorities were no more guided by 20/20 foresight than anyone else's. We did not foresee how long it would take—if indeed it ever happens—to erase the differences in academic performance between minorities, particularly blacks, and white Anglo students. Some of us, myself included, were never entirely happy with affirmative action organized by means of "goals and timetables." These did indeed too often take on most aspects of quotas, and we only accepted them because: (1) to do so came to be required by law, and (2) we saw such affirmative action as a temporary bridge to the promised land of equal opportunity.

If we did not foresee how dominant "identity politics" would become over time, we did resist the demand, repeated several times, that we establish an exclusively African American dormitory. The argument for such an innovation was that blacks had such a difficult time adjusting to life at Stanford that they needed a safe haven to which to retreat at the end of the day. Our concern, justified by events elsewhere, was that rather than a safe haven the dorm would become a recruiting aid and a fortress for the more militant, from which they could sally forth prepared to do battle with "Whitey." With some reluctance, we did agree to the creation of a "theme house," with half the beds (but no more than half) to be allocated to black students. This solution was (and remains) less than ideal; recruiting white students to share the house has sometimes been difficult, and coercion in such a situation is clearly ruled out. Some racial incidents have had their origins in a theme house. But holding the line for the proposition that Stanford must strive to remain a *university* and not a confederation of racially defined groups seems to me to have been worthwhile.

6 THE FIRST OLD UNION SIT-IN

SEPARATION OF THE ORGANIZED BLACK STUDENTS from the anti-Vietnam activists was not a conscious purpose of the Stanford administration in working to achieve a constructive outcome to the crisis precipitated by the murder of Martin Luther King Jr. But it was among the more important short-term consequences. When the next crisis came, just a couple of weeks later, the BSU was not involved. Things went badly enough without them; one winces to think what might have happened had the two causes been linked.

For more than four years, the system for dealing with infractions of university rules and regulations on the part of students—the student judicial system—had been disintegrating. The system became ever more ineffectual, while efforts to reorganize it came and went and came again. Intelligent and well-meaning people (with a few not so well-meaning) worked on and off, sometimes intensively, to fix things, but to no avail.

In quiet times, the stresses on the ill-defined "system" were bearable. There were a bewildering number of jurisdictions. Fraternity men were held accountable mostly by the Interfraternity Council. There were procedures for in-dorm violations; there was a Freshman Men's Judicial Council. But undergraduates were largely the province of Men's Council and Women's Council, which combined when necessary to form the Student Judicial Council. Let it not be imagined, however, that when both men and women were involved this necessarily required treatment by the combined councils. David Harris tells a horrific tale of how freshman Dennis Sweeney and his equally inexperienced girlfriend were found, passed out from drink on a Palo Alto lawn one predawn. He was tried by the Men's Council and given a one-quarter suspension, which was then suspended (that is, he was given an elaborate form of probation), while she was sentenced by the Women's Council to a two-quarter suspension that was actually carried out.[1]

When Stanford began creating overseas campuses, a rather jerry-built version of the home campus system was extended to them. In a much publicized case in the spring of 1964, an undergraduate named Frank Morse was given differing sentences at one point or another by the Florence campus council, the Judicial Council back at Stanford, and the dean of students, for willfully kicking in a glass panel door on the last day of the academic term. The publicity surrounding this (usually everything went on behind closed doors) stirred dissatisfaction with the ramshackle and confused arrangements.[2]

What these various bodies were to enforce was far from clear. Underlying everything was a statement by Stanford's founding president, David Starr Jordan, that came to be called the Fundamental Standard: "Students are expected to show, both within and without the University, such respect for order, morality, personal honor and the rights of others as is demanded of good citizens." This platitudinous, circular, and question-begging pronouncement might provide guidance in an era of more or less shared middle-class American heartland values. In an era of increasing cultural and ethnic diversity and growing litigiousness, it was more often a bone of contention than a beacon of light.

A sign of its perceived inadequacy was the declaration of policy on campus demonstrations promulgated in 1964. Clearly "respect for order," and so on, needed to be codified to enable the university to cope with a phenomenon unknown in Jordan's day.

It will be recalled that the Crow/Halverson report, which precipitated the crisis over Lucile Allen, was a move in the politics of reforming the judicial system; the unfortunate dean's behavior was used as evidence of a system gone awry. The masterly report of the ad hoc faculty committee that followed gave, as its concluding recommendation, "Our observations confirm the importance and urgency of the ongoing student-faculty-administration efforts to clarify and revise the Stanford judicial process."

Their reference was to a committee headed by Robert J. Wert, dean of undergraduate studies, which began working the preceding fall and, even as the ad hoc committee urged attention to its work, was about to be effectively sidetracked by the controversy over judicial competence. In late February 1965, the student legislature declared its unwillingness to oversee the enforcement of any rules or regulations that were not consistent with LASSU's own enactments. President Sterling mobilized the Committee on University Policy and the elected faculty Advisory Board to deal with the problems thus posed. Nine representatives of these bodies met with five students over the next several months, finally reaching a compromise in September 1965. Even at that, what emerged was no more than a temporary equilibrium. The Student Judicial Council was declared to have original jurisdiction in all cases other than those in which the accused chose to have the matter determined by the dean of students or the legislature declared a conflict of law. In the event of such a conflict, the university administration would have to set up some other mechanism. The group was no doubt happy to turn future developments over to the young Committee of Fifteen (C-15), which would soon become the theater in which this tangled drama played out.[3]

The Wert Committee did not disappear immediately, however. In April it produced a tentative proposal for a student-faculty appellate board to consist of three faculty appointed by the president from a list of six nominated by the Executive Committee of the Academic Council, three students appointed by the president from a list of six nominated by the president of the ASSU, and a chair, appointed by the president from the Law School faculty. Student politicians held out for the direct appointment of students by ASSU, however, and in September 1965 the Wert Committee disbanded in favor of the Committee of Fifteen. A subcommittee chaired by law professor John McDonough worked throughout the year 1965–66, and while it could not bring the parent committee to consensus, it did produce a report in May recommending the same mechanism for an appellate board that Wert and his colleagues had reached thirteen months earlier.

Given this impasse, President Sterling instituted the Interim Judicial Body (IJB) to serve as the appeals mechanism, and as the court of first instance where there was a "conflict in law" between ASSU and the university, until C-15 could find a way to break the logjam and produce a viable permanent student/faculty appellate board. The IJB consisted of five faculty members chosen by the president, with a Law School faculty member in the chair. Its creation did not cause an uproar at the time; the vacuum had clearly to be filled somehow.

McDonough himself had meanwhile reached some conclusions concerning the whole subject of campus "discipline," which are worth taking a moment to explore, even though he could never persuade his colleagues to step back long enough from wrestling with the intricacies of appellate boards and "conflicts in law" to examine his proposals seriously. They might not have solved the problem, but they would certainly have clarified the underlying issues.[4]

McDonough asked himself how the university had come to be in the position of seeking to monitor, in exquisite detail, student conduct of all sorts. The answer was, of course, the extension to colleges of the idea of a school acting in loco parentis. For many decades—indeed until quite recently, McDonough argued—this had raised no serious problems. Even suspensions or expulsions that resulted from someone having carried the "sowing of wild oats" a bit too far did not necessarily involve lasting disgrace. (One suspects that many such offenders went on in later life to make half-rueful, half-boasting references to such events.) Nor did they provoke campaigns against alleged breaches of students' rights.

· · ·

The old system was not entirely static. With the creation of the various councils—men's, women's, judicial—elements of legalism began to intrude. While for years these councils "operated largely as an arm of the Dean's Office"—we have seen this implied in the Lucile Allen case—they increasingly came to be seen as courts with procedures adapted from the courts of law off campus. Significantly, the ASSU Constitution guaranteed to an accused student "the presumption of innocence until his guilt is proved beyond reasonable doubt." The councils did not abandon their omnibus role of investigator, prosecutor, and judge, but the basis for challenging such a role was being laid.

But why was the system now under such attack? McDonough saw several reasons. First, Stanford was no longer overwhelmingly an undergraduate institution, but half postgraduate. Graduate students might or might not be wiser or more mature, but they were older and saw themselves as removed from the condition of school pupils. Secondly, undergraduates themselves often "come to us far less accustomed to accepting parental direction and authority than were their predecessors"; to them, the university acting in loco parentis was trying to roll back the clock, "an attempt to impose anew limitations from which at home they have for some time since been substantially emancipated."

Add to these changes the state of flux evident in the wider society on such matters as appropriate sexual behavior and the relation, if any, between public authority and monitoring such behavior, not to mention increased attention to the possibilities of civil disobedience, and the stage is clearly set for greatly increased dissension over the university system of student discipline. Dissenters quite naturally looked to still more "legalism," in the form of procedural safe-guards, or alterations in existing power relationships within the system.

McDonough's proposals, advanced with many expressions of tentativeness (more in the hope of disarming his potential critics than as expressions of actual uncertainties in the mind of the author, one suspects), were that the university withdraw from the overall monitoring of student conduct and recast its role under two headings, "educator" and "proprietor." Wrote McDonough:

> As [an] *educator*, it seems to me, the University's concern with a student's conduct would not be whether it conforms to the requirements of "good citizenship" generally, but only whether it casts doubt upon the student's continued entitlement to be a member of the university's intellectual community—that is, whether his continued association with us would appear to create unacceptable risks to our ongoing educational enterprise.

Thus both punishment as a concept and particular punishments, such as hours of work in the corporation yard, would be set aside, in favor of decisions about the continuing viability of the consensual arrangement by which a person becomes a student of Stanford University. The outcome might be separation, either temporary (suspension) or permanent (expulsion). To deal with an obvious question—What about offences that are not serious enough to warrant separation, but might well become so if repeated?—McDonough developed the ingenious notion of "demerits." Accumulate enough of these—a number would have to be determined in advance and for all cases—and you find yourself extruded from the university.[5]

In its role as "proprietor," the university would be doing no more or less than owners of other complex facilities, such as restaurants or bookstores, to impose and enforce regulations of various kinds. Here McDonough was not quite so clear in describing how the system would work; one infers that in many situations, outside law enforcement would simply take over. These regulations would not be especially for students—they would be the same for visitors, staff members, customers. Having removed the element of moral guidance, there would be fewer regulations, while procedurally the apparatus of quasi-criminal proceedings could be largely dismantled since as applied to students the operative questions would be just two:

> (1) Has this student failed in some important way to live up to the university community's expectations of him? (2) How serious or significant is this

default in terms of his entitlement to remain a member of the community? A student's expulsion or suspension would no longer be regarded [as] an extreme form of punishment for antisocial behavior. Rather, it would simply be a determination that the University, as one party to a mutually assumed consensual relationship, had concluded that it was unwilling to go on living and working with the student concerned.

Adoption of McDonough's rationale would surely have made it easier to focus subsequent debates on manageable issues—for example, how to construct the system of demerits. But events took over, in unforeseen ways, to give shape to the controversies and to convert a discussion of the mechanisms for dealing with student conduct into a raging political struggle that at times seemed to threaten the very future of the institution.

The argument flared up in the spring of 1967 when the IJB overturned the acquittal of Marc Sapir, a medical student and a defendant in the 1966 sit-in case who had not been a registered student at the time. The intricacies need not concern us—they were many—but the reversal gave Sapir and others an opportunity to attack the system effectively, at least from a student standpoint. Sapir said, "This decision makes in loco parentis explicit. The Judicial Council must enforce University rules regardless of whether students have a part in making those rules. It makes it impossible for an equitable student judicial system to exist."[6] The tone of the discussion can be further inferred from the statement of a member of the overruled Judicial Council, Dan Lewis, who said, "The Fundamental Standard is dead. It did not die a natural death. It was bludgeoned to death by bureaucratic stupidity."[7]

That fall, the abortive attempt at stopping the CIA from holding placement interviews set in motion the events leading to the crisis of May 1968, with consequences extending far beyond the student judicial system.

On November 20, the dean of students was informed that the ASSU Judicial Council had refused to hear the case of the nine (later ten) students charged in connection with that event, on the grounds that LASSU had rejected the university policy on campus demonstrations (an action taken by LASSU *after* the CIA episode). The dean of students turned to the Interim Judicial Body as the established court of first instance in such a situation. But the Judicial Council then had a change of heart and took the case back. It was soon clear why. After thirty hours of hearings, the council acquitted the defendants, on a divided vote and with a torrent of opinions—individual, collective, dissenting, concurring—the array was bewildering and ran to ten thousand words according to the ASSU, which took the unusual step of buying an advertisement in the *Daily* to publish the full texts, saying they "should help to bring the issues into clear focus."[8]

A pious hope, surely. The decisions cover a remarkable range of subjects and argumentation. They demonstrate what a lot of intellectual energy went into student political life in those days; scholars and Supreme Court decisions were cited, the suitability (or lack of it) of trying to base judgments on the Fundamental Standard was argued, the question of the degree to which it would be legitimate to take into account the intent of the actors in the drama discussed. At the heart of the judgment, however, was this sweeping assertion: "We find that the University Policy on Campus Demonstrations is . . . overbroad and vague. We find that, because of this overbreadth and vagueness, the Policy violates the First Amendment and the freedom of expression inherent in the idea of a University. We therefore hold the Policy to be entirely unenforceable in this case, and in any case that may come before us."

If ever a quasi-judicial ruling threw down a gauntlet it was this one. The administration was quick to pick it up; the dean of students appealed the case to the IJB. The politicization of the whole affair soon became manifest. As Herb Packer wrote a few weeks later, "An appeal is designed, of course, to review possible errors in the original proceeding rather than to go through that proceeding again. Accordingly, the record of the original proceeding is needed for the scrutiny of the appellate body. The Student Judicial Council frustrated this scrutiny by refusing to make available to the IJB the tape-recorded record of the hearing before it."[9]

Thus when the IJB held hearings, the dean had to present the case all over again. This time only one of the seven defendants obeyed the summons to attend. Probably few were surprised when the IJB found all seven guilty and recommended suspensions: five for summer quarter 1968, the remaining two, repeat offenders who had been convicted the previous year on charges growing out of the President's Office sit-in, for summer and fall quarters.

Although few may have been surprised, many were outraged. ASSU President Cesare Massarenti declared, "This sentence is like capital punishment because several of the students could be drafted."[10]

The ruling was published Friday, May 3. That noon, a rally in White Plaza led to a march on the President's Office and the presentation there of these demands: "That the recommendations of the IJB not be accepted and that the case be dismissed; That the IJB be disbanded; That a permanent appellate board be set up in the following way: It will be composed of nine members; Four members will be students, chosen by students; Four members will be faculty, chosen by faculty; One member will be chosen by the other eight from the Law School student body."

That afternoon a meeting was held involving faculty from the Executive Committee, the Committee on University Policy, and chair of other faculty committees, the four top officers of the ASSU, and two of the convicted demonstrators. As law professor William F. Baxter reported in Monday's *Daily*, one or more of the students present agreed expressly, and none disagreed expressly, with each of the following propositions:

> That the existence of the IJB was consistent with the Tripartite Agreement on which the present judicial structure and the Committee of 15 are based; that to establish the new permanent judicial body demanded would be in violation of the Tripartite Agreement; [that] the only justification for denying recognition to the IJB was frustration over the duration of C-15 negotiations; that no accusation was being made that any member of the C-15 had failed to bargain earnestly and in good faith; and that there was no genuine expectation on their part that the University would accept a judicial body containing a majority of student members.

In substance these students conceded that the demands they were presenting, under a deadline, were in violation of previous agreements and that they did not expect the demands to be accepted. They were presented, in short, not with hope of acceptance but so that they would be rejected.

Seldom, surely, have the strategy and tactics of a manufactured crisis been more devastatingly exposed while the crisis was in the process of building toward its climax.

Also in Monday's *Daily*, political science professor Hubert Marshall, chair of C-15, spoke to the issue of his group's failure thus far to conclude its work. First, C-15 had not met at all in fall quarter because the president of the ASSU, Peter Lyman, had not appointed the student members.[11] "But we have made progress in every session since the Committee began its work in January," and he had hopes of an early resolution—unless "the events of the next few days were to inflame passions to the point that agreement on an entirely new set of institutional arrangements becomes impossible."

That passions were already inflamed in some breasts was clear from yet a third letter to that day's paper, this from Tom Forstenzer, an experienced student politician and veteran of earlier C-15s:

> The sentence passed on the CIA demonstrators is vicious, but it is no more brutal than the year to year, day to day treatment of students at Stanford whenever they rock the boat. Every time an interim solution is adopted (which is the same as saying that students are barred from choosing their own representatives to such vital panels as the IJB or SES or any presidential advisory board) that patronizing dean or provost says, "Golly, gee, I wish we could do this because I'm really on your side, but we're in a bind." What he is really saying is "Go to hell."

A group meeting in Tresidder on Sunday evening voted to stage "some kind of militant demonstration" on Monday. Masserenti said he would urge all candidates running in the student body elections then underway to withdraw their candidacies, and all students serving on committees, including the Study of Education at Stanford (SES) Steering Committee, to resign, unless the demands were met. Also Sunday evening, Sterling called a special meeting of the Academic Council for Wednesday afternoon, to discuss the pending reform from the Committee of Fifteen, which was "now very close to producing agreement on a system that will satisfy the criteria of all but a very few zealots of the far Left and far Right. . . . My expectation is that by the end of this quarter we will have agreement on revised structures for rule-making and judging that can go into operation next September." He gave the defendants until Friday to meet individually with him before he reached a decision on whether to "accept, modify, or reject" the IJB's recommendations.

The president's staff guessed (correctly) that the likeliest target for a sit-in would be the Old Union, home of the Dean of Students Office and of the registrar, admission, and financial aid staffs. Late Monday morning we locked the building, "in the vain hope that burglary and forcible entry were offenses that Stanford students would be unlikely to commit."[12]

Around 1 p.m. "a handful of students jimmied open the windows, climbed in, and liberated the front door with bolt cutters. Several hundred more poured into the Old Union and the sit-in began."[13]

Some of the demonstrators "deliberately interfered with TV cameramen and press photographers," but Steve Weissman, a leader of the Free Speech Movement at Berkeley and now a graduate student at Stanford said later, "These [TV] cameras here will help us keep the building hostage. This is just the kind of publicity the University doesn't want."

Responding to some pressure for me to go to the Old Union courtyard and speak, we announced that a travel film scheduled for Memorial Auditorium Monday evening would be replaced by a three-person panel: William Baxter, C-15 chair Hubert Marshall, and me at 8:30. Massarenti announced a general student assembly at the Old Union, and some fifteen hundred gathered there at 7:30. In a series of votes, the crowd backed the demands of the demonstration but "split about 3–2 against the sit-in tactic."

In Memorial Auditorium, I supported reform but defended the IJB as "a thoroughly legitimate body," criticized Peter Lyman and Massarenti for the delay in appointing the student members of C-15, and said "the question is whether we progress toward a more rational, fairer and more effective system or a series of increasingly ugly confrontations." Marshall described the C-15's plans to create a new rule-making group as well as a reformed judicial council, each with substantial student representation, and he expressed the hope that this would lead to "an extraordinarily important de facto shift in power from the President and Board of Trustees . . . the first important step toward community government." (I'm sure I must have winced at his use of this catchphrase, then popular on the Left to denote the post-hierarchical era of participatory democracy envisioned by SDS and its supporters.)

Meanwhile inside the Old Union a vote taken around 9 p.m. went against continuation of the sit-in. Weissman said, "I think leaving is the wrong decision, but we're stuck." About fifteen remained in the building, but most headed for Memorial Auditorium where their arrival created a problem: the hall was already full, and the fire marshal told me I would have to insist that those without seats leave. In an effort to avoid a nasty confrontation over this, I took a chance and suggested that those who had asked their questions or had none they wanted to ask should yield their seats to the newcomers. Many did, and "as the demonstrators took their place, the complexion of the meeting changed markedly." In one of the few occasions on which Bruce Franklin and I encountered one another directly during these years, he criticized the question-and-answer format as reflecting the one-way power relationships of the university. I pointed out that most of the questions had been "friendly to your point of view," but when he urged that a student be added to the panel, Massarenti joined us on stage to attack what we had been saying. The tone of things as we adjourned is indicated by my ungracious parting remark, "I had hoped to thank you all for coming." About five hundred people trooped back to the Old Union and the sit-in resumed.

Was the resumption inevitable, or did the Memorial Auditorium meeting reenergize the sitters-in, after the negative vote earlier that evening? It seems likely that this was the case, though one cannot be sure. I asked myself at the time whether I had forfeited the chances of the sit-in petering out by my move to find space for the hostile newcomers. But the alternative—trying to get them to leave the auditorium against their will—was not very promising. After all, despite the vote, a core had remained sitting in throughout—rejoining them was easy.

.   .   .

At around 3 a.m. Tuesday, the Naval ROTC building was burned to the ground by an arsonist. The same wooden structure had been partially burned on February 18; neither crime was ever solved by the police. But David Harris tells how Dennis Sweeney, distressed by David's preoccupation with Joan Baez and with his making speeches around the country instead of providing leadership on campus, and others from the commune where they all lived carried out the first arson while Harris was out of town.[14]

He makes no mention of the second, more successful attempt. That it had anything directly to do with the sit-in seems highly unlikely, given the emphasis on orderly peacefulness in the Old Union, once the initial forcible entry had been achieved, not to mention the difficulties the leadership were having in sustaining even this nonviolent affair.

Tuesday the demonstration continued, with improvised seminars and discussions and with a conspicuous effort to keep the building in decent condition. At a noon rally, Weissman discounted the Monday night vote: "The vote of students in general assembly is not binding. . . . Sit-ins always are minority acts which provoke conscience." Support for the sit-in came from a variety of quarters. Several faculty spoke out, notably the future conservative, Michael Novak, then assistant professor of religious studies:

> Where one group has all the power, one must be suspicious of appeals to reason. . . . Students have very little power in the university; hence their views are not taken to be very "realistic." "Realism" is defined by those who exercise or defend present power. By sitting in, however, students create a new factor in the situation, which the "Realistic" must take seriously. In this way—and often this way alone—do human beings make progress in genuine communication. The seven convicted students should not be punished. They should

be commended for awakening us to Stanford's real responsibilities when no one else cared.

At the same time, a six-student delegation presented me with a petition bearing sixteen hundred signatures, saying, "We will follow President Sterling in the manner he uses to keep his position from being dominated by a show of force instead of student-administration compromise." Students were working to put referenda against the sit-in on the student body election ballot.

At 9:30 Tuesday evening one of the more bizarre episodes of this turbulent week occurred when David Packard showed up at the sit-in unannounced (and without advance warning to the administration). He got a surprised but welcoming reception from the demonstrators, and he told them, "We don't want the type of thing we had at Columbia. I came here to gain a better understanding in case the trustees have to decide anything in this matter—and I hope we don't. We'll keep working until we find a solution here." He supported students "having a voice in influencing" university decisions, "but not by force." After he left, Bruce Franklin chided the demonstrators for having been so receptive to this icon of the enemy who had suddenly appeared in their midst.

The more important development that Tuesday night was the C-15's meeting that reached unanimous agreement on charters for a Student Conduct Legislative Council and a Judicial Council. Divisions over the immediate crisis, however, tarnished their unanimity in support of the new mechanisms. By a vote of seven to six they rejected a resolution expressing "hope that suspensions will not prove appropriate" as a penalty in the CIA case. By twelve to one they urged Sterling to make his decision "independently of previous decisions" after consulting with the members of the IJB and the Student Judicial Council and receiving any statements from individual defendants. This was not enough for the five student members, who issued a statement hailing the committee's work as "tremendously valuable in setting up a viable judicial and legislative structure to handle student affairs and to involve students in decision-making processes at Stanford," but lamenting that C-15 had "failed tragically to meet the specific grievances which the current demonstration protests. We believe that no resolution will be found to the present impasse until . . . students, faculty and administration agree that the suspensions of the CIA demonstrators be rescinded and that amnesty be guaranteed for all students now demonstrating. Only such an agreement . . . can pre-empt the possibility of disaster for Stanford."

When it met Wednesday afternoon the Academic Council had before it a group of resolutions drawn up by the Executive Committee, backed by the administration, and hewing closely to the provisions passed by the C-15 regarding both the new councils and the treatment of the CIA case and the sit-in. This meant, of course, that the dissent on the latter points from the five students on C-15 was being ignored. On the other hand the administration was having to swallow what amounted to a trial de novo of the CIA case by the president. Furthermore, the Executive Committee voted unanimously to urge the president "that in order to avoid jeopardy to the inception of a new judicial system, no action be taken against persons for their involvement as such in the present demonstrations, on the assumption that there is a reasonably prompt withdrawal of the students without further untoward incidents." But they voted to do so in a *private* communication to the president from their acting chair. As the minutes recorded, "It was observed that it was more likely that the President would be able to act in fact on the basis of this advice than to commit himself in advance and publicly to such action."[15]

After preliminary speeches by the president and the speaker of ASSU and by me, Professor Ernest Hilgard, acting chair of the Executive Committee, moved the first of its resolutions, agreeing with the C-15 majority that the CIA case should be heard afresh by the president.[16]

Before there could be any discussion of this motion, Professor Halsted Holman moved to substitute for it with a resolution drawn up by a group of 15 Medical School faculty, which substantially enacted each of the sit-in's demands.

There were objections that only *one* of the points in the Holman resolution—that proposing amnesty for the CIA defendants—was germane to the Executive Committee's resolution No. 1. Professor Holman, displaying great parliamentary finesse, then moved to table the Executive Committee resolutions. A motion to table, as you know, is not debatable. The motion carried by a voice vote, less than five minutes after Professor Hilgard moved the first of the Executive Committee's resolutions and without any discussion whatever of the merits of that resolution.

That motion to table, which paved the way for the subsequent introduction of the omnibus Holman resolution, was, it turned out, the crucial vote of the afternoon, not merely because of its effect on the substance of what the Council enacted but because it effectively precluded any separation of issues and therefore any rational discussion of the issues. By that single action, the Council abandoned any pretense to acting as a deliberative body.

Professor Arbib then moved to amend the Holman resolution's point 3, with respect to the CIA amnesty, to give the administration leave to appeal the student judicial ruling to the "new judicial board." A call for the question on that amendment passed by a vote of 284 to 256, thanks to the fortunate ignorance that a call for the question must pass by a two-thirds vote under Robert's Rules of Order.[17]

I say "fortunate" because it became apparent that opponents of anything short of total surrender to student demands were just as determined to prolong debate when they thought they might lose as they had been to cut it off when they thought they would win. Professor Arbib's amendment—stopping short of total amnesty—carried by an affirmative vote of 346. It would appear that close to 200 members of the Council favored total amnesty. How carefully they managed to inform themselves about the merits of the case, its procedural history, or the jurisdictional basis for the IJB I have no way of knowing. I do have a small clue, though. One of the fifteen faculty members who signed the Holman resolution sent me a note the day before the Council meeting containing a number of more or less perceptive comments on the controversy, in the course of which he remarked, "I cannot comment on the issues of fact in the whole mess, for I am poorly informed on them, but I can comment on the feelings which can easily be identified in the students' reactions." Just so.[18]

Professor [Byron] Sher then moved to amend yet another point in the multifarious Holman motion by substituting the Executive Committee–C-15 interim judicial arrangement for the Holman version, which, as I have said, closely resembled the original student demand. This amendment carried by an affirmative vote of 343. Once again, some 200 members of the faculty were prepared to ride roughshod over the careful work done by the Committee of Fifteen and the position taken, after extensive discussion, by the Council's own Executive Committee.

The Holman resolution then passed by 286 to 245 on a divided vote. It was apparent, however, that some had voted who were not members of the council. Professor David Potter, the distinguished U.S. historian, moved for an unprecedented roll-call vote. Uproar ensued; I recall feeling particularly infuriated by the aspersions being cast on Potter's motives. There was no faculty member whom I loved and respected more. I recall going to the podium to say, in what I am sure were tones of cold contempt, "I think before you vote to overturn the recommendations of your administration and your own Executive Committee, you ought to be willing to stand up and be counted." The outcome of the roll call was virtually the same as the voice vote: 284 to 241. I heard later that some thought I was making note of who voted against us, for purposes of exacting vengeance later in tenure and salary decisions. Perhaps naively, I was shocked that anyone who knew me would attribute such motives to me—but no doubt I would have been better advised to have absented myself during the roll call. As Herb Packer pointed out:

> Those voting in the minority included the deans of the schools, every faculty member of the Committee of Fifteen and all but one member of the Executive Committee of the Academic Council.
>
> The Council, now thoroughly worn out [after three and one-half hours of wrangling] quickly passed the rest of the Executive Committee resolutions, defeating, however, an amendment to the resolution calling on the demonstrators to vacate the Old Union that would have called upon them to desist from further coercive tactics. That, it was thought, would have been overly provocative. And so, the Council, its mission of securing peace in our time accomplished, adjourned.

The reference to "peace in our time" was of course intended to remind his listeners of Chamberlain's defense of the Munich Accord. It was probably such rhetorical devices, rather than any actual distortions or misstatements of fact that so infuriated his critics. His account erred in one minor respect: before adjourning, the council voted overwhelmingly in favor of a resolution of confidence in the administration moved by the historian Mark Mancall. We regarded that as crocodile tears and close to meaningless in view of the actions the council had just taken.

Clearly the establishment voted almost to a man in the minority. The breakdown within schools was interesting: the largest, the School of Humanities and Sciences, voted about two to one for the Holman resolution; professors in the humanities especially favored it. Medicine, the home of the Holman group, backed it by nearly four to one. Nine-tenths of the Law School faculty voted against it, as did all the Graduate School of Business faculty. Engineering voted nearly two to one against, Earth Sciences more than four to one against. And the School of Education split down the middle, eleven for and ten against.

It seems probable that the decisive element in the faculty's majority decision was fear of "another Columbia" at Stanford—a police riot, in effect. Professor Gordon Craig, the dean of U.S. historians of Germany, wrote in his diary, "The important thing is that we have prevented another Columbia situation by yesterday's vote and taken away the SDS's following who will not support radical demands of the kind mentioned today [on White Plaza, see below]—unless another administration mistake gives an opportunity for uniting the students again. We can't predict what will happen as a result of our Yes vote yesterday; but I am sure that the result of a No vote was predictable."[19]

I received so many letters in the days following from individuals who had voted for the Holman resolution but also for Mancall's vote of confidence that I had to resort to a form response to all. Representative of this influx of mail was a letter from another history colleague, George Knoles: "The response to the Mancall resolution in my judgment was genuine; I had no mental reservations in casting my affirmative vote and I believe that few, if any others had such reservations."

The vote on the Holman resolution "was not a vote of 'no confidence'; it was a vote in favor of restoring an atmosphere in which discussions leading to decisions acceptable to large segments of the faculty and students could be made." He argued that having gone the extra mile to meet the student demands this time would result in more, not less support for the administration the next time the university faced a similar crisis.[20]

In my reply I recognized that

> many felt frustrated and confused by the chaos of parliamentary maneuver and by a pervasive ignorance as to what the real issues were. Indeed, it was because I anticipated the likelihood of difficulty in achieving clarity and coherence in that setting that I urged the Council not to tie the hands of those who must carry out the responsibility of keeping Stanford free—and indeed viable as an educational institution—in the face of physical force and ultimatum. The recommendation for full amnesty for the Old Union demonstrators did, I believe, tie our hands, and set a dangerous precedent for the future.

On a more conciliatory note I concluded that "the fact that so many of you voted for the Holman resolution, on May 8th, yet took the trouble to write so kindly to me, provides a welcome basis from which to start picking up the pieces and sorting out the issues."

Bruce Franklin rushed from Dinkelspiel, where the council had been meeting, over to the Old Union and told the expectant crowd there, "I personally feel this vote is a great big victory. . . . I urge that we accept this and leave [the Union] as soon as possible." This they shortly did, but their parting statement reflected the divisions among them over the C-15 proposals. The faculty vote, they said, proved that "our presence had been morally and tactically effective. The 'occupation' forced an understanding of the seriousness and urgency of the issues by the student body, the Academic Council, and the Administration." But the C-15 plan "leaves unamended a basic flaw in the political structure of this university: faculty and students lack the franchise to make and enforce decisions about their own lives." Only that morning, after all, the demonstrators had issued a statement calling on the Academic Council to discuss their demands, not the C-15 proposals, which they labeled "humiliating, obscurantist, and antithetical to the substance of our demands and demonstration."[21]

Ironically, the student body election results that same month showed conclusively that if the sit-in "forced an understanding of the seriousness and urgency of the issues by the student body," the understanding reached by the majority was very different from that of the demonstrators. On May 8, in the largest vote ever cast in an ASSU primary, a referendum backed by a nearly six-to-one margin the proposition that "all employers—not illegal in the eyes of the civil courts—be allowed equal access to recruiting facilities" at Stanford. A week later, in the final election, a resolution calling the forcible occupation of university buildings "unacceptable behavior at Stanford" passed by more than two to one, and another censuring ASSU President Massarenti for having advocated and participated in such an occupation passed three to two. And, just for good measure, the students rejected the candidacy for ASSU president of a topless dancer and elected instead the outgoing vice president, Dennis Hayes, who later was the founder of Earth Day in the United States.[22]

·   ·   ·

The evening after the Academic Council vote, Herb Packer and I, without communicating with one another, each wrote a short letter of resignation for submission the following day, on the grounds that the meeting had shown Stanford to be, as he put it, "ungovernable, in the literal sense of that word."[23]

In the cold light of morning, however, and again independently, we both decided that to desert Wally Sterling at such a juncture, and within a few months of his retirement, would be irresponsible. Rumors circulated, based on my over-the-shoulder response to someone (probably a reporter from the *Daily*) who ran after me as I walked from the council meeting back to Building Ten and asked whether I "could live with the outcome"; I said "no." The lead editorial in the next day's *Daily* was headlined "R.W. Lyman," and referred to "much speculation on campus that Lyman will resign because of the Academic Council vote on Wednesday. In this time of division and unrest on campus, Stanford needs Richard Lyman, and we urge him to stay." I had "made mistakes" during the three-day crisis, but "saved the University" by what I did *not* do, for example, we did not call in the police.

It remained for Sterling and me to accept the resolutions voted by the faculty, and we did so on May 10. "We have serious misgivings about some of them [the Academic Council resolutions]. We nevertheless accept those recommendations and commit ourselves to their implementation." We went on to urge speedy action to approve the C-15 proposals:[24]

> Noting the recommendation of amnesty for the sit-in, we continued: We defer to that faculty recommendation. We wish to emphasize that the faculty resolution speaks of demonstrations "to date" and accordingly we understand the faculty to support the view of the President that future disruptions will not be tolerated. It is the intention of the President to deal with any such disruptions promptly and firmly.[25]

Coming from a president who was within less than four months of retirement, and who had just suffered defeat on efforts "to deal with [a disruption] promptly and firmly" precisely because the faculty did not "support the view of the President," this whistling in the dark cannot have struck much fear in any radical breast.

The radicals, after initial jubilation and euphoria, quickly began expressing their own doubts as to the significance of their victory. In White Plaza on May 9, Steve Weissman and others complained about the faculty majorities on the proposed Student Conduct Legislative Council and Judicial Council. Weissman announced two new goals: student control of faculty tenure appointments and of presidential selection. "Students need confrontation politics so they will not be co-opted into the consensus of decision-making." The audience reaction was mixed—enthusiasm up front, silence toward the rear. Gordon Craig noted wryly, "Today, at a meeting in White Plaza, the SDS leaders indicated clearly that they will act again when an occasion presents itself and that their ultimate targets are the University Charter, the hierarchical principle, the system of tenure, etc. This was always clear, although it seems to daunt some people who voted Yes yesterday, who feel outraged at some of the careful sneers directed at them by Weissman at today's meeting."

In an interview in the alternative paper, the *Midpeninsula Observer*, Bruce Franklin said he thought "the power relationships actually did change during the course of the struggle. The fact that the faculty as a body understood that it had political power, if it wanted it, was one of the more significant developments."[26] He also said, "One of the main things we did was to create a very beautiful society inside that building. It was an alternative to the existing society, and the people began to see an extension from that, of a new kind of society in which people related to each other not as objects of exploitation, but really as brothers and sisters, or comrades, or whatever word you want to use." At the same time, Franklin sounded distinctly frustrated by the limited nature of the "struggle":

> I think we did clearly make a mistake in the kind of demands that we took into that building. I think they were basically silly demands. We had them because we were dealing with a lot of people who were concerned about the particular issues to which the demands related. I think the C15 proposal is clearly a step backward from what we have now, but I don't see what could have been done in the demonstration given the fact that the C15 was what it was and had been doing what it had been doing.

This constituted a rare admission that reform could on occasion seriously hamper the radicals' efforts to "raise consciousness." It was also illustrative of a general truth about the era pronounced by John R. Searle, a Free Speech Movement (FSM) faculty supporter turned critic: "Large numbers of students who will not demonstrate illegally against the war in Vietnam or for free speech will demonstrate illegally . . . against someone's being disciplined for illegally demonstrating against the war in Vietnam or for free speech."[27]

Another headline in the same issue of the *Midpeninsula Observer* read, "How the Sit-In Failed: War Machine Not Hurt," while a third piece warned against overinterpreting the vote in the Academic Council: "The only definite interpretation that can be made is that the students who sat in *do not* have 280 friends in the faculty who agree with the demand for student power." Rather, "votes were cast against the administration, against the professional schools, against bringing police on campus, against the turmoil that had shaken everyone out of his particular stupor."

When the Stanford chapter of the Association of American University Professors (AAUP) invited Herb Packer to be its after-dinner speaker on May 13, no one anticipated how much the political earth on campus would have moved by then. His talk was a brilliant narration-cum-analysis of the crisis, and as angry as it was brilliant. According to Packer, the supporters of the Holman resolutions "thought they were saving the university. And by their lights, they succeeded—for a few days or a few weeks. By yielding to gross physical coercion they ended the sit-in. And they taught a lesson that is easily learned: coercion pays. What do they propose to do next time it is applied? They did not face that question. And that, I submit, is the height of substantive irresponsibility."

In a private letter to a colleague later that year he stated his concerns more generally:

> Centrists like you and me and most other members of the Stanford faculty will be sitting ducks for the radical right unless we demonstrate our ability to distinguish between "legitimate complaints" and illegitimate means of seeking redress for those complaints. . . . If we believe that the university is not so corrupt that revolution rather than reform is needed, then we had better see to it that revolution does not become acceptable. That requires reform but it also requires the willingness to resist revolution.[28]

Many on campus agreed with B. Davie Napier, dean of the chapel, that Packer's speech was "hardly what is needed now." The bitter letters flew back and forth, and less than a week after his speech Herb himself was writing to the president of the Stanford AAUP, William Clebsch, about the "atmosphere of bitterness and recrimination. Many things have been said and done in the last two weeks that might perpetuate such an atmosphere. Few of us are guiltless in that respect. Certainly I am not."[29]

At the same time, he was also writing to Dick Guggenhime, a trustee and former board president, acknowledging the counsel that he and his colleagues, Robert Minge Brown, Parmer Fuller, and Ben Duniway had provided by phone during the crisis, and calling attention particularly to their support of the administration's decision that to summon police absent the backing of the faculty would be a mistake. He went on, with remarkable frankness:

> I believe that those of you on the Board who counselled moderation will have to speak up at Thursday's meeting. Any such tactic as letting the less

understanding members of the Board go on unchecked and uncorrected until they exhaust themselves will not suffice, among other reasons, because those of us who have been bloodied by students and by faculty are in no mood to be bloodied by Trustees! If we have to assume the entire burden of our own defense, things may well get said that will fatally impair our continuing relationship with many members of the Board, a result that I would greatly regret. I hope, therefore, that if you continue to think that we did not behave incompetently, you will say so early and often.

Clearly, the situation immediately after the debacle was very fragile.

·   ·   ·

A mysterious and isolated postscript to this year of mounting troubles was the arson that destroyed Wally Sterling's office in Building 10 at Stanford early July 5, with the mementos of his almost-completed nineteen-year presidency. As usual, since arson often burns its own evidence, no arsonist was ever identified. On the Left, some thought it "an effective attack on state power," while others thought it "a mistake . . . since it is not clearly connected with a political movement and since most of the people who might be educated by such an act are gone for the summer."[30]

For further insight into the kind of mind that could think of this crime as being potentially "educational," there is the poem to which the *Midpeninsula Observer* devoted its entire front page:

> *The Fire Comes Home*
>
> White gloves light no matches,
> Pull no triggers as the bodies fall.
> They scribble signatures, pat backs,
> Shake gloves with Deans of Business,
> Guiding Arbuckles to the top
> From Standard Oil of Stanford, the Peace Corps,
> Peru, Wells Fargo, on to better things
> For better living as in SRI
> Countering insurgency,
> Conjuring the McNamara Line,
> Counseling Strategic Hamlets.

A thatched hut after all is nothing much.
One of the hired men's lighters brings it down.
Can it compare with a rare book
Collection?
A wife and child or two at going rates
Perhaps worth eighty dollars—can they compare
In sterling value to this damage worth
$300,000?

In unison, bare hands reply, unite.
Now Sterling in his shirtsleeves walks among
Ashes that just now were precious things,
Fit for a showcase in some dead museum,
(They could have stood in rows
Where Stanford shows
Mrs. Robber Baron's clothes.)
When the fire comes home
White gloves blacken in the smoke and flame,
The hands that they have shaken start to shake.

This was signed by Jane Morgan. Fairly representative of the heavy irony laced with self-righteousness that passed for satire in the leftist polemic of those days, it can serve *us* as a reminder, if one were needed, of how sad it was for Sterling to have his final year in office so beclouded and himself so much reviled, Sterling, who in better days had been widely loved and admired and who had done so much to convert Stanford into a university of national and growing international repute.

The *Daily*, in its last regular issue of the year, gave him a remarkably gracious send off, considering the times and the often-encountered student tendency to take short views: "Wallace Sterling has been many things to us, from an enlightened administrator to a stalwart reactionary, but we will remember him as the man who made Stanford worth worrying about."[31] And on June 3, five hundred students, led by the Leland Stanford Junior University Marching Band, marched to the president's house to give him an LASSU resolution of thanks for his nineteen years of service.[32]

The sort of "worrying" that filled Sterling's mailbag in those days was anything but constructive, for the most part: a mind-numbing collection of letters often beginning "I am an alumni . . ." and going on to threaten never to give another cent to a university with such craven leadership, to see to it that their own brilliant and accomplished children do not even *think* about going there to college, and so on. Many expressed bewilderment that a *private* university should have trouble maintaining discipline.[33]

Sterling responded to his critics in his talk to the Campus Alumni Conference on May 18, just eight days after the "capitulation." He took heart from several developments: the recent action by the national AAUP at its annual meeting, in Sterling's words "condemning the actions of demonstrators which disrupt educational activities of academic institutions," be they students or faculty; the proposals at Stanford for an Academic Senate and for a reformed system for dealing with student conduct; and not least the votes of the student body condemning disruption and favoring universal access to job interviewing on campus.

The Stanford faculty was another matter: it "has more to do than to clarify its position on the permissibility of coercive tactics used by students. It needs also to clarify its position as to any of its own members who participate in such tactics."

As for his own role, he took a cue from the Executive Committee's private letter to him of May 8, arguing that for the sake of giving the new governing institutions—the Senate and the student legislative and judicial bodies—a decent chance to get themselves established and accepted, the campus needed to avoid "extended and rancorous divisiveness." He had therefore refrained from exercising his presidential right to ignore the Academic Council's recommendations. And he permitted himself one small barb for his alumni critics: "I made this judgment and I state this belief on the basis of my experience at Stanford during the past 19 years—an experience which has been only peripherally shared by those who charge [me with] capitulation."

7 CLASSIFIED RESEARCH, SRI, AND THE COMING OF KEN PITZER

WITH THE POLICE RIOTS in Chicago at the Democratic National Convention, a turning point of sorts was reached in the antiwar movement, though since people live their history forward, not backward, few if any sensed this at the time. A fascinating article by Maureen Kulbaitis in the *Peninsula Observer* written from Chicago September 1, wavers between optimistic and pessimistic interpretations (from the radical standpoint) of what happened there.[1] She writes, "It would seem that we have succeeded in showing the unrepresentative character of the political system and in exposing its potentially violent and repressive responses to human needs and protests." Worrying, as radicals of the time so often did, about the difficulties of relating the white radical movement to the black nationalists, she writes that "for one of the few times in the history of the white half of the Movement, we were taken seriously." There was, she thought, a new solidarity; "Radicals helped the Yippies defend their park and Yippies took to the streets with the radicals, a mass march supported the striking transit workers, demonstrators made real efforts to talk to the McCarthy people, and black militants began to respect the guts of the whites."

Yet she also detected a high level of danger that the movement would regress. "Perhaps it is significant that the last major street demonstration was led by Dick Gregory and numerous [Convention] delegates, and that those who participated sang 'We Shall Overcome' and were willing to be arrested peacefully to register their protest. It looked like the civil rights movement five years ago." There was always the problem of "'leaders who don't want to lead' [quoting Todd Gitlin from a *Ramparts* wall poster]. Strong leadership is opposed for ideological reasons, and when leaders surfaced, they were picked off by the Chicago police." She concludes with some very serious doubts: "Finally, how does one raise political issues by means of such action? Can small groups of demonstrators do anything more than peacefully picket or engage in petty high-school-type vandalism? Can large groups move beyond 'The Streets Belong to the People' and 'Pigs Are the Enemy' to more profound explanations? One demonstrator from Florida called what we were doing 'the politics of being pissed off.' And that may be as far as we've gotten."

At that, she was too close to the events to realize that what the U.S. public in general saw was not only Mayor Daley's crude stupidity and its consequences but also the same characteristics that infuriated the police (except for the body smell)—ragged, screaming, rock-throwing anarchists (as they seemed), mocking America and giving aid and comfort to her enemies.

At Stanford, it was a while before we saw anything similar, though in a way our turn would come. Meanwhile, in the spring of 1968, the trustees were trying to find a successor to Sterling who could cope with difficult times. When Wally Sterling asked me to be provost, in the fall of 1966, he told me of his then-unannounced intention to retire in a year and a half (that is, summer 1968), and he warned me not to expect "any first mortgages"—his way of saying that I must not assume that there was any great likelihood of my becoming his successor. He knew whereof he spoke; early in the search process, the president of the board of trustees, Parmer Fuller, called on me in my office to tell me that the trustees had reached a preliminary decision that I should know about: given the threats and uncertainties in academia at that time, they were going to try to find someone who had actual on-the-job experience as president of an at least roughly similar university. Among other things, that ruled me out. As an historian, I have always been bemused by the fact that in attempting to play it safe by making a conservative choice, the trustees wound up with a disaster on their hands.

As it happened, John W. Gardner, Stanford BA '35, stepped down from the post of Secretary of Health, Education and Welfare while the search was underway, thereby reigniting earlier hopes that he might be available for the job. The trustees wasted many weeks in a vain effort to persuade him, and then in the summer acted with a degree of haste that would prove unfortunate. Kenneth S. Pitzer, a Priestley Medal–winning chemist, had been president of Rice University in Houston since 1961 and had accomplished two big changes there: getting the charter amended to allow Rice to admit nonwhite students, and persuading the Rice trustees to charge tuition for the first time. When one thinks about it, both changes were so long overdue, by the mid-1960s, that having accomplished them was not necessarily evidence of outstanding ability. Indeed government and foundations were threatening to withhold support from Rice unless it ceased to be lily-white.[2]

But Pitzer was invited to the Bohemian Grove to be vetted by key trustees, apparently passed muster there, and was appointed Stanford's sixth president in August.

Since Pitzer did not feel able to leave Rice until December 1, there would have to be an acting president for the fall quarter. William Baxter, who chaired the faculty advisory committee for the search, came to my office as Fuller had done, to ask whether I would be distressed if the board appointed Robert J. Glaser, vice president for medical affairs and dean of the Stanford Medical School, and a member of Baxter's committee, rather than me. He was uneasy since it was, after all, university policy that the vice president and provost serves in the president's absence, and Fred Terman had been acting president in the spring of 1964 during Sterling's illness. I cannot say that I was delighted, but neither was I greatly surprised, since I already had evidence of the board's scepticism about me, and my appointment as provost had been attacked by a right-wing alumni group calling itself the "Winds of Freedom Foundation" because I had signed published advertisements questioning the wisdom of U.S. policy on Vietnam and China. I was also aware that, while I had received high marks from most people for my performance in the BSU crisis, the same could not be said of my part in the Old Union affair. I knew Bob Glaser quite well, and, while sitting in on his regular luncheon meetings with his department heads, I had watched him being tortured in various ingenious ways by some of those academic Grand Dukes. I knew him also to be a major figure in the world of medical education, president-elect of the Association of American Medical Colleges, and a member of various advisory bodies in Washington.

. . .

Other changes in the governance of the university were taking place that fall. In October, the student body endorsed the proposed Student Conduct Legislative Council and Stanford Judicial Council by a more than four-to-one vote. The SCLC was to consist of six faculty members chosen by the president from a panel of twelve names submitted by the relevant Academic Council mechanism, one of whom would serve as chair; five students, including, ex officio, the student body president and the speaker of the student body legislature, and three elected by the student body as a whole on a system of proportional representation; plus the dean of students or his representative, to serve ex officio without vote. The Stanford Judicial Council was to consist of a chair chosen from the Law School faculty by the president, after consultation with the dean of the Law School and with the members of the SJC; four faculty members chosen by the president from a panel of eight submitted by the relevant Academic Council mechanism; four students, chosen by a Student Selection Committee involving two faculty and four students chosen by a complex mechanism in which LASSU played a dominant role. Not until January 1969 were members appointed to these new bodies, and their early history was to be anything but placid. Yet their creation effectively ended the long controversy over such mechanisms; campus attention would henceforth be focused more straightforwardly on Vietnam-related issues, with occasional intervals of black power agitation.

Of even greater importance, given the disaster in the Academic Council in May, the long-in-gestation Senate of the Academic Council was approved by the trustees, the first elections to it were held with a respectable 68 percent of those eligible casting ballots, and, after two unofficial summertime meetings, the first official session took place September 12. Significantly, at that meeting the Senate made students eligible for membership in all Academic Council committees and urged that the same be done in all presidential ones.[3]

These votes were reported in the first issue of *Campus Report*, a new weekly periodical, launched by the administration in an effort to counter the selective reporting and editorial hostility often encountered in the *Daily*. While sometimes derided as a "house organ" and "mouthpiece of the administration," in fact *Campus Report* reflected the stern journalistic standards of Bob Beyers as director of the News Service. Not infrequently I found myself having to defend before the trustees his publication of unpleasant facts or disrespectful opinions. He firmly, even zealously, believed that the best public relations were prompt, honest, and full reportage.

The Senate consists of fifty-five elected members and fifteen ex-officio administrators (without vote). As always in the creation of such a body, issues of fairness, balance, and effectiveness made for long debates over composition. If the Senate were to be based on a straight head count of Academic Council members, the Medical School would loom large indeed, much too large for those who had uneasily to find ways of expressing their view that a school on the edge of the campus, with a small, entirely postbaccalaureate student body, ought to count for less in an all-university assembly that would be determining such things as undergraduate curriculum and overall research policies than schools closer to the "heart of the University," such as Humanities and Sciences, Engineering, and Earth Sciences. In the end an ingenious formula that balanced faculty numbers against student enrollments saved the day.

One serious danger to the success of the Senate remained; any Senate decision could be appealed to the full Academic Council by a petition from one-third of the Senate representatives, or fifty Academic Council members, or by two-thirds of the Academic Council members in any one constituency certifying that they or their constituency will be seriously and adversely affected by the decision in question—all in all a pretty easy threshold to reach. Herb Packer had worried out loud: "[The Senate] will be easily subverted . . . if those displeased with its decisions indiscriminately resort to petitions for meetings of the full Academic Council. If the faculty does not trust the administration, will it trust the Senate? I hope so."[4] For a while this risk seemed very real, but after several attempts at using the full council to overturn decisions of the Senate failed, the danger dwindled.

Our creation of the Senate was a unique achievement. Other universities had senates, but our arrangements kept the lines of communication between the faculty and the central administration permanently open by avoiding the twin dangers, that of having the president chair the meetings and therefore be removed from entering into the debates and that of leaving the administration out altogether. Stanford faculty, both then and now, have tended not to recognize their unique privilege, being able to question the president and provost on any subject, with or without notice, at every meeting. There is no way of telling how much contention and frustration we have avoided by this, but it must have been considerable.

While the plan for the Senate was being debated, ASSU President Peter Lyman had attacked the proposal as "piecemeal reform," which could "disenfranchise" students and delay progress toward true "community government of the University." The response from economics professor Kenneth Arrow was interestingly defensive: "The attempt of the faculty to reorganize itself is not intended to preclude any future reorganization of the government of the University." The Senate would have no *new* powers—that is, no powers not already enjoyed by the full Academic Council. "The argument for the Senate is the classical preference for representation as against direct democracy when numbers are large and issues are demanding of time and attention. . . . There is no attempt to pretend that the Senate is a body in which all elements of the University are represented according to their importance." Besides, there being no proposal for community government before us, it would be silly to postpone needed reforms while waiting for one to be developed.[5]

Activism did not go into abeyance during the summer of 1968. Rather it shifted to Palo Alto, where the Midpeninsula Free University (MFU), created a year earlier by the merger of the on-campus "Experiment" and the "Free University of Palo Alto," found itself thwarted by the refusal of Warren Thoits, a downtown developer, to carry out an agreement he had made to make office space available to the MFU. Demonstrations that began August 30 as attempts to persuade Thoits turned into confrontations that required the attention of the Palo Alto Police Department and drew the ire of the *Palo Alto Times*. They also split the MFU, with liberals deploring the politicization and radicals applauding it.[6]

On October 8, as Bob Glaser's fall quarter was getting under way, SDS posted a set of demands on the charred, locked front door of the board of trustees' room at Building 10. Stanford and the Stanford Research Institute were told they must "immediately halt all military and economic projects and operations with Southeast Asia." In addition, SDS demanded that "all contracts, both classified and unclassified, be made public, complete with information on the value of the contracts and the individuals performing the work." As Peter Allen put it, "This document, with its various auxiliary demands and accusations, became the agenda for protest at Stanford during the coming academic year."[7]

·   ·   ·

Classified research had been an active issue for some time. In the same week as the sit-in at the President's Office in May 1966, some fifty pickets engaged Hubert Heffner, associate provost for research, in polite dialogue on the topic, and a group of faculty, by no means all identified with the New Left, petitioned for a special meeting of the Academic Council "to consider research contracts of the University as well as University policies regarding Selective Service":[8]

> No one denied the need for review. As the Committee on University Policy put it, "It is clear that research carried out under the restrictions of security classification runs counter to the traditional academic principle of open inquiry."

Yet there might be an argument for exceptions to the principle under certain circumstances. COUP asked that the underlying questions be reviewed by the Executive Committee with a view to later recommendations to the Academic Council. Pending this review, COUP recommends that each research proposal and contract which requires security classification be reviewed for acceptability by a standing committee of the Academic Council and that recommendations of that committee be reported to the President. Further, the Committee on University Policy requests the Committee on the Graduate Division to review the question of graduate student participation in classified research and make sure that its policies and procedures in regard to approval of classified thesis programs serve the best interests of such students.[9]

A certain defensiveness, and a sense that these are real problems requiring serious, thought-through solutions, is palpable, even at this relatively early date. If Joel Smith's fourteen-item catalog of potential trouble spots for the 1966–67 year omitted classified research, that may have been because he saw the key elements of faculty governance being brought to bear on it. It must be admitted, however, that he also left out ROTC and SRI, which suggests that, despite the May sit-in, Vietnam-related issues were not yet uppermost in his mind.

At the May 17 meeting, Professor William R. Rambo, in electrical engineering, who was emerging as the chief spokesperson for the faculty engaged in classified research and Defense Department–sponsored research in general—and a highly articulate, unflappable one—reviewed the history of the subject at Stanford, pointing out the conscious decision of the university "about sixteen years ago" to refrain from creating "University-affiliated research centers which operate quite outside of the academic structure of the University" as had been done at MIT, Caltech, Johns Hopkins, and so on. Rather, Stanford insisted that research "blend with our graduate program. . . . This very involvement which is now under criticism in parts of the University was deliberately sought by us in the conduct and development of our sponsored programs—to give strength and meaning through maximum interactions with faculty and students."[10]

Even the definition of "classified research" involved difficulties, which sometimes proved useful to its defenders and sometimes to its critics. The effort to "blend" did nothing to make definitions easy. In one case, "the classification results solely from the need of the Principal Investigator to know launch dates in the Apollo program." Others are classified, not because their aims and technical objectives are secret, but because they require use of "classified background information and technical data." In still others, the program description may be classified but the actual work not.

In a startlingly frank passage in a letter to the chair of the Executive Committee, Rambo gave further insight into the murky topic: "Proposals . . . are written for a potential sponsor in the most beguiling and least definitive terms that we can manage. The consequent work generally bears little relationship to the initial proposal. How can one predict literally years ahead the ultimate course, trends, or specific goals of a freewheeling investigation?"[11]

The impact of classified work was limited. Over the fifteen years 1950–65, just 19 out of a total of 582 PhD and engineering theses in the Department of Electrical Engineering were classified, more than half of them during the Korean War. But in 1966, almost 35 percent of the research funding in electronics (centered on the Applied Electronics Laboratory, a site soon to be famous), was for classified work, and about the same percentage of graduate students "are involved to some degree in these contracts."

Although opposition to classified research often emphasized the need for openness, academic freedom could be used by the defenders as well. As Rambo said, "To deny faculty and students in Engineering the option of receiving information and stimulation from the broadest range of problem areas in the outside community is to me improperly restrictive."[12]

A research colleague of Rambo's took the offensive: "To whom can the governmental agencies turn for objectivity and intellectual competence if not the universities, and how can the universities be capable of adequate response without knowledge of all relevant matters, classified or not?"[13]

Critics of the war were not interested in the possible virtues of having *university* scientists be the ones to advise the military. Their objective was to deplore the presence of classified research at Stanford and spearhead a more general attack on the university's involvement in Southeast Asia. Their technique tended to emphasize, rather than attempting to disentangle, the seamless-web character of the university's activities. Even defenders such as Rambo, arguing against singling out classified research for attention and critical review, said things like this: "No meaningful distinctions can be drawn on the basis of the classification of our contracts (which is very largely determined by the source of our support). Travelling wave tubes based on the contributions of our unclassified research have made possible (through the developments of others) hundreds of laboratory test equipments, a communications satellite, and a great many military radio receivers on naval ships."[14] To which radicals could say, "Just so!"

Supporters and critics again found themselves in unsought agreement over such questions as the feasibility of achieving reform by reviews of research proposals. When Rambo called attention to the gap between objectives stated in proposals and the actual work under the contract, citing the use of "the most beguiling and least definitive terms" to attract Department of Defence (DOD) support, it was in a paragraph aimed at showing "that a proposal review process would not achieve its objectives." Meanwhile a group calling itself the SRI Coalition (sic—it should have been the Anti-SRI Coalition) described how "a newly studentized [!] faculty committee has been reviewing all classified contracts at Stanford, yet has accepted these 6 classified contracts at Stanford."[15]

Both sides found it difficult to maintain consistency in their arguments. Strikingly, the "SRI and Stanford" pamphlet, arguing that it would be impracticable for the university to sell off SRI while reforming its research through imposing a "restrictive covenant," points to the "difficulty of defining areas of objectionable research"—a view that such writers would normally dismiss with contempt as self-serving obscurantism on the part of the supporters of war research.[16]

It will be recalled that Bill Rambo claimed that Stanford had rejected the idea of creating "University-affiliated research centers which operate quite outside the academic structure of the University." To make such an assertion, one must either overlook or explain away the creation of SRI in 1946 as a wholly owned subsidiary of the university to support West Coast economic development through performing contract research. Here, once again, the question arises of the comparative advantages of blurring versus making clear distinctions. True, SRI was not *created* to do war-related research, though that eventually came to dominate their agenda. From a university standpoint, by the late 1960s the ties with SRI had become gossamer-thin. There were Stanford trustees who also served on the board of SRI—that was about it. A few faculty had individual ties to SRI. But the university's academic administration had nothing to do with planning or administering SRI's program—let alone paying for it. As vice president and provost, I cannot recall ever having attended a meeting at SRI. It was easy to view SRI as a creation of the immediate postwar years, when avoiding a postwar recession was a significant concern and contributing the university's name and prestige to the new venture seemed a logical step, but without implications for the academic life on campus.

When the radicals made SRI an issue in the mid-1960s, few on campus would have maintained that the university need not do nothing about the matter. Having responsibility without power is seldom an attractive option. At SRI, however, letting things continue as they were had strong attractions. The full name, Stanford Research Institute, remained a potent asset—indeed, an ever more potent one as the university's academic standing rose through the decade. Since SRI's management had nothing to ask of the Stanford administration, and nothing to fear from it either, it is hardly surprising that they regarded the controversy as a manufactured one aimed at promoting the overall effort of radicals, on and off campus, to destroy the country's war-making capacity by attacking its intellectual capital.

For the radicals, SRI presented a hugely tempting target. There was no defensive rhetoric at SRI about the damage to openness from classified research. Almost one-half of the institute's support in 1968 came from the Department of Defence. According to the critics, "6.2 million is seen as *directly* related to Southeast Asia, and \$404,000 was *directly* related to Chemical-Biological Warfare (CBW)." Better still, SRI was engaged in all aspects of "counter-insurgency," the economic and social as well as the scientific and technological. To blur the lines between particular topics under this umbrella was easy. One minute one could be attacking Stanford education professor and SRI economist Eugene Staley's role in developing the "strategic hamlet program," which involved "'an intensified population-control measure to enable [the Diem regime] to tighten its hold on rural Vietnamese by grouping them physically into manageable units.'"[17]

At the next, one would be citing, as sinister evidence of the hold that multinational companies (loaded of course with directors and executives who also served on the Stanford University Board of Trustees) had over U.S. policy, SRI's "numerous long-range studies of Southeast Asian investment opportunities" and its sponsorship of "free world business conferences recently in Sydney, Jakarta, and Singapore."[18]

The presence of CBW work at SRI provided opportunities galore. As "disease control in reverse," it was inherently repugnant to most people. The links between disseminating infectious diseases by aerosol and the massive program of defoliation then under way in Vietnam made this subject topical. Juicy quotations from SRI researchers made provocative reading. In a post–Korean War study published in 1957, they are quoted as saying, "Numerous military authorities believe that we should never again restrict our freedom of selection of weapons as we did in Korea. . . . It is detrimental to the military situation to positively assure an aggressor that a particular weapon will not be used."[19]

The SRI coalition does admit that "defining precisely what constitutes CBW research is not an easy task," and they go on to recognize beneficial uses of aerosol such as in the use of insecticides. They deal with this in a way that is typical of much New Left thinking at the time. First they counter any suggestion that the task may, in fact, be impossible by reminding us of the stakes: "But the Vietnamese have no difficulty defining the nature of CBW agents, and so it is incumbent on us to set up some criteria for acceptable research in this area." Then they say, "In looking at the work done at SRI, we must consider the source of the funds and hence the likely use to which the results of this research will be put. Our first demand, then, must be for the declassification of *all* research concerning the production and dissemination of biological and chemical materials. Only when this step has been taken will the community be able to intelligently decide which projects are acceptable and which are not."[20]

In other words, the problems of definition are postponed pending receipt of more information, which the authors of course know will not be forthcoming. Thus a daunting, possibly insoluble difficulty is set aside in favor of a demand that will sound utterly plausible and yet is certain to be rejected. So the stage is set for resorting to the streets, which, in the case of SRI, is what eventually happened.

· · ·

In faculty discussions of classified research, Rambo and his supporters readily granted two major points to the critics:

> The proposal that no classified work be accepted for academic credit is sound in my view. I interpret this to mean unclassified dissertations developed within the framework of a classified contract would be acceptable. I would hope too that the Council would reserve the right to review any special case on its merits. I certainly concur that any faculty activities offered in support of promotion or re-appointment should be subject to full and open verification. I know of no past instance to the contrary.[21]

These two concessions left at least two other problems relating to classified research. The first was the fact that the need for a security clearance might keep some students out of some lines of work being pursued by faculty, raising "the awkward possibility that two students may have knowledge that is denied to a third." Answers to this were not exactly dispositive: that some students without clearances do work in some *portions* of classified contracts, and in the case of the three hypothetical students that "the solution is not to reduce the knowledge of all three to zero."

The other major sticking point was the matter of restricted facilities. In the Applied Electronics Laboratory, three elements were restricted—one needed either a clearance or to "sign a register and be escorted by a staff member," at the very least an indignity. These were the classified documents room of the library, the area where publications were prepared, and about 10 percent of the laboratory space proper. To this problem, about the most that defenders could offer was a combination of dark hints that perhaps not all other parts of the university were universally accessible (a *tuquoque* carrying little weight without specific examples) and assurances that they were trying hard to minimize the impact of space restrictions.[22]

In 1966 the critics were not strong enough to carry a ban on classified research in the faculty. The Academic Council did create a standing Committee on Research Policy that year. But beyond that the most that the council could do was to tell the faculty investigators that they had an obligation "to exercise judgment as to whether classification is justified, to oppose classification if in their view it was not justified, and to refuse to enter [into] contracts if the government unreasonably persists in requiring classification."[23]

This voluntary system probably made some difference; the number of classified contracts declined slightly, though the total volume as measured by funding did not. But it was easily ridiculed as placing the foxes in charge of the henhouse; faculty who wanted to pursue a given line of work were unlikely indeed to turn their backs on the funding to do so.

·   ·   ·

By the fall of 1968, when SDS members posted their agenda on the Building Ten door, sentiment against maintaining the existing system was clearly increasing. The new Senate provided a mechanism for resolving disputatious issues without the potential for demagoguery and total confusion of a full Academic Council meeting. But, with its regular meetings—and its equally regular access to both the president and the provost, who made it a practice to take questions, with or without notice, near the beginning of each Senate meeting—the Senate's very existence also had the effect of keeping the political pot boiling for faculty.

Acting President Glaser enjoyed a relatively uneventful fall quarter, protected in part by the obvious fact that his ability to enter into long-term commitments was limited and partly by the sensible device of handing hot potatoes to committees. In consultation with the Academic Senate, he did revise the Policy on Campus Demonstrations, removing the disputed references to university buildings and the private residential area of the campus in favor of an emphasis on behavior. It would be a violation to (1) prevent or disrupt the effective carrying out of a university function or approved activity, such as lectures, meetings, interviews, ceremonies, the conduct of university business in a university office, and public events; and (2) obstruct the legitimate movement of any person about the campus or in any university building or facility. The new statement added a paragraph carefully and comprehensively setting out the obligations of faculty, staff, and students to identify themselves, when appropriately requested to do so—provisions without which no definitions of violations would do much good.[24]

For the rest, the biggest and hottest potato was clearly SRI, and in early November Glaser appointed a twelve-person committee, chaired by law professor Kenneth Scott, to study the matter and report back by April 15 with recommendations as to whether the university should retain title and whether it should in any event seek to alter the research program and procedures at SRI, presumably to lessen or eliminate the heavy dependence on war-related work. Five committee members were named by ASSU, five by the Senate, and two by the acting president, of which I was one.[25]

Our deliberations were lengthy and contentious, but I suspect that most observers saw the outcome as inevitable: a majority would conclude that responsibility without control was intolerable and that control was undesirable—in other words, the university ought not to be in the business of overseeing an organization doing contract research without any connection to the academic mission of the university. A minority representing the New Left viewpoint would urge that the university bring SRI under real control, for the express purpose of changing its mission to one of serving the needs of society as seen from the Left.

A third option was sale accompanied by a restrictive covenant of some kind that would fulfil the university's moral obligations without taking on the distracting burden of running the place. The SRI coalition saw practical difficulties in this, and then with a frankness that seems startling today, gave the real reason why disposing of SRI was unacceptable to them:

> But equally important is the simple fact that severance will reduce the "mental visibility" of SRI and the whole Midpensinsula defence complex to the Stanford community. SRI, the Industrial Park, and the Stanford Electronics Labs will remain where they are for some time to come. The important question is whether the members of the Stanford-Midpeninsula community treat their opposition to Stanford['s] and SRI's war research as a one-shot issue or as a first step toward reorienting the Midpensinula research and industrial apparatus towards socially constructive work.[26]

In fact, the fear that this would become a case of "out of sight, out of mind" was well grounded, as events would (after a time) demonstrate.

·   ·   ·

In November, shortly after the election of Richard M. Nixon as president, the ten volumes of the Study of Education at Stanford (SES) appeared in print. In any other time, such sweeping and comprehensive calls for reform as were embodied in this document would have commanded respect. At the beginning, when Herb Packer was appointing the three students to the steering committee instead of letting David Harris and LASSU do it, critics foresaw an establishment cat's paw, incapable of recommending significant change. They remained contemptuous. As Packer said, "The effort that we have been making has come under very very heavy attack from radical, heavily politicized students. And I think it's very understandable that that would be so. It's the old story of reform being the real enemy of revolution. They see these efforts to make the university more flexible and more responsive, but within roughly the existing framework, as terribly threatening to their desire to bring the whole structure crashing down."[27]

The SES would have reformed the board of trustees substantially; the board "should seek to increase the diversity of its membership with respect to such factors as age, occupation, cultural and racial background, and place of residence" (too many were now from California for an institution that now had national and international scope). Terms should be limited to two five-year terms, instead of the then-current ten-year terms renewable to age seventy. The trustees should hold all the board's meetings on campus, not in San Francisco, and it should reduce the number of meetings while increasing their length; many matters now requiring board time should be delegated so that busy trustees could focus on large, important questions.

The SES also urged that the undergraduate degree requirements be drastically altered, and therefore the curriculum. As the report said, "The most important of our recommendations are ground-clearing in character."[28] Its recommendations came ironically close to David Harris's demand for a virtual return to Charles William Eliot's free elective system of the late nineteenth century. Not all of the recommendations were carried out—most notably, the change from the quarter system to the semester system never took place. But general studies requirements were so loosened that I used to say that for a student to fulfil the overall unit requirement *without* fulfilling the general studies requirements along the way would require careful planning.

Publication of the report did provoke enough interest to warrant a debate on its merits before hundreds of students. An SDSer, David Pugh, speaking on the panel, says, "Take a quote from out of the SES report, 'Think freely and think well.' That sounds awful good. Where's feel? We have plenty of people like McNamara and the brain trust in the Defense Department who think very freely and very well, and my God, how many people do they destroy? Somehow we've got to get back in contact with human values."[29] George Packer continues, describing a film of this debate that has survived:

> Three seats over, my father can hardly contain himself. Pale and exhausted-looking, he rolls his eyes, purses his lips, grins, and finally says: "Independent inquiry, critical disinterested scrutiny of what is going on in life, is a very specialized kind of function that either takes place within a university or it just does not take place. And for my money, which I think on the current market may be somewhat devalued, that's what the university is all about." Questions from the student audience. What do things like freshman seminars matter when Stanford professors' research is going into F-111s and antipersonnel bombs? "Are the issues involving the undergraduate education of this university so trivial that they simply aren't worth anybody's attention?" my father asks in disbelief. "If those of us in the university are prepared to give up on that job, then I think it's a very sad day for the human race."[30]

No doubt Herb Packer's defensive tone (he's "devalued" and so on) owes much to the immediate context of a hostile audience. Anyone who has not experienced the difficulty of trying to defend one's views before a crowd made up of many who hate one's guts may have difficulty understanding how debilitating it can be. But the general situation certainly contributed, too. The enormous amount of work that had gone into SES was not wasted; many of its pages had impact, and its reform of the undergraduate degree requirements was essentially enacted—I spent much of the latter half of my presidency trying to encourage the efforts of faculty like Halsey Royden, dean of the School of Humanities and Sciences in the late 1970s, to put some structure back into the requirements.

But, whatever its successes and long-run effects, the SES landed in the midst of a campus too distracted by the war to give it adequate attention.

On December 1, Ken Pitzer arrived to take up his duties as the sixth president of Stanford. On his first working day, uninvited student guests gathered in his office, and he had his first exposure to the delights of "dialogue." Shortly after the announcement of his appointment, the *Peninsula Observer* published "The Goods on Pitzer," a well-researched exploration of his career, beginning with his work on chemical warfare for the Office of Strategic Services, the ancestor of the CIA, during World War II. At every step of the way from 1943 to 1968, they had no difficulty linking Pitzer to military and space programs in their effort to prove that he was appointed at Stanford to serve the interests of trustees invested and/or running the defense and aerospace industries. As director of research for the Atomic Energy Commission from 1949 to 1957, then as dean of the College of Chemistry at Berkeley, he was a fervent advocate of building the hydrogen bomb; from his inaugural address on, he spent his years at Rice building ties with NASA and the Manned Spacecraft Center, which was partly on Rice-owned land. All in all, the image of a "very political scientist" and a leading "defense intellectual" was easily developed; Pitzer was a director of the RAND Corporation, LBJ had appointed him to the president's Scientific Advisory Committee, and he had testified, albeit less vehemently than some, against J. Robert Oppenheimer in the notorious congressional probe of 1954, and against Linus Pauling's 1957 petition to halt nuclear testing. The *Observer* suggested that even his work to get Rice's charter amended to permit the admission of blacks, the kind of thing that got him a bad name in Houston as a "flaming liberal, like Hubert Humphrey," was hypocritical, since he also "changed Rice's historic no-tuition policy and imposed a stiff $1,200 tuition. Needless to say, few sharecroppers' kids go to Rice."[31] Less radical student voices, such as those of ASSU President Dennis Hayes and *Daily* editor Daniel Snell, were more concerned with the exclusion of students from the selection process that produced Pitzer than by the man himself.

But Snell also pointed out that Rice, with ten blacks in a student body of twenty-three hundred and no history of campus unrest, was hardly Stanford. Indeed, *Time* reminded its readers that Pitzer, upon coming to the Rice presidency, had said that his model for Rice was not Caltech or MIT but Stanford. Now, upon coming to Stanford, he said his object would be "to make Stanford as strong as Harvard and M.I.T.—put together."[32]

Clearly, Kenneth Pitzer was an easier mark for radical polemic than either his predecessor, Wally Sterling, or, for that matter, the provost, whose corporate involvements all lay in the future. Like me, he was vulnerable, fairly or not, to the charge of hypocrisy in pretending to oppose the war while defending those of its instruments over which we had some influence, like Department of Defense–sponsored research.

A handsome six-footer with rather impressive eyebrows, he could be very sure of himself, even arrogantly so on occasion, but he found direct conflict difficult. From his first "dialogue" with student radicals, he showed a tendency to giggle at inappropriate moments and to get wound up in awkward syntax and unclear expression. He was always looking for a way to reconcile opposing viewpoints, to square the circle, to have things both ways. It seemed to me that he was happiest dealing with concrete and impersonal matters; he could be articulate in discussing architectural plans for a new campus facility, whereas he fumbled in arguing the issues raised by the activists. I have always thought that perhaps his greatest vulnerability was a lack of combative instincts. Leadership requires different qualities at differing times, and sometimes some of the qualities needed are not among those generally considered admirable. As the 1960s waned, combativeness was an essential ingredient of university presidential survival.

Someone remarked to me recently that to lead a group of talented, smart, and individually strong people, two qualities are essential—clarity and irony—the former to get the message across, the latter to temper it without obscuring or weakening it. Ken Pitzer would not have scored high for these qualities, I fear, in anyone's estimate.

Having pinned its demands on the President's Office door in early October, SDS spent the fall meeting and wrangling over the best means of moving to achieve them. By Thanksgiving the frustration level was high. The pursuit of the demands "did not attract either fast mobilization or long term interest in the student body. Antagonism toward Monday evening meetings increased with calls for fewer large meetings and more small gatherings in which SDS members could get to know each other. These small meetings are now a frequent occurrence. Such a change in emphasis, however, leaves some members unhappy. They feel SDS needs the reinforcement of a confrontation to increase the confidence of members in the powers of radicalism."

Perhaps the arrival of Pitzer in December would give fresh energy to the movement.[33] But as that moment approached, SDS appeared to be in disarray. The demands pinned to the president's door on October 8 had not proven to be an effective rallying point—indeed, they were " 'a total bust' " according to some SDSers.[34]

· · ·

Regular Monday evening meetings at which tactics were debated ad infinitum lost their appeal in favor of smaller "gatherings in which SDS members could get to know each other." Beyond these, SDS concentrated on discussions in the dorms aimed at "educating students rather than radicalizing them via the shock method of confrontation politics."[35]

Soon after the Christmas break, however, three prominent SDSers, Leonard Siegel, Fred Cohen, and Mark Weiss, produced a strategy paper that argued, "Real change will come only through struggle. It is important to get non-SDS people committed to confrontation as the basic means of achieving radical goals." The paper anticipated an effort to "disrupt the normal deliberations of the board [of trustees]."[36]

On January 14, 1969, a group from SDS waited at Bowman Alumni House for trustees to appear. "The Board of Trustees is going to have an open meeting or no meeting at all!" they proclaimed. They came armed with the latest version of their October demands centering on the war in Southeast Asia, featuring specific actions this time, such as the resignation either from the Stanford board or from their respective defense-contracting corporations, of trustees Roger Lewis (president of General Dynamics), William Hewlett (as a director of FMC Corporation), and Thomas Jones (president of Northrop). Five of the nine demands related to activities at SRI; a further one directed that "all faculty resign from Defense Department boards, and that no new faculty be hired who serve on DOD boards."[37]

The trustees never showed up but were discovered to be lunching in a private dining room of the Faculty Club, just across the grove from Bowman. About forty demonstrators got into the club through an unguarded entrance, but they found themselves closed out of the room where the trustees were, with various university administrators guarding the door. The nine demands were read through a bullhorn aimed from the inner courtyard at the plate-glass windows of the dining room. After milling around in the narrow corridors, one demonstrator entered the dining room through a window and rushed to open the door for his colleagues. Scuffling ensued, and in the noise and confusion, the demonstrators poured in, ignoring warnings that they would be prosecuted for breach of the new demonstrations policy. The trustees adjourned their session and walked away, to shouts such as Fred Cohen's, "What is your right to be here, punk?"[38]

It was the first test for the new Stanford Judicial Council, and the council may be said to have staggered through it, averting disaster by none too wide a margin, thanks largely (I suspect) to the determined work of its first chair, Law Professor Jack Friedenthal. The News Service release called it "the most significant Disciplinary action on campus in the past eight years," a remarkable description, considering that the heaviest penalty meted out was "indefinite suspension, with sentence suspended and probation imposed for as long as they remain students at Stanford" together with fines of $300, $200, and $100, to three people. Twenty-six others got one-year suspended suspensions and $50 fines. Clearly, what was so significant was that the council managed to convict the defendants at all.

In doing so the published opinion twisted and turned. Defendants were indeed guilty of "a flagrant act of disruption." But, "the penalties would have been more severe had the defendants been aware of the existence of a reasonable means by which to make their views known to the trustees." Besides, they "were strongly motivated by sincerely held beliefs and felt frustrated by their apparent inability to state those beliefs to the board." On the contrary, defendants "were less interested in the orderly exchange of views than they were in the imposition of their views on the rest of the community." Back and forth the language shifted between condemnation and mitigating circumstances. The general conclusions were nonetheless clear enough: the council considered the offense to be a grave one that must not be repeated. "If every member of the Stanford community who feels strongly about an issue is permitted to disrupt the campus to impose his views on others, the result would be chaos. . . . Such actions tend to eliminate the opportunity for legitimate discussion and resolution of vital issues."[39]

.   .   .

President Pitzer's prompt acceptance of the council's judgment stressed the need to support this fledgling body as it tried to conduct a fair but thorough investigation of the episode. Hinting broadly that he found the proposed penalties too light, he took comfort from the above-cited passage about the need to avoid "chaos," and he further noted this warning from the opinion: "The Council's imposition of probation takes into consideration the threat by defendants . . . to engage in further serious acts of disruption. The Council takes the position that if during the period of probation any defendant carries out such a threat, and is duly convicted thereof; the University community has the right to insist upon his suspension."[40]

It should be added that the council, noting the interruption of their proceedings by some brief guerrilla theater, served "warning on those who would disrupt future proceedings that the Council is disposed to find in contempt persons who engage in disruption of its proceedings and to recommend immediate imposition of severe sanctions." This reminds us how campus judiciary bodies found themselves adopting the language and methods of courts downtown. It does suggest an early sense of their own institutional interests *as a council*—a promising sign for the future. Professor Friedenthal would have his hands full, however, in the spring of 1969.

8 AEL, ENCINA, AND CALLING THE POLICE

THE FACULTY CLUB DISRUPTION was not the sort of thing that rallies the un-committed middle ground of campus politics. In its editorial supporting the Judicial Council's conviction of the perpetrators the *Daily* saw SDS as "caught in a web of tight disciplinary sanctions, lack of student support, and ineffective tactics."[1]

In late January 1969, a newly organized student group calling itself the Open Campus Committee claimed twelve hundred signatures on a petition denouncing SDS tactics. On January 28, SDS members ran a Viet Cong flag up the flagpole at the Stanford Post Office. After Stanford Young Republicans and members of the Open Campus Committee tried in vain to take it down, Buildings and Grounds did so. The possibility of open physical conflict between the opposing groups made for increased unease on campus.

. . .

SDS kept pressing for an open meeting of the board of trustees to explain their involvement in Southeast Asia, a proposal that met with no enthusiasm from the trustees. When a body called the University Advisory Committee, consisting of student, faculty, and trustee members, part of the Pitzer administration's efforts to improve communications, invited the board to send five of its members to an open forum on campus, the stage was set for what turned out to be a sudden change in the climate. The session was scheduled for two hours on the afternoon of March 11.

Paul Rupert, a member of the Resistance and of the United Campus Christian Ministry, summed up what happened exultantly: "Five powerful and legitimate trustees came before the people they ruled, most of whom were trying to keep an 'open mind' or were still angry at SDS for breaking into the last trustees' meeting. But by the meeting's end, the rulers had lost control of their audience, and the people were demanding an open meeting."[2] Leaving aside phrasing like "the people they ruled," this was an accurate summation, and Rupert was a major contributor to the outcome, opening the session with a blistering attack on the trustees for subordinating the true educational aims of the university to the economic interests of the corporate world whence they came. Wrote Rupert:

> But a growing number of us look upon a different world, a world in which your interests—those of the corporations and the university—are in fact not the interests of a majority of the world's people: the poor and the black at home, the underfed, the undereducated, and the over-policed of Asia, Africa and Latin America. We came to this university to learn about that world, to discover how we and other men can best live in it. We found not an institution dedicated to finding the truth, to doing research on the fundamental human problems, to teaching democracy through its practice, but rather a research and training institute which processes men and women to fill hierarchical social roles. . . . We have had to mold our own education. And that education has led us to you: we are asking that you justify your inordinate power over the lives of men.[3]

What soon became clear to a sophisticated listener was that the trustees had absolutely no experience that would prepare them for this, or for the torrent of hostile questions the followed. They were not people accustomed to examining, much less defending effectively, the assumptions that underpinned their lives. Assertions that the university was involved in the war, on the wrong side, left Bill Hewlett puzzled: "Stanford University is an organization of the United States . . . [Applause] . . . supported by the laws of the United States and financed primarily through United States' funds. In a sense this is an American organization. It is not a South Vietnamese organization. It is not a Chinese organization. It is an organization of the United States and these services are performed for the United States of America. I hardly call that a political decision. [Roar from audience]."[4]

He denied flatly that FMC Corporation, of which he was a director, was engaged in the manufacture of the lethal nerve gas, Sarin—notorious years later as the weapon used in the terrorist attack on the Tokyo subway. But he was soon forced to admit that FMC had indeed been "asked by the government to build a plant, which they built and operated at the request of the government and they turned that over to the government about six months ago. [Loud laughter and applause]."[5]

After nearly two hours of evasions, circumlocutions, and awkward admissions, board president Fuller, pressed as to why there were no blacks on the board, said, "I guess the honest answer is that we have not gone out and looked for one. [Laughter and applause]." Rupert tried to get the trustees to promise that they would lobby, as individual board members, in favor of opening the next meeting of the board "for the consideration of the student-faculty study committee on the SRI proposal, so that we can watch you deliberate and understand that debate and then decide afterwards what course of action we'll have to take, because otherwise we're going to take some very uninformed actions. [Applause]."

At first Fuller thought the question was whether the trustees present objected to others lobbying for such a meeting. Rupert said, "What I asked was, 'Would you five people—four men and one woman—take upon yourselves the task of lobbying for an open meeting for the discussion of the student-faculty recommendations on SRI?' I'm saying very simply that I see some very bad consequences if there isn't that meeting. That is not a threat. I'm very nonviolent, so you can trust me. [Laughter] But, I have friends. [Loud laughter] And they're not all as reasonable as I am."

While this sort of playful doubletalk might not ordinarily be very appealing (and it was often quoted against Rupert later), by this time the audience had lost all patience with the trustees. When Charles Ducommon asked "whose request" it was for the open meeting, the audience yelled back, "OURS!" The session adjourned, as planned, at the end of two hours. Afterward, Joel Smith was quoted as saying what we were all thinking: "SDS is back in business."[6]

On April 3, a mass meeting involving some seven hundred people from SDS, the SRI Coalition, and "about a dozen other radical groups" met in Dinkelspiel and drew up an updated version of the now-familiar SDS demands, focusing on establishing closer supervision over SRI and on halting all classified research and all Chemical-Biological Warfare (CBW) and counterinsurgency work (mainly at SRI).[7] Nationally, SDS was disintegrating. The movement at Stanford, partly reflecting that fact and partly because adopting a fresh, home-grown label would accommodate the proliferation of splinter groups and perhaps attract the unaffiliated, became known thenceforth as the April 3rd Movement.

At the regular trustees' meeting on April 8, Ken Pitzer made what soon became a widely quoted statement: "You are being asked through your decision on SRI to say that our national priorities are wrong—that we spend too much on the military, on means to kill people, and not enough on constructive things, on helping ordinary people to live." Adopting, albeit in mild form, the rhetoric of the critics did little to advance the president's credibility. But the board did what it felt it could to ward off the pending storm, requesting that SRI's management accept no further CBW contracts, pending resolution of the questions before the SRI committee. The trustees also committed themselves to an open committee hearing on campus on the SRI committee report soon after its April 15 publication.

An overflow community meeting in Dinkelspiel the evening of April 9 showed how little impact these placating gestures had—they were not seen as more than that. Pitzer told the crowd of nine hundred (where was the fire marshal this time?), "I hope your commitment to peace extends to this campus," and he got some applause, but as the three-hour talk-a-thon wore on, it became clear that the issues were now tactical, not strategic. Ignoring pleas by several faculty leaders and by Dennis Hayes, the ASSU president who had beaten Vicki Drake the preceding spring, the meeting voted about 2–1 on a show of hands in favor of the sit-in tactic. At that point Hayes said he would support the vote.

At 10:45 that night some four hundred students poured into the Applied Electronics Laboratory (AEL). The occupation began with promises to avoid property damage and tampering with classified research files. It would be impossible for the research itself to continue, however, under such an occupation. The occupiers also voted to set up a committee to survey other buildings they might occupy, and they said they would set up picket lines at SRI, companies in the Stanford Industrial Park, and other buildings housing "war-related research."[8]

Earlier that same day, Harvard students occupied University Hall; the following morning Cambridge police stormed the building, with injuries and arrests galore. Just as behavior on both sides had been influenced by the Columbia bust at the time of Stanford's Old Union sit-in, so now the AEL sit-in took place with everyone looking uneasily over one shoulder at what had happened at Harvard.

Pitzer declared the sit-in a violation of the Policy on Campus Disruptions. On April 13, I announced that twenty-four faculty and staff members had volunteered to go into the AEL and ask students to identify themselves, with a view to Judicial Council action. "The President and I are continuing to deal with this disruption by internal means," I said. But the next day only two of the approximately one hundred protesters who were in the building when the identification teams arrived were willing to give their names; the rest responded "The April 3rd Movement." One notably and quotably declared, "We are one person. We have achieved a collective conscience." The classic rationale for civil disobedience, involving willingness to be punished for one's infractions, scarcely made an appearance.

For the first time at Stanford, there was serious public discussion of the possibility that resort to *external* means might become necessary. There was talk of the federal interest in securing classified files, and the specter of federal marshals was raised. When a deputation from Young Americans for Freedom delivered to me a letter urging the university not to make concessions under duress, I said the sit-in had "raised more moral issues than they seem willing to recognize." Remarking that the results of turning to "off-campus methods" (read: the police) elsewhere "have not been especially happy or encouraging," I indicated that turning to the civil authority is sometimes necessary, but that "we have an opportunity here to resolve this through our own established judicial mechanisms that so many people have worked so long and hard to establish."

Associate history professor Philip Dawson spoke to the sit-in of the dangers of failing to do this. "What we are attempting to do is act within the framework of these new judicial procedures for self-government. The consequences of the collapse of these new institutions [should be considered seriously]."[9]

Hours after having refused to identify themselves, the protesters voted to reaffirm their intention to leave property undamaged and classified files untouched. Opposition came from a few, notably Steve Weissman, this year a "*former*" graduate student at Stanford, who suggested, "If we are serious about winning, then we have to be serious about saying this material ought to be in the public domain. . . . American universities are going through a period of policing themselves. When they ask us to police ourselves, we're on their side." But the great majority of the protesters took nonviolence seriously; indeed, the myth of the idealistic, peaceful, educative AEL sit-in was taking shape even as it was going on. Not for the last time, I found myself trying to delineate between violence and coercion, and to ask people to count the cost of the latter:

> The student decision not to escalate tactics is significant. But the sit-in has imposed very real costs which must be borne by the entire community. It has halted work for 150 AEL employees, affecting those who are doing electrocardiograph research as much as those whose projects the sit-in opposes. Continuing payroll costs of more than $5,000 a day can be made up only from University general funds. The amount is equivalent to nearly two full-year scholarships a day. Since the students gained entry to the locked building late Wednesday night they have moved into several offices which also were locked, and removed personal correspondence from locked desk drawers. Interference with the legitimate rights of others, and general disdain for the values which keep universities open and free—no matter how high the moral imperative in which these are cloaked—do not constitute the answer to any real problems which this community, the nation and the world face.[10]

On April 13, the Steering Committee of the Academic Senate published an open letter to "Members of the April Third Movement and Other Concerned Persons," the thrust of which was that the Senate was doing its best regarding the topics of concern to the protesters and had moved to ban research on CBW on campus, but, "In our judgment, the Senate will find its attention focused on procedural rather than substantive issues as long as a major campus disruption continues." The letter closed by quoting Pitzer's "our national priorities are wrong" remarks to the trustees, adding, "We believe we share with you the deep conviction that this community's efforts should be directed entirely toward the causes of peace and human welfare." If this statement meant anything it was that the radicals were right: research and other activities related in any way to the war must be terminated in favor of an institutional mandate to pursue only "the causes of peace and human welfare." This could not have been the considered view of the Senate majority, let alone the faculty at large. But its publication showed how fragile was the faculty leadership's willingness to confront their tormenters.

The public hearing held the next day by the Academic Council Committee on Research Policy went over familiar ground and got entangled in an inconclusive argument over whether Professor Baxter, as chair of the committee, had acted innocently or with intention to deceive when he altered the title of one research project to remove a reference to "Electronic Warfare Techniques." That evening, the sit-in voted to continue its occupation even if the Senate meeting the following day took clear action to stop classified and war-related research on campus.

When the Senate did meet, it was given a letter with 123 faculty signatories saying:

> It is our strong view that the Senate should take no action having to do with the substance of the demands now being pressed by those who are illegally occupying the Applied Electronics Laboratory. It is further our view that for the Senate to respond to those demands while the sit-in is in progress would be to violate previous actions by the faculty and student body which specifically and categorically repudiate coercive tactics as a means of attaining objectives within the University.[11]

Nevertheless, after four and a half hours of discussion, the Senate instructed the Committee on Research Policy to prepare new draft guidelines "which prohibit research which involves secrecy of sponsorship or results" to be considered at the Senate meeting on April 24. There was one dissenting vote. Also, and perhaps somewhat more surprisingly, the Senate instructed the committee to explore, after April 24, "how the University can bring about a further reordering of our own research priorities and . . . a reordering of research priorities of the federal government agencies, reporting as soon as possible on these two issues." The Stanford News Service release for April 16 concluded, "It was the longest, largest, and latest session of the Senate since it was organized."

After the refusal of AEL protesters to identify themselves to faculty members, the Judicial Council moved to consider whether circumstances called for the president to use the emergency powers granted him for use under "special circumstances." After hearings April 16 and 17, to which the April 3rd Movement declined to send representatives, the council delivered itself of the most important decision it would take during these years of recurrent troubles. The "Findings of Facts" were as follows:

> 1. The members of the Council unanimously find that the actions of those persons occupying the Applied Electronics Laboratory constitute a disruption of an "approved activity" of the University under the Policy on Campus Disruption. 2. The members of the Council unanimously find that the current

case involves "extraordinary circumstances" within the meaning of Section IV of the Legislative and Judicial Charter of 1968 in that: a. There is imminent danger that external forces, beyond University control, in particular Federal troops, may enter the campus to deal with various aspects of the occupation. b. There is serious danger that the disruption will be escalated by some of those persons now occupying the Applied Electronics Laboratory. c. There is serious danger that certain individuals or groups of individuals will attempt to retaliate with force against those persons occupying the Applied Electronics Laboratory. d. A large number of persons has participated in the occupation. e. Persons engaged in the occupation have failed to cooperate with the University authorities by refusing to identify themselves when properly requested to do so in accordance with the Disruption Policy f. Persons engaged in the occupation have refused to cooperate with the Stanford Judicial Council by voting not to send a representative to participate in these hearings. g. The occupation has lasted for seven full days and the time of voluntary termination cannot be ascertained.[12]

The vote on a series of recommendations to the president of actions to be taken was divided, 5–2, the dissenters arguing that the council was going beyond its brief to tell the president what he should do, once having invoked the "internal marshal law" that enabled him to do whatever he deemed necessary to resolve the crisis. Of course, as he pointed out to the faculty in reporting the Judicial Council's actions, he could, under Section IV, have declared the existence of "extraordinary circumstances" without the council's involvement, but had chosen to turn to the council for authorization—a gamble that paid off, though it was not a very great gamble anyhow. He accepted the recommendations, even though they included closing the AEL for a week (more financial losses!). Most importantly, they declared that any student remaining in occupation of AEL after noon the next day (Friday, April 18) would be subject to immediate suspension.

.   .   .

While this was going on, members of SDS and the Resistance among the occupiers were developing a plan for escalation by seizing the building that housed the Department of Aeronautical and Astronomical Engineering. Even a threat of occupying the Aerospace building, it was believed, would bring in swarms of off-campus police polarizing the campus community. "Either we get busted or we don't," said one Resistance member. "Both ways we'll have drawn the trustees out of their hole."[13]

At the end of "a marathon six-hour meeting," however, the proposal to escalate failed: "Favouring it were a handful, perhaps 15 or 20 of a crowd of 500. They were nearly all the 'leaders' who had worked on the plan."[14]

After this, and in the face of the recommended immediate suspensions, it was not surprising that six hundred AEL protesters voted almost without dissent to "temporarily suspend" their occupation at 10:15 a.m. on Friday. Nor is it surprising that Pitzer received a standing ovation at the Academic Council for his "restraint and firmness" in coping with the nine-day occupation. Perhaps more surprising, given the Judicial Council's uncompromising condemnation, the largest political meeting yet held at Stanford, called by ASSU President Dennis Hayes, drew eight thousand students and faculty to Frost Amphitheater that same afternoon to hear various speakers discuss the outcome and to take several straw votes. There were not enough ballots to go around—obviously the organizers had not anticipated such a big turnout. Those voting were nearly unanimous (3,073 to 203) in commending the April 3rd Coalition for "helping focus the attention of the campus upon the nature of the research being conducted at the University and SRI." They urged an end of classified research by a 2–1 majority. But when asked whether they would themselves participate in another sit-in if the trustees did not "positively respond to the desires of the Stanford community regarding research at SRI by May 14," just over one-half said they would (1,633 yes; 1,438 no).[15]

The discussion was on the whole respectful, though not all the speakers were uncritical. The Nobel Prize-winning professor of genetics Joshua Lederberg did say that, while he could not blame students for finding recent developments in the nation upsetting, "If the use of bodies instead of brains is the best you can think of doing, God help us all." But it was Professor Martin Perl, a future Nobelist in physics from SLAC, who got "a lengthy standing ovation" for telling the crowd that they could expect political retaliation for their behavior, in the form of reduced federal support of research. "We may have to do less research and teach more. But we will end up a better university, and the majority of voters will respect us for it, and be on our side." Of course, telling a predominantly student crowd that they might get a bit more of the faculty's time and attention was likely to be well received.[16]

Even the BSU made an appearance, one of the very few times it came close to active participation in the antiwar movement. Chair Leo Bazile led a group of its members on to the stage to urge that SRI be brought under closer control and that it focus on the problems of East Palo Alto.[17]

. . .

Four days later, a capacity crowd of seven hundred at Dinkelspiel heard students "generally commended for their sit-in at Stanford's Applied Electronics Laboratory and particularly for ending it in a position of 'real power' by speakers at . . . the 'Day of Concern' Tuesday . . . organized by Stanford student leaders."[18]

English professor Wilfred Stone, the first speaker, set the tone: "For the past four years, the students have been the real conscience of this campus and have sparked many reforms and changes. Too few of my colleagues remember how much we owe them, and instead think in terms of punishment. It is my hope that they will come around and see this as an opportunity to develop a real feeling of community."

He thought "the faculty were sympathetic, for the most part," to the sit-in, but "urged a stop because the sit-inners had won a surprising amount of support and should end it while they were ahead." He called the sit-in's "Sunday tea a superb tactic, a kind of town meeting with the whole community talking to each other."

In legend the AEL sit-in has largely conformed to the picture painted by Stone: the peaceful, unthreatening "good" demonstration before nastier, more ambiguous protests took over. In the *Peninsula Observer*, "The sit-in (or, more properly, the open house)" was extensively discussed. Marc Sapir and Carrie Iverson smile out at the reader, above Carrie's account of how they married at the sit-in:

> Our celebration was another experiment in new forms, a re-creation of worn-out social institutions. We were married not by a priest or by a legal document of the State, but by our own community, in a simple ceremony. . . . AEL was a groping for ways of living together as a group of people involved in a struggle, for methods of organizing ourselves and methods of strengthening ourselves. It was a model for future life styles. It may not have perfected them, but we know where we are going and we are going there together.[19]

The militants on the far Left tried to see the ambiguous outcome at AEL in as favorable a light from their standpoint as possible, but they were clearly disconcerted. Steve Weissman, an odd man out at the meeting where Wil

Stone had waxed euphoric, said, "I'd like to solve our problems without head-cracking but I don't think we'll be able to." Revolution was "an eventual possibility . . . but that's in the very distant future." A writer in the *Peninsula Observer* drew a taxonomy of liberals, left-liberals, right-radicals, radicals, and revolutionaries, and said, "The struggle at Stanford is moving toward the left. This movement is not always clear—it was especially unclear in the tactic of temporarily abandoning the AEL sit-in." Then he interpreted that tactic as having been "an extraordinarily sophisticated response" to ASSU President Hayes's calling a mass meeting for the purpose of endorsing the goals but condemning the tactics of the sit-in; by quitting AEL, the protesters effectively took the tactical issue off the agenda for the meeting, leaving the top-heavy votes for the April 3rd Coalition's objectives to be its message.[20]

The lead editorial in the same issue declared:

> This was not a symbolic protest but a direct assault on the war machine. We saw one cog jammed in the research machinery that produces technology for foreign wars and domestic waste. For nine days the AEL did not produce. . . . We hope that more than the laboratory was liberated; we hope that people were freed from their illusions—the illusion that Stanford is an institution of higher learning, the illusion that the superficial morality of university regulations should override the deep morality of the political struggle against imperialist war making, the illusion that there is such a thing as concern which does not lead to action.

But the editorial also said, "We can expect nothing from the faculty. They have sold their souls for the myth of academic freedom. . . . The students must teach the faculty what is real and what is not." The paper provided some fascinating reportage, and up to a point it was honest about the failure of the radicals to get the escalation they sought: "The administration's siege-like strategy and faculty inaction made many demonstrators feel new tactics were needed. But nothing coherent emerged. There was no coordinated radical leadership. Most radicals had gone along with the moral-symbolic tone of the sit-in, keeping their mouths shut to dispel liberal mistrust of radical manipulation."

At this stage there was a consensus that action beyond AEL was necessary. But the lack of a strategic alternative and the exhaustion of the leadership made action impossible. While the administration and the trustees stalled, the AEL liberators wore themselves down with constant meetings, lack of sleep, and their own inability to decide what to do next.[21]

In a remarkable interview, Fred Cohen maintained that he and his fellow radicals were to blame:

> Because we didn't want to scare the liberals out of the coalition, we did not put forward a radical line and analysis early in the sit-in. We should have made an analysis of SRI as the central issue and the Stanford trustees as the main enemy. We should have escalated on Wednesday, by taking the space sciences building, for example. This didn't happen because we hadn't discussed escalation or the need for it in a strategic or analytical framework.

One wonders how firmly he really believed this. Later in the interview he says, "I doubt whether really militant tactics—threatening the computer center or threatening to take classified documents, or staying in the building—whether that will ever happen. The attractive thing about the sit-in was its openness and the comfortable alternative it offered to the Stanford life style. That is, of course, different from real militant action." Yet, moments later, he is anticipating that if the trustees perform as feebly at the forthcoming hearing on SRI as they did in the Memorial Auditorium session March 11, "the campus will probably blow up." What he means by that, however, is apparently only "the largest political action Stanford has seen in years, as shown by the number of people who signed the solidarity statement and voted for us at the Hayes [Frost Amphitheater] meeting." Not a blowup big enough to threaten the computer center, apparently.[22]

Remarkably, however, in all of the *Observer's* voluminous reporting there was no mention whatsoever of the Stanford Judicial Council's condemnation of the disruption or of its recommendation to the president to use his emergency powers to suspend immediately any of the "liberators" found still in the building after twelve noon on Friday. The *only* references to the council concerned its recommendation that AEL be closed for a week, which allegedly enabled the protesters to "call the faculty's bluff." That bluff, when called, resulted only in the Academic Council's standing ovation honoring Pitzer's "restraint and firmness," however. One of the most unambiguous outcomes of the sit-in, as far as the radicals were concerned, was their bitterness toward the faculty, whose protestations of "moral concern" drew nothing but contempt. As one of the leaflets published during the occupation explained, "The fact of the matter is that most professors are both objectively and subjectively members of the petit bourgeoisie. As such they share a very common idea of their class—that class struggle, if it exists at all, involves other people and springs from their irrationality. Hence the liberal idea that conflict comes from people not communicating well enough."[23] It sounds rather like Fred Cohen's explanation of the failure to escalate: the radical leaders had not been communicating well enough.

I do not think that many on campus saw the end of the AEL sit-in as anything more than a truce of uncertain duration, for all the standing ovations, congratulatory resolutions, and romanticized descriptions of what had been going on. At the Senate meeting to consider the recommendations prepared by its Committee on Research Policy concerning classified research, the dean of the Engineering School, Joseph M. Pettit, made an opening statement that constituted a surrender and a warning. Citing the "evident loss of faculty support necessary for the pursuit of this [classified] activity in a university" as the basis, he announced plans for phasing out the classified contracts at AEL. But he also urged the president and the Senate to "perceive the repeatable scenario" in which critics pick a research target, attack it on the basis of some possible applications thought immoral by the critics, dismiss arguments over tactics as unimportant compared to the issues at hand, and succeed in destroying their target. "There are many potential targets at Stanford. How many must go down before we learn how to protect ourselves?"

Welcoming Pettit's decision, Pitzer pointed out that President Nixon's science adviser, Lee DuBridge, had recently agreed that " 'it is not appropriate for secret military research to be carried on within university campuses,' " and concluded from this "that this action at Stanford implies no conflict with the policies of our federal government."

For its part, the Senate "unanimously expressed its confidence in their [Pettit's and Pitzer's] judgment in working with the faculty to achieve an effective transition." There followed six hours of discussion, culminating in passage of resolutions with few and limited loopholes. One or more researchers on a contract could have access to classified information when their project would be "significantly advanced" by this knowledge, but "the relationship between the classified data and the overall research endeavor must be sufficiently remote so that a member of the research group who does not hold a security clearance would nevertheless be able to participate fully in all of the intellectually significant portions of the project."[24]

This logic, sometimes close to hairsplitting, demonstrated once more the difficulty of legislating in this area without damage to professorial freedom. The Senate's approach also underlined the fact that the issue for these legislators was one of access and academic freedom, not of war-related research per se. Projects were not to be judged by their possible applications, but by the extent to which they conformed to the doctrines of equal access and academic openness.

In fact, as with ROTC, the decision to eliminate classified research resulted from the confluence of opposition based on the fundamental devotion to openness as the basis for all university life, on the one hand, and opposition rooted in the effort to hamper the war effort in Vietnam, on the other.

The difference was not lost on the April 3rd Movement (A3M). At a meeting seven hundred-strong held outside AEL the following day, the A3M demanded a "positive response" from the Senate "on the issue of war-related research, particularly at SRI," something "more far-reaching" than the new guidelines on classified work.[25]

But this was almost done in passing; the real thrust of the meeting was the demand that an open meeting of the full board of trustees be held on campus on April 30, replacing the hearing scheduled for that day before a five-person trustee committee on the subject of the university's relationship to SRI.

Board president Parmer Fuller rejected the demand and called the hearing "an important part of the process by which the full board can make an informed decision" on SRI. Ken Pitzer said, "The tone and the substance of your meeting suggests that the hearing may be disrupted unless your demands are accepted." He said he would cancel the hearing if he did not have assurances by 2 p.m. April 29 that such would not be the case.

To focus on SRI at this point made sense for the radicals. They had won on classified research, although not in a way that was very satisfying to them. April also saw the returns from a mail ballot of Academic Council members that would lead inexorably to the departure of ROTC; the faculty voted to deny academic credit for ROTC courses, and the U.S. Army had somehow persuaded itself that ROTC without credit was demeaning and unacceptable. So ROTC was phased out at Stanford, ostensibly by the action of the Armed Services but in fact because the Stanford faculty would no longer tolerate an academic program that purported to be academic but over which it exerted no control.

As in the case of classified research, academic objections having nothing to do with the war in Southeast Asia were a significant element in the decision. But SRI provided campus residents with an opportunity to act on their distaste for the war with minimal on-campus consequences. Still, campus opinion was very divided. Sixty-eight percent of students wanted the university to bring SRI under university control and to have a university committee redirect its research; 35.6 percent of faculty agreed. Large majorities of both students and faculty favored restraints on CBW and radiological warfare research at SRI, either by direct control or by covenanted restrictions if SRI were sold. Almost half the faculty and nearly three-fifths of students would add counterinsurgency research and research related to the Southeast Asia war to the list of prohibitions. Unsurprisingly, 41 percent of faculty but only 18 percent of students made selling SRI for maximum gain to the university and without covenanted restraints their first choice among options. Student willingness to see the university forego financial benefits, without much thought to whether they themselves might eventually suffer the consequences, is a hardy perennial of campus life.[26]

Despite this relatively more favorable terrain on which to fight, the radicals showed signs of fractiousness and divided counsels during the week of the SRI hearing. At the only meeting it held, SDS discussed its role within the Movement for four hours but was unable to decide whether to present a proposal for a formalized leadership structure to A3M. SDS members, charged with manipulation many times since they first launched their campaign against the university's activities in Southeast Asia, agreed that they should meet, but couldn't decide on whether or how to exercise leadership.[27]

Ken Pitzer quietly dropped his threat to cancel the meeting set for Wednesday, April 30, absent assurances by 2 p.m. Tuesday that there would be no disruption. In fact that day's edition of A3M's publication, "Declassified," carried a banner headline: "Any Hour Now," with eight campus facilities circled as possible targets for future activity: Encina Hall, Hoover Tower, the Business School, President's Office, Varian Laboratory, the Computation Center, Space Engineering, and that old standby, The Old Union. Meyer Library and its Forum Room, the site of the hearing, was not on the list, nor was Memorial Auditorium, where the hearing would be piped in to a bigger audience. After their March 11 ordeal, no group of trustees was prepared to risk another trial by fire in that capacious venue.

Tuesday evening the Senate spent another five hours in committee of the whole debating university-SRI relations inconclusively and refusing to make public the gist of straw votes by which it sent suggestions back to the Steering Committee for drafting. While they were thus engaged, two hundred A3M members debated tactics at a meeting in Tresidder.

In palpable agony, the outgoing ASSU president, Dennis Hayes, present in the Senate as an observer, begged his public to be patient, hinting broadly that many would like the direction the straw votes had taken and explaining why the Senate had imposed secrecy as to their content. "First, there is a real problem drafting legislation in a group of 60 people. Second, there was a reaction to reports of a threatening meeting at Tresidder." He went on:

> This decision about secrecy was a tactical error . . . because most of the University community would be pleased if it knew what had happened. . . . I've spent most of my waking hours this past month persuading the administration and faculty to ignore the tactics of students. I'm now going to have to ask students to ignore a tactical blunder by the faculty. If the Senate can be just given a chance to act upon the issues, without a disruption raging in the background, I feel confident that it will pass resolutions which we will all be able to applaud. I seriously doubt the ability of the Senate to deal positively with these issues under the shadow of some coercive act.[28]

But the Senate was a sideshow at this point. The radicals, or at least their leaders, knew perfectly well that it would not be the faculty who would decide the disposition of SRI. Though the phrase might not have meant much to students, or would have been regarded as a convenient dodge, this issue reeked of "fiduciary responsibility." SRI was a valuable property. And in the end the trustees must bear the burden of determining what is and is not an activity consistent with the fundamental purposes of the university.

The hearing Thursday afternoon was anticlimactic. Since the setting did not lend itself to a repeat humiliation of the trustee committee members, the A3M representatives walked out after a while and began a series of meetings to decide what to do next. In the afternoon, SDS members tried to address tactics, but largely in terms of abstractions—"We are in a completely different situation" from AEL, "This is a new stage of the struggle"—rather than with specific targets.

Ken Pitzer had an engagement to address an alumni audience in Los Angeles that evening and had decided to go. Breaking such an engagement on the basis of rumblings but no concrete threat seemed ill advised. Off he went, leaving me in charge.

The A3M meeting that evening was chaotic. Members of Young Americans for Freedom, the right-wing student group founded by the ubiquitous Harvey Hukari, a graduate student in communications, were on hand, heckling the majority. After three hours and at least one fistfight, the question of whether to sit in that night was called and passed. Many students seemed to be voting more against YAF than for the sit-in. Discussion of possible targets continued, and people grew more impatient to go and do what they had voted to do. The question of guidelines for the sit-in was sidestepped—a motion to "act in the most humanitarian manner possible and still accomplish our objectives" was passed.

Immediately after the final vote, seven hundred people streamed across the campus still discussing the merits of different buildings, the possible effects of the sit-in, and violence.[29] It was well past midnight.

.   .   .

It is difficult to remember just how trying it was to listen to the endless sessions of participatory democracy that led up to, accompanied, and followed after one of these "actions." Wandering sentences, all manner of crowd noises, a calculated effort on the part of the more articulate to dumb down their speech to make sure that it would not sound "too intellectual." And all the time one wondered how much there really was to decide. To what extent had it all been decided ahead of time? The radicals' reputation for manipulation, which at times caused them to operate too cautiously, from their standpoint, was not wholly unfounded. But the Movement was not a puppet show, nor were the leaders all of one mind, even about whether they were in fact leaders.

Hundreds who had been listening to A3M over KZSU all Wednesday evening, April 30, came out to see what would happen when the action started at Encina. But the sound of shattering glass and the presence of YAF with their inseparable cameras deterred most from entering the building. That said, about three hundred did so. As Fred Cohen wrote a few days later, "At that point everyone knew that the gentility of the AEL occupation would not be repeated and that the character of the Movement would never be the same."[30]

In Building Ten I met continuously through the evening with the members of the Faculty Consultative Group on Campus Disruption, appointed by the Senate to play a part in just such situations. Reports from the front were alarming to start with and did not get less so. Encina was the home of most of the university's finance departments—the Controller's Office, the Vice President for Business's Office, and the Development (fund-raising) Office. Records, many of them sensitive, filled the files of the large rabbit warren of a building. Early evidence of this demonstration's unwillingness to follow the AEL model of respect for property was the initial break-in, followed by more windows broken "to liberate rooms for meeting and sleeping."[31]

The occupiers were told that they were under immediate temporary sus-pension, pursuant to the president's emergency powers, unless they left forth-with; some did leave, but most stayed. As the evening wore on we got reports that files were being rifled and their contents carted away in Volkswagens.

The university had begun considering issues of how best to work with po-lice on campus, should that become necessary, long before any such likeli-hood existed. On February 10, 1965, spurred by the unrest at Berkeley and in particular by the occupation of Sproul Hall, a meeting took place in the Presi-dent's Office involving Fred Glover, then executive assistant to the president, Dean of Undergraduate Studies Robert Wert, Dean of Students Don Winbig-ler, Vice President for Business Alf Brandin, Bayless Manning, then dean of the Law School, and the staff counsel in the Business Office, Cassius L. Kirk. Kirk's nine-page memo of the meeting makes interesting reading, both for what those present were and were not able to anticipate.[32] Apparently Man-ning had been promoting the idea of seeking injunctive relief in the event of a protracted sit-in preventing the conduct of university business. Advice had been sought from Robert Minge Brown, trustee and university general counsel, who was clearly sceptical that a California court would grant such relief and certain that none would unless the university had first thoroughly exhausted its available internal remedies. Manning pushed the idea hard as an alternative to direct use of police to clear the building. "He pointed out that a single photograph of a female student being forcibly dragged out of a building may do irreparable harm to the University's position and public image." Even if an injunction were denied—and he was not really much more optimistic than Brown about its being granted—it would be wise to have sought it, since "by asking for an injunction, the University would manifest its seriousness and its intention to utilize court procedures rather than police enforcement procedures." A bailiff approaching a demonstrator to serve a summons to ap-pear in court was far less threatening and provocative than a policeman with handcuffs at the ready.

The memo covered many other topics, such as whether notifying a dem-onstrating student's parents of what their child was up to could be done "without sounding ridiculous." One of its most important points was Brown's recommendation that Stanford "should make advance arrangements with the County Sheriff's Office to ensure that procedures for utilization of the ser-vices of that department, in the event of an emergency, are workable and fully understood."

This by 1969 we had done; watching the disasters that came with resort to the police at Columbia in 1968 and at Harvard at the time of AEL, we needed no encouragement to undertake a serious effort to get to know the sheriff's people and vice versa. Some of the things we told them about on-campus sensitivities amused them, and some suggestions aimed at avoiding potentially provocative behavior on the part of the sheriff's deputies struck them as impractical. But it was greatly to their credit that they were willing to listen and do their best to meet us halfway. Most importantly, they were willing to tolerate the presence of faculty observers at their side. Gerald Gunther, a distinguished scholar of constitutional law and a member of the Faculty Consultative Group, described the rationale succinctly, as reported by the *Los Angeles Times*: "The purpose of sending faculty members in with each arrest team was to encourage students to leave, to prevent fear of police attack, to prevent misunderstanding afterward concerning what had happened and to give pause to those demonstrators who had hoped to follow the policy of radicalizing more students by provoking actual or apparent police brutality."[33]

To the use of this technique I would give much of the credit for the relatively successful use of police at Stanford, compared to most other institutions suffering comparable degrees of unrest.

.   .   .

As the night wore on with no sign at all that our internal mechanisms were going to work in this case, and with fears that among the items the occupiers might dig out were plans of the university's underground sewers and power lines—a potential map for saboteurs—the long-feared necessity for calling in the police seemed ever clearer. The sheriff's representatives told us that if we wanted them to clear the building, they would have to get their orders by 4 a.m.—otherwise their normal daytime duties would make it impossible for them to muster sufficient numbers. (One of the things about which we had been educated was that badly outnumbered police can make a crisis worse.) As 4 a.m. approached, we were unanimously convinced that we had to ask for their help. Psychology professor Jonathan Freedman, the youngest member of the group, said, "Don't you think we should telephone Ken Pitzer at the Hoover House, just in case he did come back from L.A. but didn't check in to see whether anything was going on?" We all thought this highly unlikely, given the tensions earlier in the day, but agreed that we should make sure. I placed the call and roused Pitzer out of a sound sleep. I

brought him up to date as succinctly as possible and said that we were unanimous and that time had run out for the Santa Clara County Sheriff's people.
He asked, "Have you consulted Leonard Schiff [one of his closer confidantes
on the faculty, whom he may have thought likely to oppose the decision]?" I
said no, but that I had been in continuing session with the group responsible
to the Senate for providing faculty input in such decisions. Pause. "Have you
consulted Sandy Dornbusch [in the same category]?" Same response from
me. "All right, then, go ahead—on your responsibility." And we did. The
police would arrive at Encina from San Jose, ready to act, by about 7 o'clock
in the morning.[34]

The decision taken, I rushed home for a couple of hours of sleep, then
accompanied my spouse and children to the street across from Encina Hall
to watch the confrontation. My wife Jing thought our kids might face questioning about their father's behavior when they got to school that day, so they
should see for themselves what happened. Faculty went into Encina to tell the
occupants that they faced imminent arrest if they did not leave forthwith.
"In a hurried but calm meeting" the one hundred or so remaining in Encina
decided to leave. According to the *Peninsula Observer*, "Many said they were
voting to leave because they considered themselves revolutionaries and didn't
believe that revolutionaries should allow themselves to get caught. Later that
day, after thinking about the effects of the sit-in on the rest of the campus,
most of them said they should have stayed."[35] But the building was vacated
without injuries or arrests, in a striking contrast with events at Columbia,
Harvard, Berkeley, and San Francisco State.

That afternoon I described in detail to a special meeting of the Academic
Council the process by which we had arrived at the decision to call the police.
I recounted all the arguments for delay and the counterarguments to each. For
example, "It was conceivable that the most serious damage had already been
done in Encina, and that calling the police was to that extent dubious as being
too late. Against that was the reported fact that the exploitation of files, and
acts of vandalism, had been more random than systematic, and the reasonable expectation that continuation of the seizure through today would imply
a more systematic effort."[36] I continued:

> A compelling reason to summon the police was simply the fact that the Encina
> occupation comes so rapidly upon the heels of the AEL sit-in. At some point,
> nearly every member of this Council will agree, defenses must be invoked

against wanton, indiscriminate and arbitrary actions designed to force University acquiescence in the views of any campus groups, no matter how high-minded. It is not a matter of patience being exhausted; it is a matter of sheer credibility. No institution, not even a university, can continue indefinitely working in an atmosphere of coercion, indeed with the *fact* of coercive interruption daily demonstrated.

Concluding my account of events, I made what seemed to me a vital point, especially given the apparent success of the police intervention:

One further word, if I may. No one is entitled to consider the clearing of Encina Hall a victory. Any time it becomes necessary for a University to summon the police, a defeat has taken place. I'm reminded of Winston Churchill's declaration after Dunkerque, when too many of his fellow countrymen imagined that Hitler was on the downward path: Wars are not won by successful evacuations. The victory we seek at Stanford is not like a military victory; it is a victory of reason and the examined life over unreason and the tyranny of coercion. To be forced into coercive acts to meet coercive acts is in itself a setback on the path that leads to our kind of victory. But surrender does not produce victory either. The French say "reculer pour mieux sauter"—draw back to jump better. Maybe that is what we have done. It is not going to be easy to jump—or even to creep—forward in the conditions facing universities today. A brutal and senseless war abroad; brutal and senseless oppression at home; a feeling of desperation among the young at their powerlessness to remedy these things—these conditions limit our chances for success. I believe in Universities, and I believe in Stanford. I have done my best to serve these beliefs. It is no disgrace, and no cause for chagrin if one's best in such times as these is not good enough. I thank you for listening, and I wish us all well as we labor to reconstruct the mutual confidence without which no human enterprise can long succeed.

Nevertheless the sense of relief in the faculty was palpable and was demonstrated as I sat down by a standing ovation. The contrast with the experience one year earlier in that same hall was remarkable.[37]

The university moved quickly to carry out the long-considered plan to seek a temporary restraining order and a preliminary injunction carrying the names of thirty-six A3M members and five hundred John Does, which prohibited further disruptions and barred named individuals (those known to have been in Encina, and therefore subject to immediate temporary suspension) from entering the "principal campus" except for purposes of cooperation with the Stanford Judicial Council.

·   ·   ·

By May 13, the eve of the board of trustees meeting at which separation of SRI from the university would be decided, the radicals had recovered sufficiently from what even they called "an abortive sit-in at Encina Hall" to mount a day-long event during which hundreds wandered through the White Plaza Carnival, practicing breaking windows in the building of their choice, smashing a police car, and knocking over dummy trustees; it cost them dearly at $.25 a hit. Other fun and games included bombing Vietnamese peasants, fitting your child for a coffin, and questioning a wheel of fortune about your revolutionary future.[38] That sort of scene, and that kind of humor, are at least as effective reminders of those days as the big demonstrations.

After the trustees' meeting, at which the decision was taken to sell SRI, without restrictions, as soon as feasible, A3M managed by attacking SRI off campus to stay active and yet avoid infringing the temporary restraining order (or, TRO). They chose a building on Hanover Street, in the Industrial Park, as more convenient to campus than the main headquarters. Rather pathetically, the *Peninsula Observer* proclaimed, "Stanford Insurgents Shut Down SRI." The encounter was fairly ugly. Barricades appeared out of nowhere—pipes, rocks, and construction materials successfully blocked traffic on both Hanover and Page Mill. With cars, trucks, and a few school buses backed up almost to Bayshore—and with SRI, Itek (which made electronic countermeasure devices), and other defense industries in the park successfully disrupted—A3M waited for the police response.[39]

That did not come until 11 a.m. A battle ensued, involving tear gas canisters heaved back and forth, and rocks smashing all the windows on the Page Mill side of the building. By 12:30 it was all over. This far had A3M traveled since the "open house" began at AEL, a scant five weeks before. Small wonder that articles and letters began to appear under headlines such as "What Happened to the April 3rd Movement?" But the energy was not there for many days like May 16, though picketing continued through the remainder of the spring, partly in hopes of making SRI less attractive to potential buyers. The Palo Alto City Council unanimously asked its mayor to draft a letter to the university protesting the use of the campus as a "staging area" for off-campus actions. And, symptomatic of the movement's fracturing, the United Campus Christian Ministry decided to deny the A3M any further use of the office space they had been using on the third floor of the clubhouse.[40] Wrote the *Daily*, "The radicals got what satisfaction they could out of saying, Stanford is no longer a 'safe' rich man's school, impervious to the social conflicts raging outside its ivory towers and green football fields. We have shown the ruling class that NO institution is safe from attack, that they will have to deal not only with those they are oppressing but with their own sons and daughters as well."[41]

The formal inauguration of Ken Pitzer as Stanford's sixth president took place on June 14. Frost Amphitheater was far from full, and a few A3M activists managed to make us all nervous by dashing around on the edges of the crowd making hand signals to one another, as if building up to a disruption. But nothing happened. The featured speaker, trustee John W. Gardner, was more prescient than festive: "We have now proven beyond argument that a university community can make life unliveable for a president. We can make him the scapegoat for every failure of the institution. We can use him as the target for all the hostility that is in us. We can fight so savagely among ourselves that he is clawed to ribbons in the process. We have yet to prove that we can provide the kind of atmosphere in which a good man can survive."[42]

One heard his remarks with special poignancy, given the time the trustees had spent trying to persuade Gardner to occupy the Stanford presidency himself.

.   .   .

In the *Los Angeles Times*, William Trombley had a piece dated April 14 (late in the AEL sit-in) comparing Harvard's with Stanford's approach to dealing with sit-ins, not surprisingly much in Stanford's favor. Even later, when we could no longer claim that we never had to summon police, such comparisons continued to be made—after all, our approach had not produced such a traumatized situation as Harvard's. William Van Alstyne, general counsel for the AAUP, who had recently taught at Stanford, was quoted as saying that he knew of no other institution that "has done as much as Stanford to make its internal processes work."[43]

Stanford's own publicity did a year-end summary for the use of volunteer fund-raisers that tried to put as good a face on things as possible. It began, "The Judicial Council in its first year proved effective, if overworked," and it offered numbers of suspensions, probations, and fines as evidence. For the many alumni who thought we ought to have been expelling troublemakers by the carload, this would be thin gruel. "Stanford has not abolished ROTC from the campus," though the Senate has voted to remove academic credit. "The University is negotiating a new contract with the Department of Defense to establish an appropriate non-credit program at Stanford." This was a bit disingenuous since by June 1969 it was pretty clear that the DOD would not accept *any* noncredit plan.[44]

In early June the chair of the Stanford Judicial Council (SJC), law professor Jack Friedenthal, whose style, which might be described as voluble patience, had stood him in good stead in achieving the significant rulings on AEL, put forth a statement on behalf of the council, calling for several changes in its charter and modus operandi. He recommended appointment of a university prosecutor who would present the cases. This would remedy the impossible situation faced by council members having to act as prosecutors and judges at the same time. "This is undesirable if for no other reason than large numbers of the University community feel that such a system is basically unfair. . . . Presence of a prosecutor would permit the Council members to enjoy a more proper role of neutral arbiter." By the same token he urged charter changes to get the dean of students out of the line of fire and free his office to do its job of supporting students. He stated that the council should be given power to determine "rules as to the conduct of its meetings not inconsistent with the Charter." Last but not least, the SJC should have "the power to subpoena any member of the Stanford community," and to impose direct, immediate sanctions on any who disrupt or fail to cooperate with its proceedings.[45]

All of this was sensible, and the need for such changes a powerful reminder of the difficulty in creating new institutions, particularly under conditions of maximum stress and polarized opinion, the conditions prevailing that hectic spring of 1968.

The Stanford administration meanwhile began preparing to respond to a subpoena from the Senate Permanent Subcommittee on Investigations, chaired by Arkansas Democrat John McClellan, demanding the university's records on ninety individuals and a dozen organizations, including SDS, A3M, and the *Observer*.

9 KEN PITZER'S DEPARTURE

THE MCCLELLAN COMMITTEE HEARINGS provided a strange postscript to our troubled year, not quite a comic aftermath, perhaps, but not a dramatic climax, either. To the extent that the hearings could be said to have had a purpose, beyond merely seizing an opportunity to exploit for political advantage the universities' difficulties in maintaining some semblance of order on their campuses, it was to promote the idea of congressional action to withhold federal research support from institutions that failed to punish students who disrupted university operations.

There was a plausible, if superficial, logic to this: Why should the taxpayers' money be used to support institutions that could not protect the activities being supported? Naturally, however, university people regarded such moves as crude threats to their integrity. University decision making in an important area would be taken out of their hands. As a precedent the legislation would be lamentable, since it could presumably be invoked any time institutions didn't behave as lawmakers, with their far-removed perspective and limited exposure to academic values, thought they should. An amendment to the HEW appropriations for 1968, introduced by a Republican congressman from North Carolina, James Broyhill, did require that federal funds be made available for the "payment, assistance, or services" to anyone convicted "of inciting, promoting, or carrying on a riot, or any group activity resulting in material damage to property or injury to persons, found to be in violation of Federal, State or local laws designed to protect persons or property in the community concerned."[1]

This provision, accepted under protest by Stanford, was, as the university then stated, "unenforceable, misguided, and without reasonable relationship to the central purposes of the Act." But the idea of such a provision retained an appeal that made it difficult to dismiss, even though in real terms it never had much impact. By May 1969, the *New York Times* was reporting, "Attorney General Mitchell has wisely abandoned his earlier 'get tough' posture and asked Congress to refrain from punitive legislation in order not to play into the hands of campus militants."[2] President Nixon, even as he signed an appropriation for the State, Justice, and Commerce Departments, noted that the government should not interfere in the "internal affairs of our colleges and universities."[3]

.   .   .

President Pitzer and I were called to testify together. He took the lead, and most of the questions were directed at him. Nearly twenty pages of the hearing transcripts cover wrangling over how student organizations were (and were not) regulated on campus. It was easy to make our system look lax; for example, we required only one signature, and that not necessarily of an officer of the organization, for registration. I said:

> We believe that a more involved or detailed method of registration would be an extremely weak weapon at best to deal with the problem, and it would have very distinct counterproductive effects. That is, it would place a weapon in the hands of the SDS which they have shown themselves very willing and eager to use every time they get their hands anywhere near such a weapon, that is, an apparent threat to the freedom of association on the campus. Student organizations come and go incredibly rapidly. They are the most ephemeral situations on the face of the earth. If you give the impression you are going to organize an attack on people for belonging to organizations, I think you hand the SDS an opportunity to create more trouble.[4]

The confrontation is well illustrated by the following exchange:

> The Chairman: Then the machinery that you have is not fully adequate to protect the other students so that the studies and the operation of the college will not be disrupted? Dr. Spitzer [*sic*]: Mr. Chairman, I don't think any university administrator will maintain that the machinery has been adequate anywhere whatever kinds of machinery has [*sic*] been tried. We do have a serious problem and we have not solved it. All we have claimed is that [they] have made some

progress towards resolving it in a way which does not create further trouble by making martyrs out of people and by enabling the radical militants to mobilize moderate opinion, which is the only point at which they become a threat.[5]

Our testimony was followed by that of Professor Friedenthal, who described the workings of the Judicial Council and the changes they were recommending—far too arcane a matter to interest the subcommittee—and Professor William Rambo, the most conspicuous leader of those faculty from engineering who had been doing classified research. Since he was also a member of the Faculty Consultative Group on Campus Disruption, he could testify with added authority about the checkered history of our attempts to deal with the problems. He defended the administration's reluctance to call in police to deal with Applied Electronics Laboratory (AEL) because it would have polarized the campus and made consensus on dealing with disruptions much more difficult. "I kid you not at all, I was personally very unhappy at the time of the AEL sit-in that our community was of such a mood that we had to endure that."[6]

The one good thing about the AEL experience was that it alerted the university to the danger it faced, enabling the administration to act "so differently and with so much more success" on Encina shortly thereafter.[7]

Throughout all this, the university got help from time to time from some of McLellan's senatorial colleagues: Charles Percy, a Stanford parent, Lee Metcalf, a Stanford graduate, and occasionally Carl Mundt. Things would have been far more difficult had the chair's performance not been so lackadaisical and inconsistent. At the very start of the hearings, after swearing us in to testify, McLellan excused himself; he had to go to his office "for a few minutes," but Pitzer should proceed with his prepared statement anyhow. It was eight pages into that statement that the chair returned. The nearest thing to a summary of his conclusions went like this:

> I don't want to cast any aspersions on the University. They feel they are doing the best they can and are taking the wisest course, but I don't believe it will prove in the long run to be a wise course, that any University will become a government beyond the law, out from the law of the land. . . . I don't think any University campus should become an island of independence where the law does not apply, and where there is substituted for the law some judicial system, as they term it, of the University, and I hope we are not moving in that direction.[8]

The whole experience left me weary and bemused by the size of the gaps in mutual understanding that were revealed. As for the antiriot amendment idea, it continued to bedevil us from time to time but essentially it failed to take hold because of the inherent difficulty of establishing clear definitions and distinctions. Would federal funds be withheld upon accusations, or only when a court of law had established the guilt of a student? Would the entire federal support for an institution vanish with the successful prosecution of a single dissident who had somehow not been punished by the university?

· · ·

During the autumn of 1969, at Stanford as nationally, the protest movement was largely dominated by the Moratorium, an effort to demonstrate the extent of the nation's opposition to the war by a massive descent on Washington, backed by protest events scheduled for the same time across the country. Intended to be a continuing affair, the Moratorium in fact culminated in the siege of the Pentagon celebrated in Norman Mailer's *Armies of the Night*. At Stanford, Memorial Auditorium and Memorial Church were both packed, while thirty-five hundred stood outside in the rain to listen. Speakers had to repeat their remarks, appearing first one place, then the other. Pete McCloskey, well-known Republican critic of the war, declared that the Moratorium "marks a watershed in the whole anti-war movement. Tonight opposition to the war has reached such proportions that it is honorable to be a part of it." But students who tried to work the commuter trains met mostly apathy and occasionally strident opposition—" 'God damn you hippie freak commie. Get out of here,' " being a sample.

But such peaceable mass gatherings were not SDS's thing. Noting, almost ruefully it seemed, that October's Moratorium "probably had more active participation than any single political event in Stanford history," Lennie Siegel saw success against the war as only possible if the Moratorium movement gained strength with each month and included such things as "expansion of the work being done with industrial production workers—to see if work stoppages are possible."[9] In November, SDS tried to help striking workers at Pittsburgh-Des Moines Steel in Santa Clara. Bruce Franklin, who liked to remind people that he had once worked as a tugboat hand back East, remarked, "Anyone who hasn't had any working experience ought to get some. I'm not saying everyone should rush out to the plant. We need revolutionaries everywhere in the society. But it's an opportunity to get rid of a lot of shit that's in everyone's head; to actually see how value is produced." To which Siegel added, "We are able to talk to them [the workers] about the fact that blacks and Vietnamese are their class allies, because they are fighting the same enemy. Unfortunately, all workers aren't like the guys at PDM. It's a long, hard struggle to win friends in the working class."[10] It turned out that even "the guys at PDM" had their limits; soon the SDS was asked, politely but firmly, to back off.

In fact, as 1969 ended SDS was floundering and in disarray. According to a *Palo Alto Times* report of a meeting attended by about sixty SDS members on November 11, one speaker said, "We must become more involved after the 15th [of November] or else the movement will die." The meeting voted to eject the *Times* reporter as a "fascist pig," one SDS member walking out with him in protest. A column in the *Daily* for December 3 speculated as to whether the then-prevailing campus apathy would yield to "the annual spring fling" this year: "After all, who isn't tired of hearing Lenny Siegel or Fred Cohen expounding? Who isn't tired of reading those boringly moderate statements by Pitzer [recently arrived to take up his presidential duties] that always seem to complement [*sic*] all sides but come down on the side of tradition? Who isn't tired of seeing the *Palo Alto Times* distort what occurs day after day? Who can stand one more Jim Schnieder call for moderation in all things except moderation?"

Meanwhile aside from the political fray, the university went on its usual way. SES recommendations began to be put into effect. An engineering professor, Peter Bulkeley, became dean of students in succession to Joel Smith, who left to become president of Denison University, while Fred Hargadon came from Swarthmore to succeed Rixford Snyder who had directed undergraduate admissions for nineteen years. The student body presidency had evolved into a "council of presidents" as a way of coping with the new insistence on female and minority representation in the highest office of ASSU, and a centrist council was coping as best it could with a polarized student body. The Ford Foundation's grant of nearly $2 million enabled the university to launch the most successful of interdisciplinary undergraduate majors, human biology. As I recall, what influenced the foundation to take such a step, including a departure from its established policy of denying any funds for endowment, was the spectacle of a founding committee that included several chairs of Medical School clinical departments, not a group generally to be found putting time and energy into developing innovation in undergraduate education. Human biology increased Stanford's reputation for entrepreneurial activity in academic matters, perhaps more than any other development of that period, and showed that as an academic institution we were refusing to be stymied by the campus unrest.

·   ·   ·

The 1969–70 academic year was dominated by the controversies around two main issues: the status of ROTC, and the relationship between the university and the Stanford Research Institute (SRI).

The debate over ROTC centered on four issues: the academic credit accorded ROTC courses; the faculty status accorded ROTC instructors appointed by the armed services; the departmental status within the School of Humanities and Sciences enjoyed by the ROTC program; and the so-called punitive clause in ROTC contracts with students enrolling in the program, by which any student who received benefits (scholarship money) from the program but then dropped out of it would have to serve a lengthy term in the armed services as an enlisted man.

All but the last of these four questions could be summed up as involving the treatment of ROTC as a regular, normal part of the academic program of the university. But ROTC was the only program in which the curriculum, awarding of credit, and appointments of faculty were all determined by an outside body, without the involvement of the Stanford faculty. Many went on to argue that many ROTC courses lacked serious academic content, standards of achievement were not high, and the academic qualifications of the teaching staff were not up to Stanford standards.

Defenders of the program usually emphasized the fact that having ROTC at major universities assured that at least some of the officers in the armed services would have enjoyed the benefits of a quality civilian education; to abandon these programs would leave military leadership in the hands of graduates of military academies. It was also pointed out that ROTC provided a useful supplement to university scholarship funds.

For the radicals who promoted the "Off ROTC" cause, of course, academic concerns about the program were secondary. It was attacked primarily as a part of the university's complicity in the Vietnam War. In abolishing ROTC they hoped to strike a blow at the war effort, though just how and why the loss of ROTC at Stanford would materially affect this effort was not clear.

The ROTC issue was slow in emerging. In May 1968, Herb Packer wrote a memo in which he tried to anticipate troubles in areas where we might take preemptive action. Of ROTC he said, "It is a mystery to me why this one has not been raised publicly. Faculty members who feel very strongly about it will now be emboldened to raise the issue directly in the Academic Council. The Executive Committee has had the matter on its agenda for some time at the instance of that flaming radical, Ken Arrow. . . . I believe that we should be looking into the possibility of converting ROTC to an extracurricular activity."

But getting ahead of the game was not easy. The attempt to find a formula whereby ROTC could be retained, but with changes sufficient to meet the faculty's main concerns, got seriously under way with the report from a student-faculty committee to the Academic Senate in February 1969, containing eight recommendations. Of these the Senate voted to support six, leaving the remaining two in limbo, largely because these last would have gone so far in the direction of reducing ROTC to the status of a student voluntary organization, like the Outing Club or Crew. Senate members recognized that to do that would be tantamount to evicting ROTC, since the Pentagon could not be expected to swallow such a drastic revision. As it was, the six recommendations accepted by the Senate would, over a period of time, have phased out all professorial rank for ROTC officers—they would no longer enjoy membership in the Academic Council or faculty. They would have phased out also departmental status for the ROTC departments, which had been departments of the School of Humanities and Sciences, and all academic credit for ROTC courses. Starting in 1970–71, there would be no academic credit for first-year ROTC students, and so on each year until there was no credit at all for ROTC courses taught by ROTC people.

For the moment the Senate was ahead of student opinion, for in a referendum on February 24 the students voted 2,106 to 1,387 that "ROTC has a legitimate place on the campus and deserves support and credit from the University for all those parts of the program the are of genuine academic interest."

In passing these strong resolutions Senate members were well aware that they were in effect initiating a process of negotiation between Stanford and the Pentagon. The university administration would take these proposals to the Pentagon and see how much, if any, of the package just voted by the Senate the Defense Department could accept. Depending on the answer, the administration would do one of three things. If the Pentagon proved willing to accept the entire package, there would be no need to remit the matter to the Senate for further action, and reform would get under way. Alternatively, the administration would decide that what the Pentagon was willing to accept fell so far short of what the Senate was proposing that there would be equally little point in going back to the Faculty Senate given that incompatibility, and ROTC would have to go. Or, a third possibility, the Pentagon would go a good distance toward what the Senate had voted but not all the way, and the president would then have to decide whether this response was sufficiently promising that it could become the basis for further negotiation.

Quite predictably, what developed was this third alternative. The armed services agreed that we would proceed to negotiate regarding the Army contract, while the other two services would sit by for the time being and watch.

What emerged was a proposal with regard to the Army to eliminate faculty rank and departmental status, but to allow Army ROTC courses to seek credit the same way that any nondepartmental course was able to seek credit, through the Committee on Undergraduate Studies. The university negotiators, led by Vice Provost E. Howard Brooks, did not make any real headway on another sensitive point, the so-called punitive clauses. Few if any observers saw these as acceptable; there were easier and fairer ways of dealing with the problem of a cadet changing his mind about wanting to be a cadet. New cadets could be given loans, instead of scholarships, with the requirement that the loan must be paid back if the recipient doesn't stay the course. It is a bit mysterious why the armed services refused to consider such alternatives, but refuse they did.

The administration passed the Army proposal along to the Senate, with the recommendation that it be approved. On January 22, 1970, the Senate voted twenty-one to thirteen to do that. But many faculty saw the proposal as drawing back from the February 1969 decision and reintroducing the idea that ROTC was a legitimate academic exercise. The Senate's decision to approve was appealed to a ballot of the Academic Council, and this vote came out almost evenly split, 390 to 373. Assuming the eleven ROTC officers who were members of the council voted in favor, the margin was six votes in a total of nearly eight hundred cast.

Shortly thereafter a student referendum came out two to one against any academic credit for ROTC, which threw everything into disarray. When the Senate met again to reconsider the matter the vote was thirty-six to eight simply to eliminate academic credit for ROTC. This vote was tantamount to ending ROTC on the Stanford campus, and everyone understood it that way. How had the Senate come to reverse itself so quickly?

The riotous activities of the month of April no doubt had something to do with it, though exactly how much is impossible to measure. The U.S. incursion into Cambodia played a part; many faculty felt some of the same desperation that students felt about finding ways to express their repugnance for that move. It seemed on the face of it not only a reversal of the administration's supposed policy of gradually pulling out of Southeast Asia but also a reversal couched in language so reminiscent of that used in the initial involvement there as to arouse maximum distrust.

In addition, senators were influenced by the student referendum. The president of the university had made a point time after time over the preceding year of stressing the earlier student vote in favor of retaining ROTC with academic credit. Were students to be listened to only when they supported the administration's preferred policies? After all, the program was defended as a service to students. If they did not want the service who was to say they must have it? Perhaps the Senate ought to have been more attentive to the interests of that minority of students who wanted ROTC, but in the emotionally charged atmosphere of "Cambodia Spring" that would have been a lot to ask.

The Pentagon, in handling the movement against ROTC on various campuses, contributed to the confusion and played into the hands of its opponents. Treating each institution separately, the Pentagon made all sorts of tricky deals that were inconsistent with each other. Sometimes they would insist on retaining academic credit, while yielding on faculty rank for the instructors, while at others it would be just the reverse. Thus on each campus it was possible to argue, "We didn't get the best deal possible."

In the end, ROTC was abolished at only a few private institutions, albeit some of the most well known. Where abolition took place, it is clear that the antiwar radicals found a tacit alliance with faculty whose objections to the program were in fact academic rather than political. In this respect, the history of the abolition of classified research at Stanford in the preceding year was recapitulated in the case of ROTC.

The spring of 1970 saw more on-campus violence than ever, before or since. It began with the uproar the night of March 31, triggered by news that the Academic Council's mail ballot had produced a slender majority—390 to 373—for giving the Army ROTC plan for awarding academic credit a one-year trial. Tom Hayden told an overflow crowd in Dinkelspiel that "the next generation of political people will have to be a generation of outlaws," but it had dwindled to about three hundred when Michael Sweeney, editor of *Chaparral*, said, "You can't have an ROTC at Stanford if you don't have an ROTC building." The crowd broke up, and most rushed to that structure, where a small group of athletes were guarding the entrance. The police arrived after the first windows were broken and two large lampposts at the entrance had been smashed. Some two hundred people then scattered and went on to break windows at the Graduate School of Business, History Corner, the Placement Office, the President's Office, the Lou Henry Hoover Building, and Aeronautics and Astronautics. Damage totaled $4,000.

The next night a masked and robed assailant poured water-soluble red paint over the head and shoulders of President Pitzer as he was having after-dinner conversation with students at Grove House. The humiliation was obvious and painful.

April and May 1970 were in a way the climax of campus unrest at Stanford, although troubles continued to plague us into 1972. Through most of April there were episodes of trashing, carried out by a limited number of Off-ROTC followers, including such vandalism as jamming locks on buildings and spray-painting the Hoover House. At times it was difficult not to see the protests as bordering on frivolous. The night of April 2, after debating whether to try to occupy the ROTC building, some three hundred protesters responded to a voice that shouted "Let's go to Pitzer's home." At the Hoover House they staged an "impersonation of Pitzer," and soon after midnight sang "Happy Birthday, April 3 Movement." A fourth successive night of marching on ROTC drew only about one hundred seventy-five people, despite an effort to recruit at a showing at Dinkelspiel of a popular movie, which drew a hostile reaction. Deciding that their numbers were too few to be effective, the marchers broke into small discussion groups for about a half-hour, then dispersed, some heading back for a late showing of the film. The business manager at Tresidder Memorial Union wrote a despairing letter to Pitzer pointing out that the administration had failed "even to back up the simple rule of no pets in residences on campus. Our patronage has declined steadily for three years because people have grown tired of competing with dogs for the food and from the sight, sound, smell and abuse they have had to take from dissident students, both black and white, who use this building as their headquarters for the planning of the destruction of this university. The dogs are much more acceptable."[11]

On April 23–24 there was a confused sit-in at the Old Union in which some fifty sheriff's deputies swept into the building without warning and arrested twenty-two people while the rest fled, hurling rocks at the police as they went. Many faculty protested the police action, and I had to point out on-air on KZSU that the police were no doubt fed up with "coming on campus in major force at major cost to the Santa Clara County taxpayers . . . only to play juvenile cops and robbers" with the rock-throwers, who were characterized by a *Daily* writer as nothing more than "a bunch of bored-to-death kids out to have a lark."[12]

During the afternoon of April 24, we had given a garden party at our home on campus for the outgoing and incoming deans of humanities and sciences, Bob Sears and Al Hastorf. That noon, Professor Barton Bernstein of history had thoughtfully given a White Plaza rally directions for getting to our house, where radicals lined the approaches to shout abuse at arriving guests, including the Pitzers. That night I returned from a visit to the police station and was talking with my wife, Jing, in a bedroom at the back of the house when there was a loud crash. Someone had hurled a big Coca Cola bottle full of red paint through our kitchen windows, narrowly missing the head of a security guard who was taking an ill-timed coffee break in the kitchen and smashing against the refrigerator. The resulting mess was spectacular; Holly, coming downstairs next morning for breakfast, took one look and exclaimed, "Wow! Would my art teacher love to see THIS!" Worse yet, in the morning we discovered two large rocks that had been thrown through an upstairs window; fortunately they fell harmless in the sewing room; Holly's bedroom, with Holly sleeping in it, was next door. No one throws rocks through upstairs windows in the middle of the night unless they intend to maim, if not kill, occupants of the house.

In some ways the most mindless atrocity took place a few days later with the arson fire that burned two wings of the Center for Advanced Study in the Behavioral Sciences, a dollar-a-year tenant of Stanford in the foothills behind the campus. Ten offices were destroyed, including the scholars' notes and other materials. A distinguished Indian social scientist, M.N. Srinivas, lost his lifework, twenty-two years' worth of study on the caste system in south India. Shock was widespread. The *Sacramento Bee* editorialized, "It was as if ignorance had struck blindly and instinctively at intelligence and humanity; as if irrationality had aimed at its natural enemy, rationality; as if purposelessness had sought out purpose to destroy." Though there was no evidence to link this atrocity to the ROTC issue, no doubt many assumed some connection.

The troubles of April and May exhausted those police departments that had been called on to help the Santa Clara sheriff restore order. Police officers from San Jose, Sunnyvale, and Mountain View all reported they could not continue providing support for Stanford and still do their jobs in their own communities.

The U.S. invasion of Cambodia in May 1970 triggered the biggest night of rock-throwing, club-wielding battle involving several hundred students and 274 police drawn from as far away as San Francisco. At least ten people were injured, and the police used tear gas to break up concentrations of rioters. The fracas wound down after 1 a.m. The ASSU Council of Presidents issued an agonized statement:

> This ghastly and horrifying clash between police and students plays into the hands of radicals who have been calling for continued vandalism and destruction. The clash occurred because of the polarization and irrationality which has prevailed on the campus for the past weeks, it occurred because of hysteria and hatred at the Union. This campus must not panic. Its problems will not be solved by hate or hysteria. We plead with students to restore a sense of rationality, so that events of the past weeks can be sorted out towards some constructive result.

But because the Cambodian invasion outraged so many, there was a lot of jockeying for position between those who still wanted to throw rocks and those advocating a shift to nonviolent tactics that would appeal to the much larger numbers now engaged. As one speaker at the Off-ROTC meeting on April 28 had said, "If we want a lot of people there [in the Old Union], we should say we're being non-disruptive and non-violent."

Across the nation, even at campuses where little active protest had thus far taken place, classes were shut down, often with the full collaboration of the professors scheduled to teach them, and protesters blocked the entrance to classrooms where professors were not prepared to forego teaching. Classes were sometimes held at faculty homes. Incompletes were made easier to take the place of final exams. All this happened at Stanford, and for a few heady days in May, the history community, the chemistry community, and so on took the place of the old-style hierarchical departments. These "communities," embracing students at all levels and nonfaculty staff members along with faculty, functioned on the basis of one person, one vote. Participatory democracy had arrived. The height of the strike was the week of May 4 through 8. On May 4, the student newspapers at ten well-known colleges and universities, including Stanford and five of the eight Ivy League institutions, published a common editorial supporting the strike. The *Daily* reported that in the School of Humanities and Sciences about 20 percent of scheduled classes met on Tuesday, with about 20 percent attendance at those that did meet. On Friday, May 8, Pitzer declared all classes canceled "to provide a period of reflection on the extensive activities and discussions of the past week and to alleviate the emotional fatigue which has become prevalent." Beyond classes shut down, blocking entrances and thus closing down administrative offices and laboratories resulted in severe financial loss for the university, as I tried to point out during a radio broadcast on KZSU on Monday, May 11. By that time hundreds of students began returning to classes, mainly to discuss how they could avoid loss of academic credit and finish their work or take incompletes.

Most of our sister institutions, which were on the semester system, were able to close for the summer with some approximation of grace, their academic year completed. Not so at Stanford, with a solid month of spring quarter left. What finally spared us further complication was the collapse of the movement nationally, shocked by the killings of four students by panicky National Guardsmen at Kent State, and that "emotional fatigue" to which Pitzer had referred after a spring filled with turmoil and sporadic violence. Later that summer the bombing of the mathematics building at the University of Wisconsin, in which a graduate student died, showed that it was not only the National Guard who could kill.

Meanwhile, Ken Pitzer's regime was coming to an end. I was neither involved in nor informed of various meetings held with the trustees, urging that they act to remove Pitzer; I have been told that concern lest I leave Stanford for a presidency elsewhere was a significant factor. In fact I was dining in New York with the presidential search committee for Wesleyan University on June 25 when I got a call informing me that Ken was resigning, effective August 31. When I got back to Stanford I had one meeting with him and then left for a month's vacation on our family's island in Penobscot Bay, Maine. I returned, and Ken took his month of vacation in August, while I took over the duties of president. I became formally acting president on September 1.

In his letter to the board president, Ken Pitzer said:

In the summer of 1968, when you asked me to consider the presidency of Stanford, I did so with the expectation that significant progress would be made at the national level in healing some of the deep divisions which beset our country, especially the war in Viet Nam. Instead, these divisions have deepened. The gulf between the campus community and society at large has widened, particularly in the last two months. Although troop levels in Viet Nam have been reduced, there is little confidence on campus about our promised disengagement from the war. As a result, pressures tending to distract and disrupt the educational process have increased significantly. The growing polarization within society also has been reflected within the campus. These trends have made it increasingly difficult to obtain the very broad and active support from all those groups who together are responsible for the well-being of the University. From a purely personal standpoint, the prospect of a more scholarly life at a less hectic pace is most welcome. Entirely too much of my effort has been devoted to a matter of purely administrative or even of a police nature. Too little time has been available for the academic matters I most enjoy—the planning and implementing of innovations and improvement in teaching and research. In a broader context, however, I have reached this decision only after the most serious thought and with a great sense of regret and disappointment. The situation at Stanford represents another manifestation of the destructive nature of the current conflict. Both on campus and in society, support for reasoned discourse and nonviolent change has steadily diminished.

Board president Parmer Fuller's acceptance of Ken's resignation gave no hint of its having been forced: "Ken Pitzer is an educator, a scholar and a friend. His feelings that the heavy burdens of administration in these days of crisis are incompatible with the basic interests of the scholar and educator are indeed understandable. Nevertheless, because I have worked so closely with him in these difficult times I have accepted his resignation not only with regret but with a sense of loss as well."

Lyle Nelson, then director of university relations, used to tell people that he had met with Ken Pitzer between his having been told that he had to leave and his writing to Fuller. At that point, according to Nelson, Pitzer had with him a draft letter to Fuller, defying the trustees' pressure to resign. Nelson dissuaded him from any such course and kept the draft just to be sure Ken did not have second thoughts. Neither I nor Nelson's widow were able to find the draft among Nelson's papers after his death, but the story is plausible. Bob Rosenzweig recalls "being told at the time that Ken Pitzer called some members of the faculty, including Bill Clebsch, [then Senate chair] from whom I probably heard it, to ask whether they would support him in an effort to dissuade the Trustees from taking their action. He was politely told that would not happen." Although there was never a statement from the board or from

Pitzer acknowledging that the resignation had been the alternative to being dismissed, the general understanding at the time was that the trustees had put very great pressure on the president to give up his office.

·   ·   ·

When I heard about the process by which the search for Ken's successor would be carried out, I was dismayed. There were to be no less than four committees, representing the trustees, the faculty, the alumni, and the students. Although it was clear that the trustees had the final authority, it seemed all too likely that getting these four groups to agree on a candidate or a slate of candidates would prove difficult and time consuming. It also seemed likely that the campus troubles might resume just as they had left off, in the fall of 1970. If there were no decision on the presidency by the time the university opened, I felt that my position would be tenuous, at best—an acting presidency held by an individual who had of course accumulated no small number of critics and adversaries in his years of involvement in the campus troubles.

There was nothing I could do about all this, and meanwhile the tasks of the presidency had to be carried on. During the summer, an episode took place that had no direct connection to the campus unrest, but illustrated the instability that had become a feature of the university's condition. Ken Pitzer had instituted a review of all the university visiting committees to the various schools, departments, and programs. It was clear that there were no generally enforced standards as to the function and modus operandi of these bodies and that some rationalization of the system would be desirable. But the president made the mistake of including the Hoover Institution Advisory Board in this review. This body was the creation of President Hoover and was designed to provide a link between various personal friends of his and the institution; his son, Allen, was a member. Not surprisingly, members of the advisory board did not appreciate being lumped together with all the visiting committees; they enjoyed a special status and wanted that recognized. Inspired, no doubt, by its director, Glenn Campbell, the advisory board asked the Stanford University Board of Trustees to approve sweeping changes, beginning with renaming the group the Hoover Institution Board of Overseers. They proposed formalizing their role in the appointment of a director whenever that position became vacant. Most important of all, they proposed removing the university president from any role relating to the Hoover Institution except that of an ex-officio member without vote of the board of overseers. The director would thus no longer report to the president but directly to the Stanford University Board of Trustees.

I saw this as a danger to the university and at some point I went to see Morris Doyle, a former Stanford board president and one of the trustees who were also members of the Hoover board. I knew that the trustees were likely to follow Doyle's advice on matters relating to the Hoover, and I urged him to reject the change in the university president's position. We met in his office in San Francisco. He tried mightily to persuade me that the proposed changes were not a threat to the president's authority, but this flew in the face of the obvious facts. I wound up telling him that if the trustees allowed the Hoover board to take advantage of the interregnum in the Stanford presidency in this fashion then neither I nor anyone else whom the trustees were likely to want to appoint as president of Stanford would accept the job.

I also sent Bob Rosenzweig and Fred Glover, executive assistant to the president, to discuss the issues with Glenn Campbell. Bob, knowing that Campbell was inordinately proud of his Harvard degrees, notwithstanding his contempt for its liberal leanings, suggested that the advisory board be renamed the board of overseers. The overseers did not govern Harvard. That was the job of the corporation and the university officers. But the overseers were kept informed of everything, and their advice was always taken seriously, surely all that the Hoover board should expect. Campbell was willing to settle for this, together with more formalized involvement of the board in the appointment of the Hoover director. The changes were enacted, minus the alteration in the director's reporting relationship, early in 1971.

10 MY PRESIDENCY BEGINS, AND
THE FRANKLIN CASE IS INITIATED

IN THE EVENT, the presidential search proceeded with incredible speed, though it also reached out widely for help; one hundred thousand letters went out to alumni, students, and faculty inviting suggestions. It seems clear that the faculty committee, and especially its chair, Professor David Hamburg, who was chair of the Psychiatry Department, led the way. Although the other committees held their own meetings and conducted interviews, it was Hamburg who orchestrated the process. At that, it was August 26 before the final element was put in place with the appointment of four Stanford staff members as consultants to the faculty committee.

The student committee, which included the four members of the ASSU Council of Presidents, as well as the firebrand former president of the Black Student Union, Leo Bazile, was understandably inclined to imagine that there must be possible candidates on the East Coast who would constitute more exciting choices than Lyman. Hamburg undertook to pay two representatives of the student committee, Bazile and Robert Grant, to make an East Coast trip on September 15–20 to explore these possibilities. Not surprisingly, they found that such potential candidates as Bill Bowen, provost at Princeton, were not in the least interested in coming out to Stanford to pick up the pieces left by Pitzer's regime.

Four days after the students' return, the trustees elected me president by a unanimous vote at a special meeting held September 24.

The university was about to reopen; freshman convocation was scheduled for September 25. Earlier in the summer, on our way back from Maine, Jing and I had an appointment with a senior fellow of the Harvard Corporation, Hooks Burr, in his Boston office to be interviewed as a candidate for the presidency of Harvard in the wake of Nathan Pusey's resignation. But the Harvard search would not reach a conclusion for some months; I could not hold off in responding to the Stanford offer in the hopes that Harvard would choose me, and in any case I felt an obligation not to leave Stanford after having put so much into working to sustain the university. I had also probably contributed, however unintentionally, to precipitating Pitzer's departure, merely by being known to be considering leaving Stanford. So I accepted the presidency of Stanford, and when the convocation took place in Memorial Church, I greeted the class of 1974 as Stanford's president.

While the faculty and trustee committees had been unanimous in their support, neither the alumni nor student committees made a report, and clearly enthusiasm was not universal in either group. The *Daily* editorial, written by Marshall Kilduff, one of two coeditors and a member of the student search committee, was fair and balanced, or perhaps one should say agonized. "Lyman is unquestionably the best man for Stanford of the nine or ten national front-runners that the search committees focused on," he wrote. "He is intelligent, articulate, honest and capable . . . [but] a man of the traditional university . . . he looks upon it as the pinnacle of modern civilization." He "can be brutally rough in conversation . . . he probably drives mild opponents far away from a possible understanding of the issues at hand. . . . Even when he took to KZSU to explain himself, his remarks showed a lofty frostiness and barely suppressed impatience with his student questioners." He sees the need for educational reform but "is almost instinctively suspicious of the hazy but heartfelt cries for 'relevance' and 'meaningful education.'" His conclusion: "Lyman is one of the few who come to power on the shoulders of so many beaming, adoring followers. He should be careful that his halo does not embarrass him." While it is not exactly clear just what that last sentence means, one has the impression that the writer is compelled to admit that the right choice has been made, given the alternatives, but wishes it were otherwise.

Perhaps representative of the "beaming, adoring followers" was my history colleague, George Knoles, who wrote to me on September 24: "The times will doubtless be difficult; but you have abundantly demonstrated in the past that difficulties fail to daunt you. . . . It is my fervent hope that under your leadership we can recover something of the sense of destiny that illuminated the vision of the university's founders and its pioneer faculty."

The *Daily* quoted a Chicano member of the search committee indicating why, on balance, the students wound up supporting my appointment: "His wife could add the warmth that Lyman seems to be lacking, and thus give him a more human look."[1] A sentiment that the *Daily* itself echoed a couple of weeks later in a profile of my spouse: "Jing Lyman is an alive sort of person with a sense of fun and a sense of purpose. She fulfills all the 'Better Homes and Gardens' clichés of the ideal suburban matron—and then in her spare time she goes out to be a person in her own right."[2]

On our way into Memorial Church for the freshman convocation, Davie Napier, dean of the chapel, warned me that radicals had visited the freshman dorms to tell residents that it was a Stanford tradition to greet the president with the Axe Yell: "Give 'em the axe, give 'em the axe where? Right in the neck," and so on. Sure enough, when I had been introduced and proceeded to the lectern to address the class, a few students in the rear of the church attempted to lead the yell, most freshmen did not pick it up, and the attempt at disruption failed dismally. I heard later that one girl had remarked that she and her classmates did not see the long-haired and bearded visitors to her dorm as the kind of students likely to be much interested in Stanford traditions.

Since my speech to the entering class was perhaps the most complete rendition of my determination to protect the university from becoming a political instrument it deserves some attention here. Granted, I said, universities were entitled to defend their interests as educational institutions and to seek to influence politics insofar as educational issues were involved. But in 1970 the political system itself seemed to be functioning badly. I said:

> The *quality* of American political life must improve, drastically and quickly.
> . . . Attention to major issues must increase, and preoccupation with trivial
> issues decrease; ways of seeking and achieving change through the politi-
> cal system must be opened up and clarified, so that they really do exist and
> people can see that they exist; the general level of involvement in politics on
> the part of millions of people who are not professional politicians must rise
> dramatically, and stay risen (it's not enough to get excited when the head-
> lines of some fresh disaster stir one's metabolism; the involvement has to be
> steady and unremitting, patient but relentless); the terrible grip of private
> selfishness, not just on the part of major corporations but among everyday
> tax-paying (and tax-resisting) citizens, must give way to a sharply increased

willingness to see money change hands and power relationships alter so that urgent public questions, such as racial equality and environmental protection, can be dealt with.

In accomplishing such changes, I continued:

Clearly college students and other university people must help. . . . If they don't, no one else will—not because they are uniquely virtuous but simply because university people *ought* to be *among* the people most sensitive to the tragic condition of the world today, and best able to by reason of their abilities and their opportunities, do something about it. Not satisfied with this, however, many university people had leapt to the conclusion that the university itself must become an advocate for change. In other words, it must be politicized. Yet to accept the view that the university must be turned into a political instrument for purposes going far beyond its institutional interest in educational matters threatens its capacity to perform its proper function in society. That function certainly includes training people to be more effective critics and advocates, of whatever viewpoint. To retain the freedom to do just that, it is essential that the university not become the captive of any particular viewpoint or ideology. . . . How long [would] such freedom last, once it became clear that universities were available instruments for the promotion of a particular brand of politics or candidates? Why on earth should we expect that a society full of powerful and wealthy interest groups will be willing to watch without doing anything while the diversity and openness of universities are abandoned in favor of institutional commitment and the production of political propaganda?

Let me be specific. If the universities allow themselves to be captured by their politically most active members, and used for political purposes, one of two things will quickly happen—and probably both. One, using the law already on the books governing corporations organized for educational purposes, those who did not like this turn of events would go to court to get the universities' tax exemption removed. (And we could not survive at all, in these days of massive deficits, without tax exemption—both on our own activities and on the gifts people give us.)

Second, and perhaps simultaneously, efforts would be made to enlist universities on the side of political interests very different from the political interests that are most active and prominent on the campus today. There is nothing in the law of nature that says a politicized university must always be politicized in favor of peace, freedom and equality. In a contest for control of the universities in which no holds are barred—a contest that takes place *after* we've abandoned the whole idea of being a refuge for all points of view, however unpopular or even distasteful, and have launched themselves instead as political institutions—who would predict that the forces of enlightenment and unselfishness would prevail? Does this mean that the university should resist all contact with politics, except perhaps to offer genteel seminars in "A Theory of the Calculus of Politics" or "The Transmission of Political Values from Parent to Child"? I believe not. Of course, the university's first duty in relation to politics, as in relation to anything else, is to *learn* and *teach* about the subject. . . . There is no reason why learning and teaching about practical politics, or about acutely contemporary problems of political action, should not take place in the University, provided only that the game is played with unloaded dice. And students who are serious about having an impact upon the direction of national policy had better be serious about doing their homework in advance.

I then proceeded to give chapter and verse demonstrating how limited student participation in politics was. There was the Republican primary next door in San Mateo County the previous spring in which the leading congressional dove, Pete McCloskey, was in a tight race against a conservative. A total of some three hundred fifty Stanford students had done anything at all to further his campaign, and only about one hundred were really active workers on his behalf—less than 1 percent of the Stanford student body. Nationally, in 1968 in states where the voting age was below twenty-one, only one-third of the under twenty-one–year-olds actually voted, versus 51 percent of those ages twenty-one to twenty-four, and 72 percent of those thirty to sixty-four. Young people appeared to be making *less* effort than anyone else to influence the politics of our day.

Urging my audience to improve on this dismal record I said, "You are accustomed to challenging the institutions of our society, mostly run by your elders, to commit themselves to change. I'd like, with all due respect to the amount that young people have accomplished in American politics, from Alexander Hamilton to Julian Bond, to challenge you to make of the youth movement in American political life something more durable, more constructive and more significant than the headline-hunting antics of Weathermen and Yippies."

"Some would argue," I continued, "that there is no point in making the effort since the system is moribund and unresponsive. Not so. It is not responsive

to you, but it is responsive to the great and growing number who are demanding law and order, fewer constraints upon police, and a crackdown on youth-
ful protest the moment it departs from the strictest standards of decorum."

Needless to say, this argument did not persuade everyone. But the developments of "Cambodia Spring" did not carry over into fall, though things
were not entirely quiet. The first major shock of my first year as president
came with the football game against the University of Southern California
in October. On the eve of the game, Jing and I returned home from a dinner
party to find a message from Bob Beyers, director of the news service, informing us that the San Francisco police had been alerted by an anonymous
phone call to a bomb threat conveyed in a note to be found in a locker at the
Greyhound Bus Station in the city. The note was signed "The Bomb Squad
(Weatherman)," and began "Football is Amerika at its fascist worst—it is the
circus maximus of the Amerikan Empire," and went on to say that unless
we canceled or postponed the USC game the next day, the Stanford stadium
would be blown up.

We had to decide quickly how to respond. Any change in the game plans
would have to be given to the newspapers by around midnight, or the word
would be too late for Saturday's morning papers. In fact, deciding was not difficult; we could not yield. So we said the stadium would be searched during
the night, and patrons arriving for the game would be searched as they entered
the stadium. On Saturday, while the capacity crowd was gathering in the stadium, I broadcast an announcement to them, describing what had happened
and what we had done to guard against an explosion and then saying, "No one
is able to ignore such threats in view of the events elsewhere in the country.
On the other hand, blackmail and threats must not be allowed to paralyze a
nation or an institution. If it ever becomes established that such tactics can
succeed, we shall have magnified enormously the capacity of a malicious few
to terrorize society."[3]

This gave people the option of departing to avoid whatever danger remained, but very few, if any, did leave. Early in the game, when Stanford
scored, the cannon that was used to signal such an event was fired; my spouse
recalls jumping out of her seat in alarm, but nothing happened, and when we
scored again no shots were fired. There was no way of knowing what, if any,
connections existed between this episode and the campus movement, but in a
way that was irrelevant; all violence and threats of violence were seen as linked
and therefore contributed to the general malaise of the time.

The victory over USC put Stanford on a trajectory that led to our appearance in the Rose Bowl on January 1, 1971, our first since 1951. Since we had lost our last two regular season games, we were decided underdogs to Ohio State, an undefeated powerhouse coached by the redoubtable Woody Hayes. There were jokes about how the Stanford team, a bunch of effete intellectuals, called signals in Latin, and the easygoing Stanford approach—no segregation of the players from the rest of the world and its temptations in the days leading up to the game, as Ohio State practiced—led superficial analysts to conclude that we were not serious about winning. So the victory when it came—the score was 27–17—was all the more stunning. Lenny Siegel produced a suitable slogan: "Go Red! Smash State!" But it is unlikely that very many of his fellow-radicals were even paying attention. For the rest of us, the boost to morale was short-lived.

On January 11, 1971, Henry Cabot Lodge, U.S. ambassador to the UN, was scheduled to speak in Dinkelspiel under the sponsorship of the Hoover Institution. The speakers who were trying to introduce the program were subjected to a cacophony of heckling, chanting, and booing. After a few minutes Campbell, the director of the Hoover and moderator of the meeting, decided that Lodge would be unable to speak, so he closed the meeting. Conspicuous among those doing the heckling was said to be English professor H. Bruce Franklin, the Maoist faculty member who had, until then, always managed to fade into the background whenever protesters exposed themselves to the risk of arrest. The *Daily* story of the incident did not mention him. But reports we received in the President's Office this time led me to conclude that Franklin had overstepped the line and should be disciplined. According to our tenure policy a faculty member could be disciplined for "substantial and manifest incompetence, substantial and manifest neglect of duty, or personal conduct substantially impairing the individual's performance of his appropriate functions within the university community."[4] Clearly Franklin's behavior fit the third of these three categories.

According to our tenure policy at the time, a faculty member charged with misbehavior was to be informed privately of the fact and given the chance to accept discipline privately. If he wished to appeal the decision of the president, he had the right to a hearing before the Advisory Board, an elected faculty group whose normal duties involved passing on all appointments and promotions to tenure. It seemed clear to me that in informing Franklin of the charges against him I would have to state the penalty I proposed to inflict, since otherwise he would have no basis for deciding whether to accept the discipline quietly or go public with an appeal.[5] So I said that he would be suspended without pay for one academic quarter.

I had no doubt that he would choose to appeal, and indeed his responses throughout the "Franklin case" were defiant and contemptuous of the entire process, not surprisingly. After all, if one believed in the necessity of a revolution in U.S. society, then a matter such as university status would seem trivial and not deserving of anything better.

The two weeks that followed the Lodge incident constituted the last period of fairly sustained and sporadically violent antiwar protest at Stanford. This was occasioned by the rumors and then the fact of the South Vietnamese invasion of Laos, backed by U.S. air power. In some ways this paralleled the campus reaction to the Cambodian invasion the previous spring, but protest in 1971 never managed to spread sufficiently through the campus population to become a successful strike that would bring normal activity to a halt. This fact, that protest was limited to a smaller section of the campus body politic, no doubt accounts for the often chaotic and nihilistic nature of events—several cases of arson included. On February 6 alone there was arson aimed at the Free Campus (that is, conservative) Movement, Molotov cocktails tossed into the ROTC office, three false fire alarms from widely scattered locations, and moments later a fire in a trash barrel behind Ventura Hall and a false alarm at the Boathouse.

The Advisory Board's opinion provides a succinct narrative of the next couple of days:

> On Sunday, February 7, the invasion of Laos by South Vietnamese troops with U.S. air support was officially announced. At 8:00 p.m. in Dinkelspiel Auditorium a crowd of some 800 people attended a performance by the San Francisco Mime Troupe sponsored by the Stanford Community Against War and Fascism. Before the Mime Troupe began to perform, it was announced that Laos had been invaded. A telegram sent from Ann Arbor, Michigan, by Madame Binh, head of the North Vietnam delegation to the Paris peace talks, was read which called for "mobilizing peace forces in your country." The Coalition Against the War in Indochina distributed a flyer entitled "It's Official!! Laos has been invaded," which spelled out Madame Binh's message in detail and called for a rally in White Plaza on Monday, February 8. Leaflets were distributed by an anti-war group called The Inquisition, demanding that the University "release all information on the uses of the Computation Center" and that war research at the Center "immediately be halted." In this leaflet a Stanford Research Insti-

tute computer program known as "Gamut-H" was described. The program was said to simulate the logistic of the deployment of helicopters and ships and the leaflet asserted that "the work is directly applicable in Indochina."

After the performance, at about 10:30 p.m., over 200 persons protesting the Laos invasion broke about 100 windows in several buildings, including the Graduate School of Business, Undergraduate Library, Post Office, Engineering Corner, Terman Engineering, Placement Center, Cubberley Education, Lou Henry Hoover Building, and the Inner Quad. In addition to campus police on duty, 35 sheriff's deputies were brought on to the campus briefly after the first reports of property destruction, but the trashing quickly subsided and the deputies were not deployed. Windows in two Stanford University police cars were broken when spotlights from one of the cars were focused on 15–30 demonstrators hurling rocks into the Lou Henry Hoover building. Fights broke out between demonstrators and members of the Free Campus Movement who were attempting to halt the trashing. The University Computation Center was evacuated at 9:30 p.m. after a telephone bomb threat was received, but after a search people re-entered the facility. (This was not the first threat to the Center. In the spring of 1970, a part of the computer complex in Polya Hall was the target of arson, but quick action averted serious damage.)

On Monday, February 8, the noon rally was attended by about 800 in White Memorial Plaza. The leaflet from The Inquisition on the SRI war-related computer program together with a flyer entitled "Do It!" was distributed. "Do It!" encouraged the formation of tight affinity groups to "do whatever actions you feel ready to do" and stated "last night's action was the first in a series in response to the invasion of Laos." It anticipated trouble with police and with "right wing fascists," and gave suggestions for handling such trouble.

An "Open Letter to the Stanford Community" from The Inquisition also became available at about this time. It stated that the Computation Center was being used by Stanford Research Institute for "war research." Six demands were made in the letter, including making public the identity of all non-Stanford users of Stanford facilities and phasing out of all Stanford research funded by the Department of Defense; attached to this letter was a reply made by Provost Miller to some of these demands.

About 100 antiwar demonstrators left the rally and then went to the near-empty Faculty Club dining room searching for members of the Stanford University Board of Trustees. The group then left for the Graduate School of Business where at 1:25 p.m. about 150 persons jammed into the ground level lobby, blocking entrance to a room in which a trustee committee was meeting and holding the committee virtually under siege for 45 minutes. At 1:45 p.m. C.D. Marron of the Santa Clara County Sheriff's Department declared it was an unlawful assembly, with the group chanting back: "Power to the People." The crowd dispersed when a squad of sheriff's deputies appeared. One plain clothesman suffered a head laceration when hit by a thrown rock. At 2:30 p.m. about 24 police dispersed some 300 demonstrators who had reassembled outside the ground floor of the Graduate School of Business.

At about 2:45 p.m. part of the group of demonstrators headed for the Old Union. About 150 persons arrived at the courtyard, and 50 of them proceeded into the Union lobby. A meeting was then called in the lobby, and the Old Union was selected as a "strike center." At 5:30 p.m. about 20 Santa Clara Sheriff's deputies moved into the rear (West) of the Union, sweeping about 40 remaining occupants into the courtyard. Simultaneously some members of the San Jose Tactical Squad moved to the front (East) of the Old Union. At about 5:45 the San Jose units left the scene. Subsequently, however, numerous squads of Santa Clara County and San Jose police patrolled the campus on foot as well as by car.

On Tuesday, February 9, there was an afternoon meeting in the Physics Tank, following the Stanford Judicial Council hearing, in which a "Cambodia-type strike" protesting the invasion of Laos was planned. In the evening, beginning at 8:00 p.m., a three-hour session was held in Dinkelspiel Auditorium, attended at the peak by approximately 800 people.[6]

At this meeting the focus was on the war and on possible means of impeding Stanford's contributions to the war effort. Thus would the protesters ally themselves with the Pathet Lao and the National Liberation Front in Vietnam. Action at Stanford would provide examples for other campuses. There was repeated emphasis on the Computation Center as a target, both because of its alleged war complicity and its vulnerability. Various means of putting the center out of service were mentioned as possibilities, including destroying it. While cautionary notes were struck, people applauded any reference to coercive or violent activity. There were frequent references to a "mobile strike." Janet Weiss, law student and a prominent radical leader, described what this would involve:

> I've heard that at some places they've used a tactic of shutting down one building with a large group of people, and then going and shutting something else

down so that nothing is shut down continually but things are shut down, you know a lot of things are, are shut down at different times, and maybe that's the kind of strike that would work here, maybe that's the kind of thing that would keep people doing something, keep them involved in it, so that you don't feel like you're just sitting there all day, bored and cold.[7]

Toward the end of the meeting it was clear that too few people remained to mount an effective action, so a noon rally at White Plaza was announced for the following day.

That rally, attended at its peak by about seven hundred people, was both a resumption and a replay of the previous evening's meeting. Two student body leaders, Robert Grant and Larry Diamond, urged actions in the community beyond the campus, but most wanted to focus on the campus and shutting down key facilities. Opinion was divided between attacking the Hoover Institution and attacking the Computation Center. The latter tended to be favored, and in the end it was declared that a show of hands, mainly in the front of the crowd, had decided on the Computation Center. There were a number of speakers, but Bruce Franklin spoke last. Much of his speech was analytical and general, contrasting the sacrifices involved in an industrial strike with the lack of anything comparable when the term is used to describe efforts to shut down university facilities. "We're just ripping off the term strike when we talk about striking at Stanford. This isn't a strike. We're not risking anything. It's a voluntary boycott—a shutdown of some of the activities of the University as a demonstration of something."

He also cited with relish polls showing that, although a majority of Americans wanted to get out of Vietnam, the support for doing so was highest among grade school graduates, next highest among high school graduates, and lowest among the college educated. In closing he argued that at least Stanford people should be willing "to begin to shut down the most obvious machinery of war, such as, and I think it is a good target, that Computation Center."

A crowd of one to two hundred proceeded from White Plaza to the Computation Center, which was closed by telephone order from Provost Miller minutes before they arrived to find the building locked and two campus policemen guarding the front door. Access was easily gained by scaling the gate and forcing open the rear entry. For nearly two hours, demonstrators moved in and out of the building and milled about inside it, taking various actions to shut down the computer, but doing only about $800 worth of damage. There had been no decisions taken in advance about what to do to "shut down" the facility, and we who were gathered in Building Ten to monitor events and decide whether to invoke police power to clear out the demonstrators were left to ponder the likelihood of major destruction, there having been instances of such at other institutions. I later told the *Daily* that the decision to call in the police at this point was "just about the most agonizing decision I've ever had to make," given "the expressed willingness of at least some of the people to undertake destruction of the computer."[8]

Professor Franklin had met his class at 1:15 but found that almost all the 150 enrolled students were at the Computation Center. He suggested that the class be held at the center, but when he got there his students were mostly inside the building and the class was not held. Franklin himself remained outside the building, talking to various people, until the police arrived.

Bruce Wiggins, Stanford director of public safety, arrived soon after the occupation of the building began, and around 2 o'clock he telephoned to inform the Santa Clara County Sheriff's office of the occupation. Representatives of that office arrived soon after, and at 3:00 p.m. it was decided that Wiggins should return to the center and declare the occupation a violation of Stanford regulations. He declared that accordingly the occupiers should vacate the building immediately. Since this produced no result, police were summoned to clear the building, which they did, the demonstrators departing as the police arrived. There were no arrests. The police lined up outside the building, and the crowd was declared an illegal assembly and ordered to disperse.

It was at this point that Professor Franklin began shouting arguments against the illegality of the gathering and urging faculty members who were present as witnesses to remain to protect against a violent police charge. The extent to which his arguments were directed at police or at the demonstrators, and the extent to which he urged the latter not to obey the police order to disperse were disputed in the hearings the following fall, but the majority of the Advisory Board concluded that indeed he had addressed the demonstrators, trying to persuade them not to disperse. When several police moved to arrest Franklin he escaped, and a "police charge" then took place, dispersing the demonstrators and ending the affair.

A rally was held at the Old Union courtyard that evening to decide what to do next. A number of speakers addressed a crowd of about three hundred fifty. Some argued for relatively limited action and a single demand, to leave Southeast Asia, but most urged more militant responses to the presence of police on campus. Professor Franklin spoke twice. In his first speech he concentrated on drawing connections between abusive police behavior in the United States and the war in Southeast Asia, supporting the Black Panther argument that all were part of a worldwide struggle against imperialism. His second speech came at the end of the rally. According to his own affidavit in the Advisory Board hearings, he "said that we must learn from the peoples of Southeast Asia that when confronted with an occupation army, we must respond with the methods of people's war."

Bob Beyers, of the Stanford News Service, described what happened: "Professor Franklin suggested that people go back to their dormitories, meet in small groups, decide to do whatever they wanted to do as late at night as possible so as to bring more police onto the campus to help out their brethren in other communities. At this point, in Beyers' view, the nature of the meeting changed dramatically, leading him to expect that illegal or disruptive incidents would follow."[9]

As they did; immediately after the speech, Free Campus Movement members were beaten up, and fights and trashing took place at various points near the Old Union. Later that evening came the only instance during our time of troubles when gunfire played a part; someone (we never knew who) wounded the teenage son of history professor Philip Dawson, not seriously but ominously.

Reviewing the events of February 9–10 and Franklin's role in them, we decided to enter three more charges against him, to accompany the Lodge incident charge and to change the proposed punishment from suspension to permanent dismissal from the Stanford faculty. Needless to say, this became the focus for much attention on campus for the rest of the 1970–71 academic year. Arranging for the hearing before the Advisory Board proved cumbersome and time-consuming; each time one side was ready to proceed the other found reasons to delay. As a result, the actual hearings did not start until fall quarter.

Just a day after the uproar of February 10, the *Daily* was headlining "Apathy Hits Movement," and protest returned to peaceful means; on February 16 one thousand people marched from the campus into Palo Alto protesting the war. My wife Jing was among the marchers. As it happened, an alumni gathering was held in San Francisco the following day, and Jing remembers being peppered with hostile questions there concerning her participation in the protest. Later in the spring there were sporadic outbursts of violence, not all connected with the war, but no general movement aimed at shutting down the university such as we had come to expect in the spring quarter. On April 26 there was a bomb blast in the attic of the President's Office at 3:50 a.m.; I recall sitting upright in bed at the sound, a good half-mile away in the Hoover House. Six Molotov cocktails were found in an attic across the Quad from the explosion; earlier that night a sniper fired five shots at the PG&E substation on Panama Street, and the following day a set fire did considerable damage in a dormitory lounge at Junipero House. I was quoted at the time, saying, "Terrorism tends to be a tactic taken by a protest movement that does not have a mass following."

But the only other episode of note was unconnected to the war. An African American custodian in the Medical Center was dismissed, and protests erupted throughout the Bay Area, demanding his reemployment. I was on the East Coast when a small group occupied the administrative offices of the Stanford Hospital and barricaded themselves in. As it happened, that portion of the Medical Center was in Palo Alto, not the unincorporated area of Santa Clara County; therefore it was the Palo Alto police who were called in by the provost, acting in my absence, to break up the sit-in. We had not had dealings with the Palo Alto police comparable to our extended discussions with the Santa Clara County sheriff's people, so they were less prepared for the peculiarities of policing on campus. Although they had some sheriff's deputies with them, by a mutual help arrangement, it was Palo Alto that was in charge. Bob Rosenzweig, John Schwartz, the university prosecutor, and Tom Gonda from the Medical School met with representatives of the police chief and thought they had his agreement, should he have to move to end the occupation, that the police would force the sitters-in out the doors leading into the Medical School, rather than those leading into the hospital. When the police moved, however, they did the opposite. In any case, a barricaded sit-in is generally the harbinger of violence, and so it was on this occasion. When the protesters burst out of the offices they had been occupying and attempted to escape arrest, a general fight took place that resulted in some thirty-five injuries and twenty-three arrests. Many of those hurt or arrested had no connection with the university or its Medical Center. Damage to the offices amounted to some $100,000. All in all it was one of the messiest episodes of our time of unrest and a reminder that minority issues remained volatile. Just to add insult to injury the Palo Alto police conducted a raid on the offices of the *Daily* a couple of days after the sit-in, searching the files for evidence concerning that event. Felicity Barringer, then editor and later a *New York Times* staff member, went to court seeking an injunction against such raids, and the case finally reached the Supreme Court before being decided in favor of the police. I made it clear that I had not been consulted before the raid and would have argued against it had I been.

All through the spring there were meetings, arguments, and demonstrations over the former employee, Sam Bridges. The case was full of ambiguities, the university saying that he was fired for shortcomings in job performance, the protesters claiming he was let go because he was outspoken in criticisms of the hospital administration. In May the National Labor Relations Board found that he had been dismissed for "reasons related to work performance," and by the quarter's end protests were finally fizzling out.[10]

All in all, my wife and I were glad to see the end of the academic year, and we escaped that summer to academic meetings in Nara, Japan, and visits to all the Stanford overseas campuses.

On May 27 the *Daily* published articles summarizing my first year as president. On the whole the judgment was surprisingly positive: "Lyman's decisive style, his forthright willingness to deal with problems, and his articulate leadership have become central in the maintenance of the university's integrity."

There were critics. "Especially in the black and radical segments of the student body Lyman, while respected as an adversary, is regarded with deep suspicion." Faculty were more supportive, except for a few who found me inadequate as a leader in opposing the war; I was also criticized for "putting people on the defensive." Staff were happy: "Compared with the uncertainties of the recent past, the reliability and self-assurance of Lyman make working conditions more secure."

The writer quoted Willard Wyman, former special assistant to the president, as a summary: "Stanford has come dangerously close to the rocks recently, and Lyman is now in the process of cautiously getting the ship out to sea before he begins steering it on his own course."

11 THE FRANKLIN CASE AND AFTER

ON SEPTEMBER 28, 1971, the *Daily* published a special section on the Advisory Board hearings set to start the next day in Physics 101, which as configured for the hearings seated 122. There was also closed-circuit television in two other physics classrooms, seating a total of 350. At first the hearings were crowded, though the audience soon dwindled. KZSU also broadcast them, and when they tried to stop they were deluged with angry phone calls calling on them to resume coverage, which they did. Franklin saw the hearings as an opportunity to educate the community, as well as attack administration witnesses. At the quiet opening session he spoke for two and a half hours, giving a "lengthy Marxist analysis of the University and the State."

The university brought four charges against Franklin. The first concerned his alleged leadership role in the disruption of Henry Cabot Lodge's visit in January 1971. The other three all concerned the events of February. The first involved the White Plaza rally at noon on February 10.

During the course of the rally two principal courses of action were discussed, one being to work in the nonuniversity community to bring about changes in government policy, the other being to disrupt university functions and business. Professor Franklin intentionally urged and incited students and other persons present at the rally to follow the latter course of action and specifically to shut down the university Computation Center.

The second stated that "students and other persons were arrested for failure to disperse after orders had been given to clear the area around the Computation Center. Professor Franklin significantly interfered with orderly dispersal by intentionally urging and inciting students and other persons present at the Computation Center to disregard or disobey such orders to disperse."

The third involved Franklin's speeches during the Old Union Courtyard rally the evening of the same day: "Professor Franklin intentionally urged and incited students and other persons present to engage in conduct calculated to disrupt activities of the University and of members of the University community and which threatened injury to individuals and property. Shortly thereafter students and other persons were assaulted by persons present at the rally, and later that evening other acts of violence occurred."

Perhaps ironically, since the charge relating to the Lodge incident was what got the prosecution of Bruce Franklin under way in the first place, this was the one charge rejected by the Advisory Board in its findings. The administration's witnesses proved unreliable, misidentifying Franklin and disagreeing about exactly what his role had been. Perhaps I should have known that this charge would be difficult to sustain; a friend of ours, Harlan Cleveland, who was then president of the University of Hawaii, dropped by my office at the time to report that he had been present in Dinkelspiel, and it was his opinion that the director of the Hoover Institution, Glenn Campbell, had given up too soon and declared the meeting disrupted when with a bit of persistence Lodge could have spoken. The Advisory Board did not find that there was clear evidence that anything would have been different had Professor Franklin not been involved; others would have heckled and shouted. While the board did say, "The Board cannot accept the view that the interruption of University functions—let alone their disruption—is part of the appropriate function of a faculty member at Stanford," it concluded that the university had failed to prove that Franklin's involvement warranted punishment.

The administration's ability to prove its case regarding the Old Union Courtyard speeches was greatly weakened by a ruling from the chair during the first day of the hearings. We attempted to add witnesses who could testify as to Professor Franklin's own involvement in the assaults and fighting that followed the rally, but Professor Donald Kennedy supported Franklin's objection that to do so would constitute an additional charge against him, and the deadline for filing charges had expired. Kennedy's colleagues supported him, though I was told later that they did so only because they were hesitant to question his performance in the chair so early in the proceedings. In all the arguments as to the meaning of "people's war" when applied to campus activities, it was unfortunate that we could not demonstrate in the most direct way what Franklin himself thought it meant.

By October 12 the administration had completed the presentation of its case, and Franklin began his defense with another two-and-one-half hour speech, winding up with a motion to dismiss the charges. This the board rejected, though again the chair, Professor Kennedy, said, "Some members of the Board are by no means convinced by the evidence presented that there was a causal relationship between Professor Franklin's speeches and events that followed either of the February 10 rallies," thus anticipating the verdict reached by the two dissenters from the board's final conclusions, Professors Kennedy and Robert McAfee Brown. Since his own ruling had so hampered our ability to demonstrate that "causal connection," at least as regards the evening speeches, this seemed ironic to me.

The *Daily* was hardly an unbiased witness to the hearings, but I would not dispute its description of their early stages: "Franklin has certainly won any struggle for domination of the hearing sessions. His constant objections and insistent questioning have attracted most of the attention in the mock courtroom. And observers of the hearing, including most reporters, agree that the suspended teacher has frustrated and challenged many administration witnesses."

By October 27, however, Kennedy was expressing frustration at "repetitious and barely relevant testimony" for the defense, and looking for ways to move the proceedings forward after twenty-two sessions. The hearings finally ended on November 5, but supplementary briefs were not filed until December 17, so a decision could not be announced until after New Year's.

Meanwhile Stanford had gone to its second successive Rose Bowl in Pasadena, this time upsetting the heavily favored University of Michigan team. While we were watching the game from the stands someone managed to spill a box containing a half-dozen large cups of Coca Cola on me. We did not know it at the time, but I was coming down with pneumonia, diagnosed when we returned to the campus. While I was sick in bed at the Hoover House, the football coach, John Ralston, came to tell me he was leaving to coach the Denver Broncos. And on January 6 the *Daily* announced the Advisory Board's decision supporting Franklin's dismissal, which the paper called "Outrageous," in part because students had no role in the process, yet the decision to support Franklin's dismissal "deprives students of a stimulating, intellectual alternative." The *Daily* had to admit, however, that the decision was met with a good deal of apathy among students; Ralston's departure to the Broncos "got about the same amount of attention—maybe more." About sixty marched to the Hoover House, yelling "Fire Lyman, Not Franklin." My mother, visiting us over the holidays, was somewhat shocked to find her son thus abused and perhaps endangered by a hostile crowd.

In the end, the Advisory Board unanimously found the charge that Franklin had incited the disruption and Computation Center shutdown on February 10: "Professor Franklin could reasonably expect that an occupation of the Computation Center would involve great risks to the computer and to the members of the Stanford community who rely upon it, including the staff of the Computation Center. It should be emphasized that the research and education of many people throughout the University were in jeopardy."

Professors Brown and Kennedy, "although in accord with much of the descriptive account of the majority report," nevertheless dissented on several grounds to both of the other charges concerning February 10. They found persuasive Franklin's claim that he was urging faculty observers not to leave the scene outside the Computation Center in case the order to disperse were followed by a police charge on the demonstrators, and that he was arguing against the dispersal order as illegal, something a citizen is entitled to do. As to the evening speeches, much turned on how one interprets the phrase "people's war." The dissenters thought that more emphasis should be placed on the effort to recruit hitherto uninvolved students in the protest by going back to the dormitories and educating the residents.

When it came to sanctions, the board gave careful consideration to possible mitigating factors and to the special nature of dismissal of a tenured faculty member. It placed strong emphasis on Franklin's view of the world and of the role played by the United States in it. The majority understood that his behavior was consistent with his view of the world, but it also saw how fundamental this view was and therefore how unlikely it was to change. Seeing "rehabilitation" as one possible outcome of punishment, the majority found it unlikely that Franklin could be "rehabilitated." Use of this word gave the radicals a handle; the rest of the year they called themselves the Rehab Movement.

The majority were careful to point out that Franklin's political views were irrelevant; no one should be penalized at all, let alone dismissed, merely for holding political views at variance with the majority of the community. They also saw their decision regarding penalties as especially significant in view of the paucity of case law on such questions at issue here. Tenure "is not merely a protection of the individual against unwarranted attacks from the institution, but also a device to guarantee the maximum protection for the institution from outside political forces. Tenure thus protects freedom for the full range of scholarly inquiry, and both the institution and the individual have a large stake in its continued good health."[1]

Yet the rights of the institution must still be weighed heavily. The majority concluded that "a lesser penalty [than dismissal] would fail to recognize the fundamental nature and severity of Professor Franklin's attacks on the University of which he is a member."[2]

Professors Brown and Kennedy, dissenting, stressed that suspension without pay was itself a severe penalty, and that Professor Franklin might well be better able to judge just how far he could go without infringing on the institution's rights and those of its other members in future, with this conviction and penalty in his experience. Stressing the importance of tenure in a way not very different from the majority's version, Brown and Kennedy pointed to the possibility that, given Stanford's dismissal of Franklin, "less well-buffered institutions may become more vulnerable to outside pressures to get rid of controversial faculty members. . . . We see substantial costs in Professor Franklin's loss to the institution; they are measured externally, in the form of corrosive effects on academic freedom, and internally in terms of lost challenge and the subtle inhibition of dissent."[3] Accordingly, Professor Kennedy recommended suspension without pay for two quarters, and Professor Brown recommended for one.

In an addendum to the minority opinion, Brown argued, "Speech that goes 'up to the line' of what is permissible is extraordinarily important speech both to the university and to society, since it is through such speech that new insights are often born. If there is the slightest possibility that an individual, called to account for speech that transgresses permissible boundaries, will more clearly respect such boundaries in the future, he deserves to be given that chance."

It is difficult to see how the kind of speech we had heard from Franklin carried with it any "new insights" beneficial to society, and there was scant comfort in the notion that there might be "the slightest possibility" that he would not transgress in future. But Brown concluded, "Stanford University will be less a true university without him and more of a true university with him. I fear that we may do irreparable harm to ourselves and to the cause of higher education unless, by imposing a penalty short of dismissal, we seek to keep him as a very uncomfortable but very important part of what this University, or any university, is meant to be."[4]

Later that month the board of trustees, unsurprisingly, voted twenty to two to dismiss Franklin, the two dissidents being Denis Hayes, the former ASSU president, and Ira Hall, the only black trustee at the time. About one hundred twenty protesters, including Franklin and his wife, demonstrated in the San Francisco street outside the building where the trustees were meeting.

In a full-page interview with the *Daily* on January 24 I discussed the concern widely expressed that the Franklin dismissal might lead other institutions to dismiss troublesome faculty members without adequate procedures:

> I cannot help questioning the benefit of the sort of self-fulfilling prophecy that we are getting from a few faculty and some leaders of the "rehab" movement . . . where they say this will unleash the storm elsewhere. Their own reading of the decision is more likely to encourage people to that than a direct reading of the decision. . . . Simply to condemn the decision sweepingly, as Daniel Ellsberg did in Memorial Church, is extremely unlikely to produce any good result in West Podunk State, if that's what you're really worried about.

I also responded to those who argued that we ought to rely on the criminal code, rather than developing policies and procedures of our own: "There are too many things that ought to be the basis for prosecution on campus but are not covered by the criminal code, such as disruption of classes or research."

The Stanford chapter of the American Association of University Professors entered the fray late, writing to the board of trustees to ask them to delay a decision until they had consulted with "leading members and representatives of the academic community throughout the nation," a suggestion that was both impractical and somewhat insulting to our board. Why should they involve others, less close to the issues at Stanford, in their decision making?

The American Civil Liberties Union (ACLU) of Northern California, which was to undertake an appeal to the civil courts on Franklin's behalf, submitted an amicus curiae brief. Perhaps ironically, the brief was more sympathetic to the charge regarding Lodge's appearance than to the other three charges, just the reverse of what the Advisory Board concluded. It quotes, "If the Board concludes that Professor Franklin intentionally engaged in concerted activity designed to silence Ambassador Lodge—that is to prevent him from speaking at all—then it is the Civil Liberties Union's position that some discipline would be appropriate."

Concerning the speeches on February 10, however, the authors of the ACLU brief admitted they had "not studied the testimony relevant to the context in which the speeches were made. The Union believes, however, that viewing the speeches in isolation they themselves are so clearly within the protection of the First Amendment that it would be highly improper to discipline anyone for delivering them." The brief was signed by the director of the ACLU/NC and by Professors Alan Dershowitz of the Harvard Law School, who was then a fellow at the Center for Advanced Study at Stanford, and Paul Brest and John Kaplan of the Stanford Law School. It is clear from the decision of the Advisory Board, however, that the speeches were only actionable because of the context; considering them "in isolation" was not helpful.

The Northern California American Civil Liberties Union helped Franklin to take the university to court in the years following his dismissal. In 1978, a trial court determined that Stanford's standard for dismissal of a faculty member was not, as the plaintiff had claimed, unconstitutionally vague, but that the third charge, involving the speech at the Old Union in the evening following the computer-center occupation, had not been sustained. The court therefore remanded the case to the Advisory Board to determine whether, given only two sustained charges, dismissal would still have been the appropriate penalty. In 1980 the Advisory Board determined that it would, and the trustees backed that decision. The case was finally put to rest when the appeals court decided unanimously in 1985 in favor of the university.

A headline in the *Daily* on May 11, 1972, read, "Protesters Wander Campus." This pretty well describes that spring. There were various rumbles, some arrests, and Bruce Franklin addressed a crowd of three hundred on the anniversary of the Kent State deaths, but nothing remotely resembling the uproar of the preceding several springs occurred. In mid-May, I and some fifty faculty members flew to Washington to try to tell Congress and President Nixon that they should not underestimate the protests against his escalation of the war with the mining of North Vietnamese harbors. I found myself explaining to the Faculty Senate that my Washington visit had been to inform government leaders of campus attitudes rather than to protest the war as president of Stanford—a bit of tightrope walking that was probably unconvincing to most.

James Reston of the *New York Times* was the commencement speaker that year. Police had discovered a cache of small arms in the foothills behind the campus, and Reston and I were urged not to do the traditional march from the top of Frost Amphitheater to the stage, through the crowd of thirteen thousand, but to allow ourselves to be led in from behind the stage. I recall Reston's shock at this; he knew, of course, about the campus protests across the country in those years, but he had not realized the dangers we were facing.

The final event of the season came about on June 19: a set fire destroyed one wing of Encina Hall, the biggest administration building on campus. No one claimed responsibility, and like almost all the other arson cases this one was never solved. But no one could miss the familiar faces of just about every radical ever seen on campus, in the huge crowd that gathered to watch the firemen battle the blaze. The damage remained unrepaired for years, standing as a kind of mute testimonial to the campus unrest long after the emotions involved had faded. As I stood across the street from the fire that night, I was reminded of the episode when Richard Brinsley Sheridan, eighteenth-century dramatist, politician, and owner of the Drury Lane Theater in London, was sitting at a table in the café across the street from the conflagration that was destroying his theater. An observer asked him what he was doing there. "Cannot a gentleman enjoy a glass of wine by his own fire?" he replied.

The Danforth Foundation had run a program of grants to hard-pressed university presidents who had survived at least five years of the troubles to take a term's leave of absence, provided only that they did nothing job-related during the leave. The university was to match their grant. I was awarded one of these, the foundation kindly counting the three years I had served as provost as if they had been presidential.

Accordingly my spouse and I spent the fall quarter in London, where I found that I could once again live a normal life of reading and going to museums without the excitements of the preceding five years. As I told the *Daily* after my return, "I vastly enjoyed the opportunity to be an intellectual dilettante." Toward the end of the term, as we were getting ready to return to Stanford, we decided we should go out to the overseas campus at Cliveden, just west of London, for dinner with the students. It was a depressing evening; the students, who had of course left Stanford months earlier, retained the mood of hostility toward authority, and particularly presidential authority, that had then prevailed on campus. As we drove back into London Jing and I thought unhappily about having to go back to such conditions as those that led her to cut my hair in the Hoover House so that I would not have to be badgered by critics as I sat, a captive audience, in the barber's chair at Tresidder Memorial Union (TMU). Contributing to our somber mood was the news that Herb

Packer, my colleague and valued friend, discouraged by his inability to recover from the loss of capacity he had suffered from a stroke a couple of years earlier, had committed suicide in a San Francisco hotel room.

Much to our surprise, when we got back to campus and 1973 began, we found that civility had broken out all over. The mood was completely changed. Stanford had, somewhat belatedly, returned to the kind of normalcy enjoyed by most other campuses after the shock of Kent State and the bombing of the Mathematics Building at the University of Wisconsin two years earlier.

12 TRYING TO MAKE SENSE OF
THE CAMPUS UNREST

DESPITE SCORES OF ATTEMPTS to interpret the troubles of the late 1960s, there is no consensus as to what caused them. No interpretation that is limited to a single country can suffice, since there were outbursts around the world. Only the United States was involved in Vietnam, yet Japanese and British and French and German students rioted and rebelled. Our civil rights upheavals no doubt affected others; racial conflict crops up just about everywhere at one time or other.

By the same token, no explanation that is based on timeless tensions, such as generational differences, can explain why the struggles in the late 1960s were so traumatic. Analyses of the student activists at the time showed them to be "comparatively intelligent, stable and unprejudiced" rather than alienated.[1]

The crosscurrents of the 1960s complicate things. What was the relationship between the counterculture of hedonism and liberation from the trammels of earlier cultures, often laced with psychedelic drugs, and the political rebellions associated with SDS or the Black Panthers? Rampant sexism among radicals fed the beginnings of women's liberation. And while the mid-1960s saw the emergence of the Free Speech Movement at Berkeley, the period also saw the start of that resurgence of right-wing politics embodied in Barry Goldwater's nomination in 1964. At campuses such as Stanford, SDS overshadowed the Young Americans for Freedom, but the latter were the more telling harbingers of the future.

In many ways, Stanford's experience was the same as that of other campuses. The speed with which things changed was remarkable. As David Harris wrote later, "The entire course of the Sixties would be littered with strategies that had been given six months to succeed and then abandoned for something a notch more obstreperous."[2] His own student body presidency burned itself out in a matter of weeks. The occupation of the electronics labs in the spring of 1969 seemed to establish the nonviolent, inclusive, and communitarian ethos of the New Left, only to give way to violence and trashing at Encina a couple of weeks later.

The same self-destructiveness that was noted elsewhere was visible at Stanford on the far Left. As has been said of the Weathermen, there was "a moral urgency that precluded consideration of political effectiveness and a desire to display one's personal commitment, especially if it involved risk or injury."[3] There was the distrust of hierarchy that made it so difficult for leaders to be effective; "participatory democracy" was supposed to replace leadership with consensus, even if it meant that deciding what to do next required endless— and endlessly tedious—meetings.

But Stanford had a unique history as well. No other university had climbed such a steep curve in quality and reputation as began at Stanford under Sterling and Terman. This contributed powerfully to our problems with alumni. Graduates of the earlier decades found it hard to recognize their beloved alma mater in the academic powerhouse that was emerging on Leland Stanford's Farm. Many of them realized that they would never have been admitted to this new Stanford. But this did nothing to appease their wrath when their own children were not accepted for admission. It was therefore not just boarded-up windows and raucous sit-ins that alienated these alumni; the rapid ascent of the institution to world prominence shook them too. What is remarkable is the fact that all the upheavals of the late 1960s and early 1970s did not halt that ascent; the prestige of the university suffered very little and has since risen to unprecedented heights.

History, contrary to popular belief, does not repeat itself, though some turns of the unending spiral do resemble others. In May 1977, there was a sudden outburst of protest over issues of South African divestiture; the Old Union was once again occupied, and in one night 294 people, mostly students, were arrested. I visited the office of Jim Siena, legal adviser to the president, the next day, and we speculated as to whether we were about to descend into the maelstrom again. But the whole thing blew over in a trice—there simply was not the context for a repeat performance. I think many of those arrested woke up rubbing their eyes and reminding themselves that they did, after all, want to go to law school.

That said, universities have been spawning grounds for riot and strife, and sometimes revolution, for centuries and in many countries. Young people have energy to burn. Many tend to act first and think later. The urge to tell your elders that the whole system is a fraud and in one way or another to act accordingly is never entirely dormant. The campus, with its concern for free debate and its cherished self-image as the place in all of society most tolerant of deviance and controversy, is a natural home for protest.

For more than a century now faculty members have been trying with ever-increasing success to get out of the role of disciplinarian that the early American College assigned them. They are also slow to take alarm at student excess. Today's administrators are unlikely to be any more able to make the center hold than they were in the late 1960s.

Some barriers were broken in those years that have never been restored. Civility returned, for the most part, but formality did not, for better or for worse—mostly I would agree that it's for the better, but there is more to be said for adhering to some prescribed forms of behavior than our culture is generally willing to admit.

Although by 1970 there was widespread agreement that violence, even in pursuit of what the perpetrators considered noble goals, was not to be tolerated, if we could figure out ways not to tolerate it, there was far less readiness to condemn coercive tactics, such as preventing the university from functioning by blocking entrance to its facilities. However irrational political processes may be, they are not made any more rational by that sort of behavior. As the historian, Crane Brinton, observed long ago, people cannot live indefinitely at the height of revolutionary circumstance.

Rationality itself was widely scorned in the 1960s and suffered setbacks. It has never entirely regained its place in its supposed Temple, the University. This is not the time or place to explore the extent to which the keepers of the flame in academe have decided that rationalism is an eighteenth-century hang-up, to be avoided even if to do so may weaken the limb on which your tenured professorship perches. But one need not be an admirer of the late Allan Bloom's polemic to find in this some cause for concern.

Finally, what were the results of all that turmoil at Stanford? As always, cause and effect are hard to trace in history, which is why history is not a science. Most of what might be considered "effects" of the campus unrest are things that would have happened anyway, but more slowly, in some instances much more slowly, without this stimulus. Governance at Stanford was not revolutionized, but it was substantially altered. Among the new elements were an expansion of the board of trustees by one-third, to make room for eight trustees directly elected by the alumni, and the addition of faculty and student representation to most board committees; an elected legislature for the faculty for the first time (the Senate of the Academic Council); a revised and much more formal system, with heavy student involvement, for both legislating and enforcing rules of student conduct; the elimination of ROTC and classified research; a sweeping reformulation of academic requirements for the baccalaureate degree growing out of the Study of Education at Stanford; changes in the dormitory and other arrangements for student living that would have been regarded as totally inadmissible just a few years earlier; the opening of Stanford Memorial Church to all faiths; and a divestiture by the university of SRI. In addition to these structural changes, the demographics of the campus population began to evolve from the overwhelming WASP dominance of the past toward the multicultural panorama of the future. The quota limiting the number of women undergraduates that dated back to Mrs. Stanford's day disappeared; before long more than half of incoming students were women.

Campus radicals would hardly have been impressed; even at the time they opposed some of these changes. The new judicial arrangements were no sooner proclaimed than they were denounced on White Plaza. The new Senate was attacked by David Harris's successor, Peter Lyman (no relation to me; he was later head librarian at UC Berkeley) as a missed opportunity to move in the direction of community government, since it made no provision for student members.

In fact, quite ironically, considering the dreams of a university freed from bureaucracy and red tape, the Stanford that emerged from the time of troubles was characterized by more formal structures for decision making, with more explicit recognition of particular interest groups than existed previously, and a greatly increased involvement of lawyers. Operations of the university have come to resemble far more closely the way things are done downtown then they did before the protests of the 1960s. This should come as no surprise, for few things are more familiar in history than the triumph of unintended consequences.

Beyond all these specifics, radical ideas and practices born of the 1960s have had enormous impact on America, sometimes in unrecognized forms, ever since. As Maurice Isserman and Michael Kazin suggest in their interesting essay, "The Failure and Success of the New Radicalism," in *The Rise and Fall of the New Deal Order, 1930–1980*: "The New Left was shaped by and came to embody a profound dislocation in American culture, and, in the end, it had more impact on the ideas that Americans had about themselves and their society than on the structures of power that governed their lives. Young radicals articulated a critique of 'everyday life' in the United States, which was, in time, taken up by millions of people who had little notion of where these ideas originated."

Some of the attitudinal changes are clearly benign: for instance, the fact that, as Isserman and Kazin note, "Since the mid-1970s, any prominent public figure who has castigated blacks as people, even with humorous intent, has quickly lost reputation, employment, or both."

Others are less so. Without falling into the trap of blaming the 1960s for everything that has gone wrong since, one can argue that American politics has never recovered from the blows it suffered at the hands of the Sixties radicals. Of course more recently it has been the Right that has made disillusionment with, even contempt for government its stock in trade. But the New Left of the Sixties got there first. Their contempt for ordinary politics, with its compromises and evasions, has by now become epidemic in the United States, to the point where many people believe that the only way to deal with any really important question of public policy is somehow to take it "out of politics." Students of the rise of fascism in Europe may be forgiven for finding this worrisome.

.   .   .

On a personal note: toward the end of my Stanford presidency I was driving to work one day and picked up Moe Abramovitz, the distinguished economist, to give him a ride to his office. As we approached the Inner Quad I remarked that I did not think my presidency would be remembered for any very interesting architecture in new buildings. "You won't be remembered for buildings," he replied. "You'll be remembered for having saved the university."

A couple of years ago two of my successors, Don Kennedy and Gerhard Casper, both made the same remark about saving the university at a trustees' dinner. But to save something presumes that you were in danger of losing it or seeing it destroyed, and it is pretty clear now that no American university was destroyed, or even very seriously damaged over the long run, by the turbulence of the 1960s. I think we did some things better at Stanford than at most other institutions; in particular, our development of ways to lessen the traumatic effect of calling police to campus was significant in saving us from the total collapse experienced, however briefly, at places like Harvard and Columbia. I think I contributed to sustaining faculty morale by managing to articulate the proper purposes and parameters of a research university. I also avoided the mistake, so characteristic of Ken Pitzer, of looking for solutions that would please everybody; pleasing everybody was not an available option in those troubled times. In fact there was some benefit from that fact: since one could not hope to please everybody, one might as well do what one thought most likely to succeed. Of course we paid attention to what seemed to be the most likely immediate consequences of a given course of action. But we did not always let that calculation determine what we would in fact try to do.

·   ·   ·

The Stanford administration was blessed with many talented people, some of whom were quite explicitly asked to keep the place running while a few of us spent most of our time on crisis management in one form or other. During the provostial interregnum between Fred Terman's departure and my arrival, Howard Brooks and Bob Wert held the office together admirably. Brooks played a part in the crisis management when he was Stanford's representative in the abortive negotiations with the Pentagon over ROTC. He would have been happy to have been in a position to do more to help, but I assured him that it was essential to have at least some people in the top levels of the administration who were not consumed in the day-to-day confrontations. In 1971 he left Stanford to become provost of the Claremont Colleges, held various offices there in the 1980s, and retired as president of Scripps. Bob Wert became president of Mills College and arranged for me to get an Honorary Degree from Mills in 1972.

Raymond F. Bacchetti, with whom my administrative career began when he was assistant dean of the School of Humanities and Sciences and I an associate dean, always provided wise counsel and was the central figure in developing our sophisticated approach to budget planning. He was also the chief instigator of extending affirmative action recruitment to American Indians. After leaving Stanford he served as a program officer at the Hewlett Foundation.

Bob Rosenzweig, whose part in the BSU crisis of spring 1968 has been described, is another who held an important post in higher education after leaving Stanford: he served as president of the Association of American Universities in Washington from 1983 to 1993. Seldom has a PhD in political science been put to better use, although in that role he sometimes had trouble concealing the fact that he was smarter than most of the people he was working for—as indeed had been the case at Stanford. When I became president and needed a successor to myself as provost, I was bemused by the fact that three of my staff, Rosenzweig, Brooks, and Bacchetti, were eminently well qualified to be provost except for one awkward fact: they were not members of the faculty. Even the dire straits in which the university and its faculty found themselves in these years was not sufficient to break down the barriers created by the academic culture.

One of the more unusual career paths was that of John J. Schwartz, who came to an assistant professorship in physics at Stanford armed also with a law degree. When, responsive to Jack Friedenthal's suggestion, we created the position of university prosecutor in cases before the Stanford Judicial Council, we recruited John to take this on. The position was created to remove the conflict of interest embodied in the dean of students and likewise that of the council itself. Bright, somewhat sardonic, energetic, and fearless, John took on all comers, both then and subsequently during Stanford's travail over indirect costs in Don Kennedy's presidency.

Finally, William F. Miller, who came to Stanford as professor of computer science in 1965, became vice president for research and then served for most of my presidency as vice president and provost. In 1978 he left Stanford to become president of SRI International. He served as acting president during my absences, notably when the hospital sit-in took place and then during my Danforth leave of absence. He promised when I started that leave to preserve radio silence while I was gone, and he did so. I said at the time that this was an appropriately humbling experience, since it demonstrated how far from indispensable my presence on campus was.

No doubt other universities had similar officers, and no doubt their efforts on behalf of the university were similarly underappreciated by the faculty. Never, surely, had higher educational administrators been put under greater stress than in those years. They could not save the day if their leader, the president, was unable to play his part, and the same was true of the faculty. Once the faculty had looked into the abyss and become thoroughly aware of the dangers involved, "saving the university" became relatively easy. Its destruction was never as likely as we sometimes thought it to be. As I have remarked, Stanford's strength actually increased, despite the fears and the turmoil. We've long since ceased to need such claims as that of being "the Harvard of the West." Just being Stanford is enough.

REFERENCE MATTER

APPENDIX

Report to the Academic Council
by Provost Richard W. Lyman
May 1, 1969

I HOPE THAT THE COUNCIL WILL FORGIVE ME for any lack of rhetorical verve that may derive from having been up all night.

It occurred to me as I was considering what needed saying this afternoon that a good many Deans, Provosts, and Presidents have gone through something resembling this experience over the past few years. To cite a particularly melancholy example from the very recent past, my longtime friend and fellow historian, the distinguished scholar and Dean of the Faculty of Arts and Sciences at Harvard, Franklin Ford, went through it. His remarks made the *New York Times*. They did not, apparently, persuade the Harvard Faculty. I shall be happy to forego the former state of felicity if I can also escape the latter result.

I hope—I profoundly hope—that the Council will recognize the deep reluctance with which I, in full consultation with the President's Faculty Consultative Group, took the decision at 4 a.m. today to summon the forces at the disposal of the Sheriff of Santa Clara County to the campus for the purpose of clearing Encina Hall, which had been occupied by members of the April 3rd Movement since 1 a.m. There are probably rumors—there usually are in such situations—to the effect that I have been yearning for the opportunity to do something more or less like this for some time, perhaps even since last May. It is perhaps a mistake to dignify such rumors with a denial, but that is a risk I believe I must take. At no time, until I picked up the telephone in my office at 4 this morning to call the President at his home and report the recommendation unanimously reached by the Faculty Consultative Group, the Dean of

Students, the Associate Provost, and myself, did I urge or recommend that police be called to Stanford.

Why, then, last night? Why did we conclude, not only that there was a necessity to call in the police, but that that necessity was pressing and immediate, that it must be carried out then, rather than waiting a day, perhaps invoking the in some ways preferable instrument of a civil restraining order, and meanwhile continuing to hope that the invocation of the President's emergency powers to place students on immediate temporary suspension might produce more results in the course of today than it did last night.

Before proceeding to give our answer to that very legitimate question, I should remark that we did invoke those emergency powers and did make every effort to make them effective last night. When it had become clear, out of that protracted, bitter, and repellent argument within the April 3rd Movement yesterday afternoon and evening—which I assume many of you heard, at least in part, over KZSU—when it had become clear that a firm decision had been taken by them to occupy another building, we began calling upon faculty members to come to the President's Office and accompany the Dean of Students and the Associate Dean of Students in attempting to carry out the steps, suggested by the Stanford Judicial Council in its statement of April 17th, steps necessary to bring the emergency powers into action.

And at this point let me underline the obvious. The faculty who rallied to that call and spent the entire night, first working to effectuate the emergency powers, then working to do everything possible to assure success in the use of police, those faculty demonstrated the highest form of unselfish devotion to the University and its preservation. The job they undertook was not only extremely repellent to most faculty, it was also potentially dangerous, and they deserve the thanks of everyone who cares about Stanford, certainly including all who may disagree with any or all of the steps undertaken last night with the cooperation of these faculty volunteers. There's been a lot of loose talk about people putting their bodies on the line. I know a group of distinguished and honorable Stanford faculty who showed their willingness to put their bodies, and a lot more besides, on a most difficult line last night, and I salute them. The same must be said, and with heartfelt emphasis, about the members of the Faculty Consultative Group.

The faculty members who had come to the President's Office accompanied Joel Smith and Bill Wyman to Encina, first to fulfill the requirements for determining that there was indeed a breach of the President's emergency regulations involved in the sit-in; second to give proper warning to those involved that such a violation had been determined; and third to help identify as many as possible of those who were persisting in that violation. At the notice of immediate summary temporary suspension some occupants of Encina vacated the building. But most remained, and the rifling through files that had characterized the occupation from its inception continued.

In a very real sense, the University's on-campus remedies, designed to end a disruption, were then exhausted. We could have waited to see whether the actual delivery of letters addressed to individual students, informing them of their suspension, might have made some difference; actual suspension, even temporarily from this University has, after all, been so infrequent an occurrence, especially arising out of a disruption, that there was some reason to think that few would believe it until they actually experienced it in person.

That possibility, along with every other conceivable reason to *refrain* from calling in police, was canvassed in the Faculty Consultative Group during its intensive exploration of this matter between about 2:20 a.m. and 4 a.m. today. I return to my question: Why did not these various and weighty considerations cause us to reach some other decision than the one we in fact reached?

First, the difference between being told you're suspended and receiving a letter to that effect seemed to us at best marginal. The Violators' utter contempt for the entire institution of on-campus judicial due process had, after all, been demonstrated not only last night but throughout the sit-in in the Applied Electronics Laboratory the week before last. Indeed, few aspects of our current crisis are clearer or more critically significant than this contempt. We have tried—President Pitzer has tried, the Judicial Council has tried, *you* have tried, to the utmost of your ability—to make the on-campus procedures work. The careful labors of faculty and students in creating the Stanford Judicial and Legislative Charters last year have been dismissed by the SDS and by many, if not most, members of the April 3rd Coalition, as a hopeless, if not downright silly exercise in liberal self-delusion, aimed at suppressing dissent rather than achieving justice. At least tacit acceptance of that view, in the form of unwillingness to assist in *making* that machinery work, has been more widespread than I like to think, and it has contributed its bit to the decision taken this morning to call upon the civil power for the purpose of supplementing on-campus judicial and enforcement measures. This Council, by its approval of the Statement on Community Responsibility a few weeks ago, recognized that the alternatives available to us are stark and few: make the campus system work, or call in outside elements to restore a tolerable degree of peace to the campus.

A second reason why we decided to call upon the Sheriff's Office was the character of the Encina occupation. From the outset it was violent; students who attempted to stand in the doorways and peaceably block the entry of demonstrators were roughly shoved aside and in some cases manhandled. Locked doors, both on the exterior of the building and, later, inside were broken open; so were windows. Once inside, the demonstrators opened desks and files in many parts of the building and were seen seizing documents from those files. Given the fact that Encina contains not one but a wide variety of sensitive and important repositories of information, this was highly ominous. In the Planning Office, soon broken into and occupied, is kept information on the routes of sewers, steam lines, power lines, and the like, without which we might well spend an interesting if unprofitable decade or so conducting amateur archaeological expeditions in an attempt to rediscover where these things are. In the Payroll Office is information the nature and significance of which I need not pause to describe. The very machinery for paying all University employees is in jeopardy when Encina Hall is occupied by hostile and unpredictable forces. Serious disruption of the General Secretary's Office would imperil the means by which a private university sustains itself through gifts—a crassly materialistic matter, one may say, but crucial to our capacity to function as a University. And so on.

The point was made last night that it was conceivable that the most serious damage had already been done in Encina, and that calling police was to that extent dubious as being too late. Against that was the reported fact that exploitation of files and acts of vandalism had been more random than systematic, and the reasonable expectations that continuation of the seizure through today would imply a more systemic effort. Also, such sensitive areas as the inner portion of the General Secretary's Office and the Administrative Data Processing computers were as yet unoccupied (though three attempts were made to enter the former, each being repelled by a firm warning that such occupation would mean immediate police action). These warnings were delivered in person by George Gregory, a member of Mr. Cuthbertson's staff, at my specific direction some hours before the police were called—in fact, before the target was definitely determined to be Encina.

Continuing risk to vital information and vital University functions was a strong consideration, then.

Linked with that was the fact, of which we have been aware since we first discussed possible police action on the campus a year ago, that the Sheriff's Office can best act in the early hours of the morning. The presence of large crowds, including many not directly involved in the demonstration, has been a potent cause of confusion in other campus police actions around the country. Such confusion contributes to the likelihood of personal injury. It cannot be contemplated lightly.

I should also make clear that the intention of the police, and of ourselves in asking for their help, was to clear the building, not to accumulate victims of arrest. This is amply borne out by the result, as you know: no injuries, no arrests. To ensure that we were as well prepared to obtain this result as possible, we have had numerous conversations with Sheriff Prelsnik and his people over the past twelve months. Their understanding of campus problems, and of the sensitivity to police action that exists on campus, has always been of the utmost help to us. Their cooperation in our plans to involve faculty as observers going along with arrest teams, and as general observers, is something for which we're also most grateful. Like most of us, policemen would rather operate on their own terms and in their own established fashion. The Sheriff of Santa Clara County has understood and accepted the need for limitations on this autonomy of action.

A further reason for our decision lay in the fact that the Encina occupation comes so rapidly upon the heels of the AEL sit-in. At some point, nearly every member of this Council will agree, defenses must be invoked against wanton, indiscriminate, and arbitrary actions designed to force University acquiescence in the views of any campus groups, no matter how high-minded. It is not a matter of patience being exhausted; it is a matter of sheer credibility. No institution, not even a University, can continue indefinitely working in an atmosphere of coercion, indeed with the *fact* of coercive interruption daily demonstrated. Substantial numbers of University people, from distinguished members of this body to employees in many branches of the University service functions—and most certainly including students—have complained that without effective deterrence to disruptive forces, life at Stanford would soon become intolerable, and the University's essential functions would cease to be performed, or their performance would be damaged so severely as to threaten our capacity to consider ourselves an effective institution.

On the other hand, an effective effort to curb such forces would restore credibility in Stanford's determination and capacity to run its affairs and carry out its educational mission.

I could continue with further analysis of the complex and probing discussions and reasoning that led to our decision this morning, but I shall not. The Faculty Consultative Group was unanimous in its conclusion that this course of action was not only justified but necessary. Dean Smith, though understandably reluctant to abandon the hope that the on-campus judicial machinery might work to produce an evacuation of the building, supported the decision and brought to the discussion preceding it those qualities of lucidity and breadth of judgment for which, amongst other things, he will be so badly missed when he leaves Stanford at the end of this year.

One further word, if I may. No one is entitled to consider the clearing of Encina Hall a victory. Any time it becomes necessary for a University to summon the police, a defeat has taken place. I'm reminded of Winston Churchill's declaration after Dunkerque, when too many of his fellow countrymen imagined that Hitler was on the downward path: Wars are not won by successful evacuations. The victory we seek at Stanford is not like a military victory; it is a victory of reason and the examined life over unreason and the tyranny of coercion. To be forced into coercive acts in order to meet coercive acts is in itself a setback on the path that leads to our kind of victory.

But surrender does not produce victory either, whether in war or in the personal struggle that each and every one of us carries on from the cradle to the grave. The French say "Reculer pour mieux sauter"—draw back to jump better. Maybe that is what we have done. It is not going to be easy to jump—or even to creep—forward in the conditions facing universities today. A brutal and senseless war abroad; brutal and senseless oppression at home; a feeling of desperation among the young in their powerlessness to remedy these things—these conditions limit our chances for success. I believe in universities, and I believe in Stanford. I have done my best to serve those beliefs. It is not disgrace, and no cause for chagrin if one's best in such times as these is not good enough. I thank you for listening, and I wish us all well as we labor to reconstruct the mutual confidence without which no human enterprise can long succeed.

NOTES

Introduction

1. Edwin E. Slosson, *Great American Universities* (New York: Macmillan, 1910), 112.

Chapter One

1. *Time*, November 9, 1962.

2. Frank J. Taylor, "Stanford's Man with a Midas Touch," *Saturday Evening Post*, December 3, 1960.

3. At Stanford, the board chair bore the confusing title of "President of the Board of Trustees," leading to confusion with the university presidency.

4. J.E. Wallace Sterling, "Memorandum to the Board of Trustees of Stanford University" (November 17, 1948), 2, SC 216, J.E. Wallace Sterling Papers, Stanford University Archives. Quoted in Frank Medeiros, "The Sterling Years at Stanford," *Sandstone and Tile* 4 (summer 1985): 6.

5. The once-famous Stanford Binet Test was his creation.

6. I discovered this in December 1963, as I was about to become an associate dean of the School of Humanities and Sciences; the Dean's Office was in a flurry of preparation for this submission.

7. See Rebecca S. Lowen, *Creating the Cold War University* (Berkeley: University of California Press, 1997), 169–74. The author laments these developments, but does not ask herself whether the alternative—trying to hold the scales even between the old and the new biology—would have made any sense for an ambitious institution with limited resources such as Stanford.

8. The exclusion of women from this picture was, of course, typical of that era.

9. Jesse Oxfeld, "Slice of cheese pizza at Tresidder Union: $2.75, Econ 1 textbook: $123.56, Undergraduate tuition: $29,847, Bloomingdale's across the street . . . Priceless," *Stanford Magazine*, July/August 2004.

10. C. Stewart Gilmore, *Fred Terman at Stanford: Building a Discipline, a University, and Silicon Valley* (Stanford, CA: Stanford University Press, 2004), 356–59.

11. What he actually wrote (in a letter to David Packard) was, "Stanford, which has always been a good university, is trembling on the edge of becoming one of the small number of great ones." See Frank A. Medeiros, *The Sterling Years at Stanford: A Study in the Dynamics of Institutional Change* (PhD dissertation, Stanford University, 1979), 186.

12. *Time*, November 9, 1962.

13. Fred Terman, "Stanford's Academic Goals and Academic Needs," *Stanford's Minimum Financial Needs in the Years Ahead* (November 10, 1959), quoted by Medeiros, *Sterling Years at Stanford*, 134.

14. Medeiros, *Sterling Years at Stanford*, 199.

15. Rixford K. Snyder to Frederic O. Glover, November 29, 1965, SC 216.

16. Medeiros, *Sterling Years at Stanford*, 10. From a transcription of a talk in Salt Lake City in 1958. Note the assumption, which would not be made today, that "equality before the law" was a reality, whereas "equality of opportunity" might not be.

17. Ibid., 11.

18. Gary Nash, *Herbert Hoover and Stanford University* (Stanford, CA: Stanford University Press, 1988), 154.

19. Robert N. Sayler (President of ASSU) to President Sterling, May 18, 1962, SC 216, Box 5, Folder 21.

20. Sterling to Sayler, May 23, 1962, SC 216.

21. Hand-typed memo, Glover to Sterling, January 23, 1963, SC 216, Box C5, Folder 16.

22. *The Stanford Daily*, January 25, 1963.

23. Ibid. (the *Daily*'s paraphrasing).

24. Ibid.

25. Rosencranz to Sterling and Morris M. Doyle, March 2, 1963, SC 216.

Chapter Two

1. Stephen Weissbluth, Chair, Stanford Peace Caucus, to *The Stanford Daily*, April 17, 1963.

2. Ibid.

3. "President Sterling's Statement on Vigil Policy," April 26, 1963.

4. Ibid.

5. Peter C. Allen, "Demonstrations at Stanford, Autumn 1965–Spring 1971," 6, SC 157.

6. Steven A. Jarvis to Lyle M. Nelson, May 3, 1963.

7. Alex Maurey, Kit Havice, and Stephen Weissbluth, "Spokesmen for the Peace Caucus," letter to President Sterling, May 1, 1963.

8. Allen, "Demonstrations at Stanford," 7, SC 157.

9. *San Francisco Chronicle*, June 17, 1963.

10. Allen, "Demonstrations at Stanford," 8, SC 157. The total was forty, "all who could be handled by available funds."

11. "The Report of the LASSU Committee on Religion," SC 216, Box 23, Folder 16.

12. In the early years, Mrs. Stanford had the legal right to amend the Founding Grant by her own fiat. See Orrin L. Elliott, *Stanford University: The First 25 Years* (Stanford, CA: Stanford University Press, 1937), 25. She formally yielded her powers to the full board in 1903. See Elliott, *Stanford University*, 460.

13. Sterling to Daniel Schwartz, Chairman, LASSU Committee on Religion, February 4, 1964.

14. No copy of this draft appears in the relevant folder of the Sterling Papers.

15. Sterling Papers.

16. Richard W. Lyman (RWL) to Sterling, March 11, 1964.

17. RWL to Sterling, April 12, 1964.

18. Glover to Sterling, June 25, 1965.

19. Glover to Sterling, September 22, 1965

20. *The Stanford Daily*'s paraphrase, October 19, 1964

21. Clark Brown, ASSU Vice President and Legislative Speaker, to Sterling, November 15, 1965.

22. RWL to Sterling, November 16, 1965.

23. The President's Committee on Religious Activities to Sterling, November 16, 1965.

24. This is based on a four-page handwritten text in the Sterling papers—he did not speak from partial notes on such important occasions at the board.

25. Joel P. Smith to Sterling, September 6, 1966, Sterling Papers.

26. See Kenneth M. Cuthbertson to Robert Minge Brown, December 29, 1975, Sterling Papers.

27. This account relies much on the report of the Executive Committee of the Academic Council, dated February 12, 1965, SC 050, Allen Controversy Papers. Unless otherwise indicated, quotations are from this document.

28. The Crow/Halverson report published in *The Stanford Daily* on February 4 went far beyond anything in the ad hoc committee document, alleging that, in leading up to her proposal for reporting on English classes, Dean Allen had charged, "The young professors arouse the freshman girls sexually, as well. They concentrate deliberately on the erotic aspects of literature, in part because those who are unmarried use literature as their sexual outlet, and in part because they wish to seduce the girls in their classes. The Dean said she knew of several recent cases where professors had succeeded in seducing students," going on to say the faculty used "their grading power" to "intimidate a girl who will not comply with their wishes." The language here is that of the report's paraphrase; it does not purport to be a direct quotation of Dean Allen.

29. Members were Gerald Gunther (law), Kenneth J. Arrow (economics), and Sanford M. Dornbusch (sociology).

30. "Reply of Lucile Allen to Report of Ad Hoc Committee of the Executive Committee of the Academic Council of Stanford University," "dated at Stanford University this twenty-third of February, 1965." SC 050.

31. Frederic O. Glover memo to Sterling, February 12, 1965, SC 050, Allen Controversy Papers.

32. Gerald Gunther, Marc Franklin, and Bayless Manning memo to Sterling, February 12, 1965 (but probably actually sent the next day), SC 050.

33. Sterling to Robert L. Sutherland, April 13, 1965, SC 216.

34. *The Stanford Daily*, February 4, 1965.

35. *The Stanford Daily* is missing from the Stanford University Archives' microfilm.

36. *The Stanford Daily*, April 19, 1965. The reference is, of course, to the Free Speech Movement and its aftermath. The author of this reference to "men of general good will," interestingly, was a woman, Nancy Steffen, a reminder of feminism's limited reach in 1965.

37. John Timothy to Sterling, May 30, 1964.

38. I chaired one session, and although I was critical of the war policy, I was among several who would only agree to participate if some balance were maintained in the speakers' roster.

39. Allen, "Demonstrations at Stanford," 9.

40. Application in SC 216.

41. Quoted in *The Stanford Daily*, May 13, 1966.

42. Leaflet from the 1966 sit-in, SC 216.

43. *The Stanford Observer*, June 1966.

44. John D. Black to Stanford Committee for Peace in Vietnam, May 17, 1966, SC 216.

45. *The Stanford Daily*, May 20, 1966.

46. *The Stanford Observer*, June 1966.

47. Ibid.

48. *The Stanford Daily*, May 23, 1966.

49. Typed text, SC 216.

50. "Why We Sat In" (leaflet advertising White Plaza rally for May 23), SC 216.

51. Sterling to Peter J. Flaherty, June 3, 1966, SC 216.

52. Typescript in SC 216.

53. In view of the administration's objection to the seminar idea, the Judicial Council rescinded the original sentence in November, and finally in December, six months after the first hearings, it imposed a new sentence: probation plus a requirement to write a paper on civil disobedience. The administration decided not to appeal,

despite the open-endedness of the additional penalty. See H. Donald Winbigler to Professor Joseph T. Sneed, Chairman, Interim Judicial Body, January 4, 1967.

54. Glover memo to Sterling (reporting telephone conversation), May 31, 1966. See also the angry and puzzled letter to the president from another senior trustee, Richard E. Guggenhime, May 31, 1966.

55. Joseph W. Vickers to Morris Doyle, May 23, 1966, SC 216.

56. Lyle M. Nelson to Mrs. and Mrs. Paul F. Busch, June 7, 1966, SC 216.

57. Statement read at 2:30 p.m., May 21, 1966. Text, with no names, in Sterling Papers. According to *The Stanford Observer* (June 1966), it was written by Keith Lowe and read by Barry Greenberg.

58. David M. Brown (first-year law student), "Letter to the Editor," *The Stanford Daily*, May 25, 1966.

59. SC 216.

60. *The Los Angeles Times*, June 11, 1966.

61. David Harris, *Dreams Die Hard* (New York: St. Martin's, 1982), 36.

62. Ibid., 41.

63. Ibid., 81.

64. Ibid., 84.

65. Quoted by Gina Berriault, "The New Student President," *Esquire*, September 1967.

66. Harris, *Dreams Die Hard*, 87.

67. Ibid., 97.

68. Ibid., 124.

69. Ibid., 133–34.

70. Ibid., 134.

71. *The Stanford Daily*, April 20, 1966. Harris's recollection years later also exaggerated his position on both the board of trustees and fraternities, both of which were to be reformed but not abolished, according to the responses in the *Daily*.

72. *The Stanford Daily*, April 20, 1966.

73. Harris's account of the episode in *Dreams Die Hard* is muddled from start to finish. He pictures himself as having opposed the draft entirely during his campaign— "I said I thought no one should be drafted, but if they were, then no one should be allowed to remain exempt." He misdates the sit-in and then speculates on the administration's motives in not evicting the protesters based on this misdating. He omits any mention of the counterpicketers, and he says nothing about how the sit-in ended or with what result.

74. Harris, *Dreams Die Hard*, 135–36.

75. Dated May 12, 1966. Copy in SC 216.

76. *The Stanford Daily*, October 13 and 17, 1966.

77. *The Stanford Daily*, February 23, 1967.

78. Harris, *Dreams Die Hard*, 157.

79. *The Stanford Daily*, January 16, 1967.

80. *Esquire*, September 1967, 154.

81. Ibid.

82. Ibid.

83. Ibid., 153.

84. Quotations are all from *The Stanford Daily*, February 23, 1967.

85. Harris, *Dreams Die Hard*, 224.

86. Ibid., 234.

87. Ibid., 215.

88. Ibid., 261–62.

89. Ibid., 289. Harris was paroled on March 15, 1971. He and Joan Baez separated three months later.

90. Ibid., 251–52.

Chapter Three

1. Incredible as it now seems, Sterling left it to us to determine which of us would take which position. Packer had no interest in administration per se, but he wanted the status of the vice provost's position from which to chair the imminent Study of Education at Stanford.

Chapter Four

1. See *Supra*.

2. Michael Novak, "Humphrey at Stanford," *Commonweal*, March 24, 1967, 7–8.

3. *Time*, Editorial, February 23, 1967.

4. Winthrop Griffith to Lyle M. Nelson, Director, University Relations, March 6, 1967.

5. J.R. White to Richard E. Guggenhime, February 24, 1967, SC 216.

6. Lyle M. Nelson to Sterling, February 28, 1967, Sterling Papers.

7. February 22, 1967.

8. Stanford News Service release, February 24, 1967.

9. Sterling Papers.

10. Peter C. Allen, "Demonstrations at Stanford, Autumn 1965–Spring 1971," SC 157.

11. David Harris, *Dreams Die Hard* (New York: St. Martin's, 1982), 196–97.

12. Leaflet, "A Call for Active Opposition," Sterling Papers.

13. Harris, *Dreams Die Hard*, 208.

14. Allen, "Demonstrations at Stanford," 17, SC 157.

15. *The Stanford Daily*, October 31, 1967.

16. Mimeographed statement in Sterling Papers.

17. *The Stanford Daily*, November 1, 1967.

18. *The Stanford Daily*, November 2 and 3, 1967.

19. Tim Haight, "The 'War' Is Not Lost," *The Stanford Daily*, November 17, 1967.

20. RWL to Richard Helms, November 28, 1967.

21. Helms to Lyman, December 13, 1967, Sterling Papers.

22. Robert R. Sears to Sterling, November 10, 1967.

23. Abbreviations in the original.

Chapter Five

1. Robert M. Rosenzweig to Sterling, October 20, 1964.

2. Copy of Stanford's responses in Records of Vice Provost Robert Rosenzweig, 1963–1974, SC 091.

3. *Palo Alto Times*, April 22, 1967.

4. Open letter to "Friends" from Mid-Peninsula Friends of SNCC; it is undated, but it announces a forthcoming meeting on May 17, 1967.

5. Memo, no addressee, dated February 1, 1967.

6. Sterling letter to Mrs. Wilks, August 8, 1968, from her initial letter of complaint.

7. David G. Clark, Administrative Assistant in the Provost's Office, memo to RWL, March 19, 1968.

8. Ibid.

9. Rambo to Sterling and Lyman, April 10, 1968.

10. This account is based on typed texts of my Memorial Auditorium notes, the Sterling/Lyman statement of April 9, of the BSU's demands, and of my "Response" on April 11, all located in the Stanford University Archives, together with the reports in the *Daily* and the account in George Packer's *Blood of the Liberals*. The latter focuses, of course, on his father's role and is generally accurate, as far as I can tell, though it seems to me that he errs in saying that the university representatives on the deck that Tuesday night "wanted to agree to most of the demands . . . *but they didn't want to appear to be giving in, or turning over university decision-making to a group of students*" (243; my italics). I believe that a desire to save face played a remarkably small part all through that tense week. George Packer's statement has the effect of trivializing our desire not to agree to things that would prove impossible or undesirable in the event, such as proportional representation or subcontracting pieces of university administration to the BSU, which was not only a "group of students," but an organization with its own hierarchy, modes of operation, and agenda.

11. April 13, 1968. Stanford University Archives has a (permission-only) microfilm copy.

12. Fuller to J.R. White, April 20, 1968.

13. James E. Simmons to RWL, April 20, 1973.

14. In early 1969 I got it changed again, to Assistant to the President for Black Affairs, to make sure he had clear entrée to the nonacademic parts of the university.

15. Michael Sweeney, "Koff and a Black Dilemma," *The Stanford Daily*, February 10, 1969.

16. Stanford News Service release, February 20, 1969.

17. Simmons to Pitzer, July 28, 1969.

18. "Black Students Say Only Activist Tactics Pay Off," *Palo Alto Times*, April 16, 1968.

19. Another oft-encountered attack came from the opposite quarter, when Asian Americans would ask, "How come you count us when reporting to HEW but not when it comes to affirmative action recruitment?" To this I responded that we reported them because we were required to by law and did not recruit them because they did not need it—without any help from affirmative action their numbers were growing as fast as those of any other minority, and they were statistically overrepresented at Stanford. Needless to say, this answer did not draw applause.

20. At Stanford, for geographic and demographic reasons, the category "Hispanic" has generally (and even officially) meant Mexican American.

Chapter Six

1. David Harris, *Dreams Die Hard* (New York: St. Martin's, 1982), 21.

2. An irrelevant but irresistible factoid: Frank Morse later married one of President Sterling's daughters.

3. The fact that Smith was writing a four-page concise history of the Stanford judicial system for the enlightenment of C-15 is a reminder of a perennial problem running through this story: decision-making bodies kept changing personnel, especially students, with a resulting loss of institutional memory.

4. The basis for this description is the text of a talk by McDonough, dated February 15, 1967, and included with the 1966–67 minutes of C-15, Stanford Archives.

5. Alternatively, a predetermined number of demerits would trigger a judgment as to whether you should be extruded.

6. *The Stanford Daily*, May 22, 1967.

7. Ibid.

8. *The Stanford Daily*, February 29, 1968.

9. "An Address by Herbert L. Packer to the Annual Meeting of the Stanford Chapter of the American Association of University Professors—May 13, 1968," 4.

10. "Old Union Sit-In," draft press release, Stanford News Service release, 6, SC 133, Box 21. (Unless otherwise noted, quotations from the sit-in are taken from this document.)

11. No relationship as far as I know. Lyman, like David Harris before him, resigned

his office midterm. He went on to become head of the library and of information services at the University of California at Berkeley. Vice President Cesare Masserenti succeeded him as ASSU president.

12. Packer, "Address," 7.

13. George Packer, *Blood of the Liberals* (New York: Farrar, Straus & Giroux, 2000), 245.

14. Harris, *Dreams Die Hard*, 226–27.

15. "Minutes of the Executive Committee of the Academic Council, May 8, 1968"; confidential letter from Ernest Hilgard to Sterling, May 8, 1968.

16. In much of the following account of the meeting I quote extensively from Herb Packer's angry address to the AAUP chapter five days later, for the simple reason that for the most part I cannot improve upon it.

17. I cannot explain why neither Herb nor I, both well versed in Robert's, did not call attention to this at the time. Whether in the near-chaos of that meeting we failed to think of it, or we thought of it but decided not to stop something we wanted to see happen, I honestly do not know.

18. Unfortunately, Herb could not resist omitting the sentence that completed his correspondent's point—and makes the quotation substantially less telling from Packer's point of view: "They [the students] sense that the administration distrusts their abilities to self-govern." Packer quotes the passage in full in *Blood of Liberals*, 248.

19. Craig Diary, May 9, 1968.

20. George H. Knoles to RWL, May 15, 1968, SC 328, Box 1, Folder 9.

21. "Open letter to 'the Faculty of Stanford University,'" May 8, 1968, SC 122, Box 214, Folder: "Demonstrations, General, 1965–70."

22. It seems to me that George Packer's analysis is at least somewhat misleading when he says, "Although several votes in which thousands of students took part during and after the sit-in condemned its tactics by majorities of two to one, *they also supported the demands*" (*Blood of Liberals*, 246; my italics). Votes in the mass meetings held in the Old Union courtyard may have done so, but the six-to-one support for open recruiting, in a supervised election by secret ballot, was anything but supportive of the *purposes* of the CIA defendants and illustrates rather dramatically how far the majority of students were from the general position of SDS and its allies.

23. Quoted in Packer, *Blood of Liberals*, 250. My recollection is that I used the same word in my draft.

24. Doing this before LASSU met to consider these proposals that evening was "the main point," according to a memo summarizing the week's events that I sent to the trustees on May 13.

25. "The Sterling-Lyman Statement," *The Stanford Daily*, May 10, 1968.

26. *Midpeninsula Observer*, May 20–June 3, 1968, 4.

27. "A Foolproof Scenario for Student Revolt," *New York Times Magazine*, December 29, 1968.

28. Quoted in Packer, *Blood of Liberals*, 251.

29. Ibid. George Packer's phrase "By June" is misleading; the date of the letter was May 18. Repentance, if that is what it was, though political calculation strikes me as more plausible, came in just five days.

30. *Midpeninsula Observer*, July 15–29, 1968.

31. *The Stanford Daily*, May 31, 1968.

32. "Chronological Summary of Demonstration Activities at Stanford University," in Peter C. Allen, "Student Demonstration Papers," SC 157, Folder 15.

33. There is a huge stack of these letters and telegrams in the Sterling Papers, SC 216, Box C-6, Folder 16.

Chapter Seven

1. *Peninsula Observer*, September 9–22, 1968. The "*Mid*" was dropped in the summer of 1968.

2. *Peninsula Observer*, August 26–September 9, 1968, 10.

3. *Campus Report*, September 18, 1968.

4. "An Address by Herbert L. Packer to the Annual Meeting of the Stanford Chapter of the American Association of University Professors—May 13, 1968," 16.

5. See *The Stanford Daily*, November 4, 1967, for Lyman's criticisms; October 11, 1967, for Arrow's reply.

6. *Peninsula Observer*, November 18–December 1, 1968, "Politics at Last: Free U Confronts Self Over Downtown Liberation."

7. "Demonstrations at Stanford, Autumn 1965–Spring 1971," 26, a "rough draft" in Stanford Archives, SC 157.

8. Stanford News Service release, May 5, 1966. H. Donald Winbigler memo to Members of the Academic Council, May 9, 1966.

9. COUP, "Recommendation on Classified Research," May 5, 1966.

10. "Remarks on Classified Research presented by W.R. Rambo to the Academic Council on May 17, 1966," Rambo Papers, SC 132, 1939–1992.

11. Rambo to Kenneth Arrow, June 3, 1966, SC 132.

12. "Remarks," May 17, 1966.

13. W.R. Kincheloe Jr. to Kenneth Arrow, June 6, 1966, Rambo Papers.

14. Rambo to Arrow, June 3, 1966.

15. "Stanford and SRI," a twenty-five–page pamphlet, no date but from internal evidence either late 1968 or early 1969, 23. This is quite an impressively researched and well-written document. SC 420, Box 1, Folder 1. The Rambo paragraph is in his letter to Kenneth Arrow of June 3, 1966.

16. "Stanford and SRI," 24.

17. "Stanford and SRI," 11, quoting Douglas Pike of the U.S. Information Agency.

18. Ibid., 14.

19. Ibid.

20. Ibid., 9.

21. Rambo to Arrow, June 3, 1966.

22. Ibid.

23. Peter C. Allen, "Student Demonstration Papers," 26, SC 157, Folder 15.

24. Robert J. Glaser, MD, "To the members of the Stanford Community" (open letter), October 7, 1968.

25. It is noteworthy how completely the resistance to allowing student government to appoint the student members of university bodies had evaporated by this time. The appointments to the SES Steering Committee were the last in which the administration resisted this and made resistance stick.

26. "Stanford and SRI," 24.

27. Quoted in George Packer, *Blood of the Liberals*, (New York: Farrar, Straus & Giroux, 2000), 257.

28. SES *Report to the University*, vol. II, "Undergraduate Education," 3.

29. Packer, *Blood of the Liberals*, 258.

30. Ibid., 258–59.

31. *Peninsula Observer*, August 26–September 9, 1968.

32. *Time*, August 30, 1968.

33. *The Stanford Daily*, November 26, 1968.

34. Ibid.

35. Ibid.

36. Stanford News Service release, January 28, 1969. The paper was produced "on or before January 10."

37. *Peninsula Observer*, January 20–27, 1969, 24. A participant in the events of January 14 wrote the piece.

38. "SDS Militants Invade Lunch, Rout Trustees," *Palo Alto Times*, January 15, 1969.

39. Quotations from the council's decision are taken from Stanford News Service release, February 28, 1969.

40. Statement by President Kenneth S. Pitzer, February 28, 1969.

Chapter Eight

1. *The Stanford Daily*, March 3, 1969.

2. *Peninsula Observer*, "through March 31," 1969, 9. The *Observer*, chronically underfunded, was struggling; its dating of issues was somewhat erratic.

3. Ibid., 9–10.

4. Ibid., 12–13.

5. Ibid., 10.

6. Ibid., 13; regarding Smith, see page 12.

7. Peter C. Allen, "Demonstrations at Stanford, Autumn 1965–Spring 1971," 30, SC 157.

8. Stanford News Service release, March 10, 1969.

9. Stanford News Service release, March 14, 1969.

10. Stanford News Service release, March 15, 1969.

11. Stanford News Service release, March 16, 1969.

12. "Comments of Kenneth S. Pitzer at Special Meeting of the Academic Council, April 18, 1969."

13. "Radical Losing Control of Stanford Sit-In," *San Jose Mercury News*, April 18, 1969.

14. Ibid.

15. Stanford News Service release, April 20, 1969; *Peninsula Observer*, "through May 6," 1969, 3.

16. Stanford News Service release, April 18, 1969.

17. Ibid.

18. Stanford News Service release, April 22, 1969.

19. Issue "through May 5," 1969, 11. A photograph of the "ceremony" appears on page 1. The building was kept open to all. One laboratory became the nursery for very young children of protesters. Another served as the "Red Guard Bookstore." Names were distributed widely—the Eldridge Cleaver Room, the Che Guevara Room (see William Rambo testimony before the McLellan Committee, Peter Allen Papers). One is reminded of Bruce Franklin's rhapsodic description of the Old Union sit-in the year before.

20. *Peninsula Observer*, "through May 5," 1969, 10.

21. Ibid., 18.

22. Ibid., 21.

23. Ibid., 6.

24. Stanford News Service release, April 25, 1969.

25. Ibid.

26. The poll, carried out under the direction of Professor Nathan Maccoby, was reported in a Stanford News Service release, April 28, 1969. I have touched on only a few of the many and complex findings.

27. *Peninsula Observer*, "through May 19," 1969, 3.

28. Stanford News Service release, April 30, 1969.

29. *Peninsula Observer*, "through May 19," 1969, 4. According to the *Daily*'s report (May 1, 1969) that "final vote" was to occupy Encina.

30. "Erosion of Smooth Society," *The Stanford Daily*, May 6, 1969.

31. *Peninsula Observer*, "through May 19," 1969, 3.

32. Kirk to Glover, February 11, 1965.

33. "Discipline on Campus Tougher than Believed," *The Los Angeles Times*, June 23, 1969.

34. I should point out that I have no way of knowing what advice these two would in fact have given, had they been asked, although I am tolerably certain about Ken's motivation in asking. I should also point out that, although the added qualifier, "on your own responsibility," struck me at the time as unfortunate, he had been rudely awakened by bad news; later that day at the Academic Council meeting he made appropriately positive comments about my performance and left it to me to describe how we had reached the decision without him.

35. *Peninsula Observer*, "through May 19," 1969, 4.

36. See text, Appendix.

37. Radicals often quoted my remarks about defeat in a triumphant tone, illustrating, however unintentionally, how little they truly understood the point that I was making.

38. *Peninsula Observer*, "through May 26," 1969, 1 and 3.

39. Ibid., 3.

40. *San Jose Mercury*, May 21, 1969, re: City Council; *The Stanford Daily*, May 20, 1969, re: UCM.

41. Ibid., 10.

42. SC 420, Box 1.

43. *The Los Angeles Times*, June 23, 1969.

44. "Volunteer Fact Sheet," September 23, 1969, Peter Allen Papers, SC 157.

45. Peter Allen Papers, SC 157, Folder 2.

Chapter Nine

1. *The Stanford Daily*, May 23, 1969.

2. Ibid.

3. *The New York Times*, December 20, 1969.

4. Hearings Before the Permanent Subcommittee on Investigations of the Committee on Government Operations, United States Senate, vol. 56, "Riots, Civil and Criminal Disorders, and Disruptions on College Campuses," SC 157, Box 1, Folder 7, 8152.

5. Ibid., 8172.

6. Ibid., 8317.

7. Ibid., 8271–72.

8. Ibid., 8350.

9. *The Stanford Daily*, October 28, 1969.

10. *Stanford Chaparral*, November 6, 1969.

11. Philip G. Duffy to Kenneth S. Pitzer, April 20, 1970, President's Office files of complaint letters, SC 215.

12. *The Stanford Daily*, April 3, 1970.

Chapter Ten

1. *The Stanford Daily*, October 5, 1970.

2. *The Stanford Daily*, October 19, 1970.

3. *The Stanford Daily*, October 12, 1970.

4. "Decision Advisory Board in the Matter of Professor H. Bruce Franklin, January 5, 1972," 9 (hereafter, "Advisory Board Decision").

5. I explained this reasoning to the Academic Senate since some saw unfairness in my establishing the penalty before the decision, so to speak. *The Stanford Daily*, January 29, 1971.

6. Advisory Board Decision, 39–41.

7. Ibid., 46.

8. *The Stanford Daily*, January 24, 1972, 4.

9. Advisory Board Decision, 101–2.

10. *The Stanford Daily*, May 19, 1971.

Chapter Eleven

1. Advisory Board Decision, 132.

2. Ibid., 148.

3. Ibid., 144.

4. Ibid., 148.

Chapter Twelve

1. *The New York Times*, June 19, 1967.

2. David Harris, *Dreams Die Hard* (New York: St. Martin's, 1982), 215.

3. Winifred Breines, "Whose New Left?" *Journal of American History* 75, no. 2 (Sept. 1988): 528–45.

INDEX